FORBIDDEN KINDER

THE 1932 MASS TRESPASS RE-VISITED

Trespass veterans at Bowden Bridge quarry 1982. L-R Arthur Schofield, Benny Rothman, George Sumner, Walter Leigh, Jimmy Jones and Bella Costello

FORBIDDEN
KINDER
THE 1932 MASS TRESPASS RE-VISITED

KEITH WARRENDER

consultant editors
Roly Smith & Tom Waghorn

Willow
PUBLISHING

Willow Publishing, 36 Moss Lane, Timperley
Altrincham, Cheshire WA15 6SZ

ISBN 978-0-946361-48-9

Book design Keith Warrender, printed by the Buxton Press

Dedicated to the memory of all who took part
in the 1932 Kinder Mass Trespass

*Front cover: From a set of photographs of 1920-22 walks on Kinder and Bleaklow
by Donald Berwick, from the Peak and Northern Footpaths Society. Inset: The Kinder Trespass*

CONTENTS

FOREWORD

KATE ASHBROOK

It is with acute embarrassment that I quote my predecessor at the Open Spaces Society, Lawrence Chubb. In the July 1932 edition of the society's Journal, under the heading 'Mass Trespass', he writes (without mentioning the Kinder Trespass):

Demonstrations arranged with the object of asserting claims to rights where no reasonable claim can be advanced are entirely disapproved by the Society and by all serious ramblers, Rambling Clubs and Federations.

After fulminating about the evils of trespass he concludes:

If Access to Mountains or to any other tracts of land is to be secured for the public, it will be secured not by violent but by reasonable methods, leading perhaps to legislation in due course; and forcible disregard of legal rights will only hinder success.

His view, which was shared by many established groups, was of course thoroughly misguided, for the Trespassers had no intention of violence and were merely demonstrating with their feet that open country should be free to everyone. It did not take many years for the Ramblers' federations to recognise this, but it did take many years to effect change - and even that was limited.

Forbidden Kinder sets all this down as never before. Not only do we have here a variety of descriptions of the Trespass itself, from those who took part and their descendants, we are also presented with details of many of the Trespassers' lives, and of others in the struggle for access. The book concludes with short essays by current figures for whom Kinder the battle, and Kinder the mountain, have a place in their hearts. The scene is set, the context explained, the significance explored, and the aftermath related.

Keith Warrender

Kinder reservoir from Kinder Scout

There are differing views on what the Trespass actually achieved, but it is evident that the five Trespassers did not suffer their months in jail in vain. The severity of the sentences angered conservative ramblers, changed people's minds, and strengthened their resolve to campaign for increased access. Kinder is now an icon to our movement and we salute the courage and determination of those Trespassers led by the indefatigable Benny Rothman, a dear friend and comrade.

If only we could say that the Trespassers' work is done. But it is not.

Right now, we face greater threats to our rights and freedoms than at any time since the Second World War. The Westminster government is determined to extend trespass as a criminal offence, which will penalise gypsy, Roma, and traveller communities, and could entrap innocent wild campers. It is cracking down on our rights of peaceful protest. It is rewriting the Human Rights Act and the rules for judicial review, moving power from the judiciary to the executive.

It is failing to apply the public money which goes into farmers' pockets to encourage those farmers to provide more access - despite numerous promises from ministers. While, mercifully, it is still working on the England Coast Path it has no further plans to extend access rights - yet we have the right to walk on only eight per cent of England. What about access rights to woodlands and to water for instance, both foreshadowed in the Countryside Act 1968, more than 50 years ago?

So, in this ninetieth anniversary year of the Kinder Trespass, we must reignite the Trespassers' torch, create a mass movement, and march into a future where the people hold greater rights and freedoms over more land. What the Kinder Trespassers began, we must complete.

Access and walkers' rights campaigner **Kate Ashbrook** has been the general secretary of Britain's oldest national conservation body, the Open Spaces Society, for nearly 40 years. She is a former president and three-times chair of the Ramblers, and now a vice-president and member of the Ramblers' board of trustees. RS

Rock on Kinder almost resembling a piece of modern sculpture

Keith Warrender

INTRODUCTION

A new look at the 'half-minute battle'

The usually peaceful Sandy Heys Moor below Kinder Scout was the scene of imminent confrontation on Sunday 24 April 1932. A handful of keepers and others drafted in for the day moved forward with sticks raised, shouting at a huge crowd of advancing ramblers to turn back. The two sides eyed each other, neither wanting to give way. The 'half-minute battle', as it was later described in court, was about to start.

How had it come to this? The location of the incident was significant. They were on the lower slopes of 'Forbidden Kinder' - the high moorland that could only be accessed with written permission, and guarded zealously by the landowners' gamekeepers. Anyone caught on the plateau and this moor would be quickly and sometimes forcefully escorted off the land. On this day the ramblers were deliberately trespassing and prepared to face the consequences.

It had not always been this way. People remembered walking freely over Kinder in the first half of the nineteenth century, but then Kinder landowners began insisting their grouse-shooting interests should be protected from the ever-growing numbers of walkers. They believed, without any real evidence, that the presence of walkers disturbed grouse nesting grounds. As a consequence, Kinder became the 'Forbidden Mountain' for ramblers, and would remain so for nearly ninety years.

Valiant efforts were made by country access campaigners to get Parliamentary Acts passed, but the landowners were not prepared to compromise. Ramblers were frustrated that there was no public access to the great high moorland areas such as Kinder and Bleaklow. Walkers from the surrounding cities and towns of the Peak District came in their thousands, but were confined to limited tracks and footpaths, and could only look from a distance at the 2088ft high Kinder - the area's highest point.

The old-established rambling organisations continued to lobby Parliament and to hold annual rallies at the Winnats in support of legislation. They also did good work in maintaining and opening up footpaths and much else, but the great prize of freedom to roam the Dark Peak moors of Derbyshire eluded them. Despite the stirring rhetoric at the Winnats gatherings, change seemed far off, yet by the early 1930s, rambling had never been more popular as people sought escape from the grim conditions of the surrounding towns and cities. Pressure for more access to the mountains and moorlands was building.

If the rambling organisations would not go beyond achieving change through lobbying Parliament, others were plotting a different approach, to drive the process forward. And so on that Spring Sunday afternoon in 1932 Benny Rothman and hundreds of mainly young people from Lancashire and Yorkshire came onto this moor to hold a mass trespass - but would their actions finally bring breakthrough?

This book re-examines what happened next and everything connected with the protest. The Kinder Trespass is an iconic event in the campaign for access to the countryside, known to many through websites and publications, but how much of what you hear and read is correct? I want to reassure you I'm not trying to re-write history - the Trespass did occur and people were jailed. However, many of the things said about the incident are either untrue or not the whole truth, or more has been uncovered. Even though it is a subject which has interested me for many years, it continues to throw up surprises.

I have devoted part of the book to the largely unknown people who took part in the Trespass, including those who ended up in prison. With the exception of Benny Rothman and a handful of the trespassers, little is known about the hundreds who marched onto the slopes of Kinder. Through tracing some of their families I have come across many remarkable stories, as well as discovering important new information about the Trespass. I am most grateful for all their help and I will not give too much away here, except to say that some of the trespassers went on to be successful in business, others were involved in politics and campaigning for justice, and some gave their lives in the war against fascism in Spain. The search for the trespassers led into the world of professional football, speedway and even espionage.

In this story of how the previously forbidden Kinder became free for all to enjoy, you will also discover more about the roots of the dispute. I've tried to give a balanced view of the situation around the Trespass and so you will find portraits of some of the access campaign pioneers as well as an insight into the landowners and their gamekeepers.

The names of the great ramblers' leaders Tom Stephenson and GHB Ward crop up frequently but I've not gone into detail about them because their lives and work are extensively covered elsewhere. But the book does contain fascinating stories of their campaigning colleagues: Stephen Morton, Phil Barnes and Edwin Royce.

Everyone will have their own opinion about the place the Trespass holds in access history, but I've tried to answer some of the questions which critics of the Trespass pose, such as its impact on the campaign for access and the claim that it has become the 'mythical Trespass', and also to assess whether the Trespass really was forgotten for decades. I also examine the central issue of whether the presence of walkers was such a problem on the grouse moors.

You will find that Benny Rothman's account of the Trespass is not included. Benny's story remains the key eye-witness statement in our understanding of the Trespass, and it is still to be found in the book *The Battle For Kinder Scout*, along with lots of other information about the protest. However, you will discover much more about Benny's life and work in this new book in a moving portrait by his son Harry, who also generously gave me access to a huge collection of family photographs.

I'm grateful to John Beatty for his impressive photographs and I must also thank Nial and Philip Barnes, Janet Capstick, Jan Gillett, Peter Ames Greenall, Eva Lawson, Thomas Noel, The North East Labour Society, John and Philip Poole, Judy Skelton, Ian Watson and the Manchester Evening News for their kind permission to use their photographs

The book is part anthology and there is a full list of acknowledgments of all the contributors at the end, but I would like to mention a number of people. Firstly, my grateful thanks to Kate Ashbrook for her thought-provoking foreword and her general support for the book, and to the families of the Trespassers from around the world who so enthusiastically shared great insights into their lives, as well as supplying excellent photographs; to Terry Howard and David Sissons who answered my many questions particularly regarding Sheffield ramblers, and the help with my enquiries from David Toft of the Hayfield Kinder Trespass Group.

My appreciation for everyone who has written articles for the book, to Cynthia Hitchcock and Judith Warrender for their proofreading and to anyone else I may have inadvertently forgotten to mention.

I'm grateful to those who have contributed their wide range of experiences on Kinder and their views about the present and future for the countryside in the final chapter.

Finally, I must express special thanks to consultant editors Roly Smith and Tom Waghorn, for all their hard work, both for their written contributions and their wise advice and encouragement during the preparation of this book - referred to by Tom as KT3. It is my hope that this book will enable you to understand more clearly what happened at the Trespass and will also contribute towards its being remembered and celebrated for many years to come.

Keith Warrender

Please note, throughout this book Communist Party is abbreviated CP, Young Communist League YCL and British Workers' Sports Federation BWSF

Kinder becomes 'the forbidden mountain'

For centuries, most people who lived at the foot of its slopes had no desire or need to go onto Kinder. No doubt some energetic and curious locals climbed up to see the dramatic landscape for themselves, and there are tales of secret meetings on Kinder between landowners arranging how the plateau land could be divided up.

There were other visitors, for before Kinder became the 'Forbidden Mountain', generations of walkers had freely explored its slopes and plateau. A correspondent of the Manchester Graphical Society journal wrote that in the 1820s and 30s they were never challenged nor troubled as they explored Kinder. It was known to them as 'King's Land' or more appropriately 'No Man's Land' where people had the perfect right to cross in any direction. In the 1824 Sheffield Independent newspaper *Vignettes of Derbyshire* series, it described how, without any mention of keepers: 'From the tops of Kinder Scout, Bleaklow Stone and others among the highest in our district, we have looked upon the vallies beneath, blooming in all their pomp and glory...'

By the early 1840s some of the original footpaths had been lost with the enclosures, but the freedom to explore Kinder continued, as shown by an article in the *Manchester Courier* in 1843. In a series entitled *Railway Rambles* the writer, in rather flowery style, described the climb up to the plateau and then invited readers to linger there and enjoy the sights.

Amateur self-taught naturalists, geologists and botanists among the mill workers were also drawn to Kinder, as well as those who wanted to escape the dreadful conditions of the towns and cities. Mechanics' Institutes from surrounding areas also organised rambles and tours of the district.

Capstick Family

Sidebotham's refectory was reputed to have been the best stone cabin in the High Peak, with two rooms covered in stone slates, and standing on a green mound.

John Sidebotham, a cotton spinner and manufacturer, was well-known in the hunting circles but squandered his wealth by gambling. His cousin, Col William Sidebotham, took over the Lodge.

The cabin was demolished by keeper Sydney Capstick after vandalism. The stone plaque was removed in the 1960s and the ruins were blown up. The damaged plaque is now in the hands of the National Trust who are intending to restore it to a site on Kinder. Keeper, Sydney Capstick's son, Roger, is second right.

Signs of change

Change of ownership was imminent in 1868 when a thousand-acre section of Kinder was advertised to let as grouse moor by Thomas Hyde Marriott, a wealthy landowner from Sandbach. Since the mid-1850s there had been significant developments in grouse shooting with the introduction of the double-barrelled breech-loading shotgun and the new method of beaters driving the grouse out of their nests towards shooters hidden in a line of butts. This greatly increased the numbers of grouse shot and made it a more lucrative business on high moorland areas such as Kinder.

With the increasing numbers of ramblers wanting to walk over Kinder and the growth of grouse-shooting, a mixed response from landowners towards walkers was noted. The *Derbyshire Times* published a description in 1872 of a peaceful walk with a stop at Kinder Downfall for lunch, sitting on a bed of ferns and grasses and admiring the scenery below.

But that same year in the *Manchester Guardian*, in the earliest sign of trouble, a correspondent warned readers after his experience of being attacked by keepers and their dogs as he and his party tried to ascend Kinder, and then being forcibly ejected off the moor.

The letter prompted this reply from Walter Armitage of Huddersfield, a champion of farmers' rights:

Sir - It is quite clear there is a proper way of seeing Kinder Scout. The gentlemen who shoot there have perhaps as high an appreciation of the beauties of the district as the previous correspondent. From his letter your correspondent has been churlish about the pleasure party who had been allowed to ascend the hill. Therefore, let him and all tourists bear in mind that if they wish to visit Kinder Scout, there is such a thing as asking permission, and that if they venture to make the ascent without obtaining it they may be subjected to some inconvenience. If the publishers of guide books will kindly intimate as much to tourists I am sure they will not only do good to that enterprising but occasionally thoughtless body, but they will confer a boon on those who have the right of shooting over the wild Derbyshire hills.

The original incident also brought this reply from 'MOUNTAINEER' in the *Manchester Guardian*:

Sir - I was somewhat struck by the hints which it threw out to the unfortunate walker and to the public at large that they must not dare to ascend Kinder Scout without permission. I myself, with several friends, have frequently made this mountain a place of holiday resort, unmolested by gamekeepers... Scarcely a week before the 12th we indulged in a ramble upon these romantic heights for upwards of three hours; and last summer, on the very day that grouse shooting began, we made the ascent without suffering any inconvenience, although surrounded by shooting parties with their keepers and dogs. All the guide books speak of the place as being free to the public but as this idea seems to be a delusion, I would ask your correspondent from what quarter permission is to be sought before one perpetrates such an outrage as the ascent of the Peak.

MOUNTAINEER September 2, 1872.

William Gibb's shooting parties

The liberty to walk across Kinder unheeded was recalled in a letter to the *Hyde and Glossop Weekly* in 1876 by correspondent 'JBE of Marple'. This was James Booth Elverston, a Manchester cotton and linen merchant who recalled how he used to ramble freely over every part of Kinder Scout. But he had noted a change when William Purvis Gibb became manager of the Kinder Printing Works about 1873 and walkers began to be excluded from Kinder.

James Elverston was in a good position to know what was happening on Kinder. Not only was he an experienced walker, he was also a founding member of the Peak District and Northern Counties Footpaths Preservation Society, and its honorary treasurer. Many readers will know that it was this footpath society which successfully negotiated the reopening of the path between Hayfield and the Snake in 1897.

To be fair to Gibb, exclusion from Kinder began a year or so before he became manager, but he did make sure his shooting interests were protected. William Gibb succeeded his brother James as manager and although he was liked by the mill

Willow Publishing

Visitors at Edale Head c1900

owner and friends, Sam Garside in his history of the print works, had little good to say about him, writing that Gibb was originally a working machine printer who wormed his way to the top of the company.

Gibb was pertinacious, overbearing, stubborn, not to say stupid. His temper and disposition were most difficult to deal with. I never knew him to admit an error in his life, nor make the faintest admission that you could possibly be right. He never gave way. In matters of controversy, he would do all the talking, and his talk had much blustering in it. You could never get a word in edgeways; and at the end of an hour's wrangle you would find yourself yielding the position, without ever having the chance to defend it. No matter what the subject was - prices for printing, new machinery, sampling, or business matters of any kind, or politics, religion, sports, fishing, or shooting, he knew more on these matters than anyone present; and to dispute his dictum was to draw upon yourself a torrent of words.

Gibb lived the life of a country gentleman, residing in a large house and grounds at Kinder Bank, Hayfield, where he had stabling for two horses, a coachman and large expanses of greenhouses.

He was fond of flowers and always had an expensive buttonhole. He was extravagant both in his own personal affairs but also with the company finances. He only spent half the week at the works, but was said to have a good eye for colours and shades, and always demanded high-quality goods.

Gibb co-rented most of the grouse-shooting moor on Kinder from the owner. It was then that the practice of using keepers to patrol the grouse moors came into prominence. Walkers were no longer welcome, even though Gibb insisted that his keepers had never turned anyone away from Kinder - but this was simply untrue. There was further consternation in Hayfield that people were even being stopped from using the old-established Hayfield to Edale route. At a meeting in Hayfield in 1876 to form the Hayfield and Kinder Scout Ancient Footpaths Association, Gibb also suggested that a committee should meet to establish rights of way over various footpaths around Kinder. Gibb, who came from Lanark, took shooting parties on Kinder, then in 1885, perhaps with his health failing, he was leasing a cottage and 800 acres of grouse shooting on Kinder for two guineas a week or thirty guineas for the season. He died aged fifty-one in December 1886.

Stop all tourists on Kinder

The landowners' benevolent attitude to walkers had changed, and the new Kinder limits were indicated by an 1873 *Nottingham Journal* article, when a party found themselves on the slopes of Kinder near Upper House, which would later come into the ownership of James Watts. The group were stopped by a keeper who told them he had strict orders to stop all 'tourists' from ascending the moors above, unless they had a permit from those who rented them for shooting. The keeper was courteous, but firmly insisted they could go no further and escorted them off the moors. Even in 1896, others such as Charles Tallent Bateman, a friend of Kinder owner James Watts, still mistakenly believed that walkers were allowed on Kinder providing they kept off the skyline and did not interfere with the grouse-shoot.

Willow Publishing

Warning to excursionists

Visitor and walker numbers to the area increased with the opening of the railway line to Hayfield in 1868. Notices instructed the many visitors to keep off Captain White's Park Hall estate on the Kinder slopes unless they had permission. In 1875 there was a sudden increase in newspaper notices from an anonymous owner which warned ramblers in no uncertain terms to keep off Kinder. One read 'Notice to excursionists - Kinder Scout, together with all the adjoining moorlands and inlands, is strictly preserved. Trespassers will be prosecuted with the utmost rigour of the law'. A similar notice in 1877 also urged excursionists to keep to public paths. Then in 1880, it was advertised that permission could be obtained to ramble over the Scout or picnic there by contacting Joseph Walton at the Royal Hotel, Hayfield. Also, for moderate terms, there was shooting for several guns over 800 acres of grouse moor.

The *Derby Mercury* summed up the situation in 1876, writing *Upon the moors, the 'sacred grouse' claim precedence, and woe to the unlucky tourist who shall stray in the 'religious solitudes' where they breed during the close season.*

The first edition of the guide book *Kinder Scout with the foot paths and bridle roads about Hayfield* was published in 1877. It was so popular it was reprinted in 1880 but advised readers not to go onto Kinder. Abel Heywood's 1880 *Penny Guide to Hayfield and Kinder Scout* does not mention any restrictions on accessing Kinder, even though Heywood was a Vice President of the Peak District and Northern Counties Footpaths Preservation Society and knew that walkers were barred from Kinder.

An 1875 article entitled *How to See The Derbyshire Peak*, originally published in the *Gardener Magazine* echoed the visitors' disquiet at the closure of Kinder:

I would above all things advise you to put down in your list a trip to Hayfield and an ascent of Kinder Scout. The owner of the fine mountain that bears this name is not an angel; he is not, even such a genial gentleman as the owner of a mountain ought to be, and, in the endeavour to look like a curmudgeon, he has actually shut the mountain up. But you can scour the Scout if you mean it, and stay at the snug hotel at Hayfield. Should you fail to reach the head of Kinder, you may nevertheless do well for entertainment here for the scenery is everywhere fine and the views from the heights extensive.

Willow Publishing

Harry Rothman

KINDER SCOUT.—NOTICE TO EXCUR-
SIONISTS.—KINDER SCOUT, together with all the adjoining Moorlands and Inlands, is strictly preserved. Trespassers will be prosecuted with the utmost rigour of the law.

Above: James Watts and friends on a Kinder walk
Left: 1875 warning notice to ramblers

Louis Jennings in his 1880 *Rambles Amongst the Hills* highlighted the problems of the visitor to Kinder:

> The first discovery which my inquiries brought to light was that the Kinderscout is regarded as strictly private property, and that it is divided up among numerous holders, almost all of whom are at loggerheads with each other and with the public ... There are said to be certain public rights of footway, but they do not appear to lead to the best points, and even in regard to these there are constant disputes. Moreover, they are hard to find amidst a labyrinth of heath and ferns, and it is not unusual for the game keepers to turn strangers back even when they are upon the paths which are supposed to be fairly open to all.
>
> The owners of the moor are jealous to the last degree of their rights, and quarrel over the few birds which by some accident are still left as though the cause of empire were at stake. This arises from the foolish way in which the district has been parcelled out among small holders, in patches not much larger than a table-cloth. One man's allotment is actually under two acres in extent, and his only chance of getting a shot is on the days when his neighbours are out shooting, and the grouse are driven over his field. Then he stands waiting for a chance, and if he can manage to bring a bird down on his little patch, he has had a fine day's sport, but if the bird drops outside his boundary, he goes home with an empty bag.
>
> The stranger in these parts would naturally pay very little heed to local troubles and bickerings if he did not speedily find that they materially interfered with his freedom. If you go to the right you are liable to be warned off; if to the left, to be threatened with an action for trespass. You get permission from three or four different holders, and find that there is still another who bars the way. While mentioning these facts, however, I am bound to add that personally I experienced no inconvenience whatever.

The situation had become frustrating for ramblers - the once free moors were 'no-go areas'. The campaign to get access was soon under way in 1884 with an attempted Access to Mountains Bill, but with the exception of those who either had permits or simply trespassed, Kinder would remain officially forbidden to walkers for nearly ninety years before they could freely traverse the plateau.

Origins
of the Kinder Trespass

The core of the protesters on the Kinder Trespass were members of fifteen clubs from the Lancashire district of the British Workers' Sports Federation and supported by a further two from Sheffield. However in the pre-publicity it was made clear that everyone was welcome, including other rambling clubs.

The BWSF claimed there should be a right of way over areas of great beauty such as Kinder Scout where there were no public footpaths. All the old established rambling clubs disagreed with the protest and refused to take part, although some of their members did. But what were the British Workers' Sports Federation's origin and motives?

Footballs
not cannonballs

The BWSF was jointly founded in 1923 by the Labour Party, the National Clarion Cycling Club and various trade unions in order to take part in the International Socialist Federation's activities. Their early slogan was 'Footballs instead of cannonballs'. The London Federation was successful in establishing football leagues and providing good pitches.

The BWSF participated in an International Workers Olympics in 1925, then in 1927 a Federation football team was invited to go on a two-week playing tour of Moscow, paid for by the Soviet Government. By 1928 most of the BWSF had been taken over by communists, although the Dundee District secretary claimed his branch was not affiliated to any political organisation nor religious creed. The BWSF took part in the 1928 Moscow Spartakiad and by 1930 had three thousand members.

About 1929, local groups were formed in Moss Side, Stockport, Manchester, Eccles, Swinton and other areas using cycling, rambling and physical culture as a means to promote their political beliefs. The Cheetham branch, to which Benny Rothman belonged, was essentially a rambling and camping club comprised of about twenty-five Jewish members. Benny became secretary of the BWSF Manchester Committee in 1930. Groups such as this attracted working class youth who wanted to escape at weekends from the miserable conditions of towns and cities. For Jewish youth it was also an opportunity to get away from the restrictions of immigrant life.

'Bosses' organisations'

The Young Communist League began their Red Sports Clubs in 1923 as a rival to existing youth organisations such as the Boy Scouts and Girl Guides which were considered bourgeois and bosses organisations. The BWSFs aim was to influence young people through sport and rambling. By 1933 it had an estimated membership around Manchester of about three hundred, approximately 40% of whom were members of the Young Communist League. According to Benny Rothman, most of the BWSF were ramblers with leftish leanings.

Federation split

Clarion members withdrew from the Federation in 1928 followed by Labour Party members and union members to form the rival British Workers' Sports Association, while the BWSF continued to organise sports and campaign against growing restrictions on camping. Benny Rothman remained with the BWSF until about 1933 but by 1935 it ceased to exist. In a 1932 article in *The Worker Sportsman* magazine Benny was encouraging readers to join the BWSF, both to agitate for better conditions for working-class outdoor men and women and to fight the war preparations against Russia and China.

Clough Head Farm camp 1932 with Benny Rothman (right) doing the cooking. The marquee (left) was home-made, and the bell tents (right) were hired.

B. W.S.F. LANCS EASTER CAMP Arrangements.—Camp address, Tomlinson, Clough Head Farm. Hayfield. One mile (20 min.) from Stones Head. Rambles to Camp, Thursday midnight, meet 9.0 p.m., Tram Clock, Piccadilly. Friday, meet 9.0 a.m., Piccadilly. 9d. return.

BWSF Camps

The camps would have been the first introduction to camping for many, and contact with the opposite sex a big attraction. One of the campers who later joined the 'Black Shirts' was predictably scathing about the BWSF camps, describing them as a place of 'bedlam, sexual immorality, filthy jokes, drinking and communist depravity'.

Benny Rothman admitted his main job was to keep the sexes apart. He and Harry Mendel had a long stick which they used to lift the sides of tents to make sure that same sexes were sleeping in the single bed accommodation.

Miserable first night

The first Easter camp was held in 1930 at Arthur Tomlinson's Clough Head Farm, Rowarth near Hayfield, and according to Benny Rothman's 1931 newspaper article, (see next page) the preparation had been last-minute and the first night had been miserable because of thick snow. Many had gone to the camp ill-equipped for bad weather. Campers walked around all night trying to keep warm, and some collected wood for camp fires. Benny added that things went much more smoothly over the

following days. One hundred and eighty came to the camp from twenty towns and districts, with thirty tents pitched over the four days. There was an Irish stew night and musical evenings, and some from the camp helped to extinguish a local fire by torchlight.

At the 1931 camp, the guests were told that they were part of the struggle against war, while other organisations were heading towards future conflict. Many of Benny's motor trade colleagues were regulars at the camps.

1932 camp

The 1932 Easter camp was again at Clough Head Farm, Rowarth and there was also an organised ramble to the camp from Manchester, meeting at the tram clock, Piccadilly at 9am, for a cost of 9d return.

A Whit Week camp was held at Rosehill, Marple with sixty people attending. Organiser, Lance Helman, reported that they had suffered four days of continued rain but a good time was had by all, and there had been a few illnesses treated by the on-site doctor and nurses. A sailor came to the camp on the Saturday to give a lecture on the 1931 mutiny in the fleet at Invergordon, when about a thousand naval personnel demonstrated over paycuts of up to 25%. On the Sunday night after the sing-song a resolution was passed: 'Not a gun, not a ship against the USSR and we will defend the workers' country to the last drop of blood'. It was during the 1932 camp that the key incident with the keepers on Bleaklow occurred which sowed the seeds of the Kinder Trespass - see Benny Rothman's account next page.

In 1933 the camp moved to Jesse Eyre's Ringstones Farm, Rowarth, with Lance Helman the organiser at Easter. Martin Bobker was the contact for the 1934 Whit and August camps which were promoted as 'bigger and better than ever' with organised rambles, open-air swimming, camp fires and sports. The following year, a peace camp was held at Wortley near Sheffield.

Above right: Camp sites around Rowarth. Below: Former Trespassers at the Wortley camp: back row, second left, Jud Clynes. Front row, Max Clynes with Angela, his future wife behind.

The plan to trespass
BENNY ROTHMAN

I was the secretary of the BWSF for the north. We were a working class sports movement and were part of a national organisation, mainly centred in London with some groups in Scotland. In London, they were mainly people who were interested in football and other sports. In Scotland it was similar but in Manchester, for various reasons, we were more of an open-air movement and did a great deal of camping and rambling.

My interests were camping, cycling and rambling, which I'd been doing regularly at weekends with lads from work from about 1925 onwards. So through the BWSF we started to run camps, generally at places like Marple or Rowarth. They were run on a shoestring, and some of the equipment was very rough and ready - a lot of ex-army stuff and big pans for boiling spuds, an old marquee we'd got from somewhere. There was no money, and we ran savings clubs so that people could go to them. Some of the people who came were hard pushed even to borrow a blanket from home, let alone a sleeping bag.

We froze and got wet occasionally, but there was a very good atmosphere at these camps. We had a good comradely spirit, and in spite of the fact that our facilities were so much inferior to some of the other more organised groups, we were quite a magnet. We'd have fifty or sixty people at a weekend, all ages from fifteen to over fifty, and we introduced a lot of young people to the outdoors. Our weekend activities were mainly rambling,

with sing-songs round the campfire at night. One of my jobs was segregating the sexes - quite a job of course, and to what extent we were successful I don't know, but we had to try hard because the Local Authority could come round to inspect for cleanliness and behaviour and would be on the lookout for any excuse to close down the camp, so we never gave them any.

It was at the discussions round the fire at these camps that the first glimmerings of the wholesale process of theft by which these Derbyshire moors fell into private hands came about, but the Mass Trespass itself grew out of one particular incident. We were running a camp at Rowarth in 1932, and some of the London section of the BWSF were there. I think there were six or seven of us, including a couple of youngsters from London, set out for a ramble on Bleaklow. When we got to Yellowslacks, we were met by a group of keepers who accosted us in a very nasty threatening way, telling us they were going to knock hell out of us.

We turned back - there was no point in having a pitched battle because we'd have lost. We went away very crestfallen and angry, naturally. When we got back to the camp we were incensed to have been humiliated in front of our visitors, to be turfed off like that. I should have known better because on Bleaklow, which is the biggest stretch of open moorland in Derbyshire, if you wanted to get onto it, you'd got to trespass, and then you faced not only the

continued next page

landowners' keepers who could be very rough, who'd think nothing of beating you up if you were on your own - but also the waterworks keepers who were determined to keep you away from the various reservoirs in the area, in the belief that the water would be polluted if anybody walked in the vicinity - or that was their story.

Anyhow, I should have known better than to try to get them over Bleaklow. I'd been there many a time, of course, but it was round a holiday period when it was lousy with keepers, and at least, I should have taken them along one of the few public footpaths that go across Derbyshire. These had been established through the efforts of our predecessors.

After the camp closed and we got back to Manchester, we got our heads together and decided that keepers could stop half a dozen or ten of us, but they couldn't stop a big crowd and so we planned a mass trespass across Derbyshire and we picked Kinder Scout.

Many years later I was in Hayfield speaking to one of the young Peak Park wardens and he was very interested as to why we chose Kinder and I couldn't give him a very direct answer except Kinder is the highest point in Derbyshire. It was a challenge. It was something that you saw every time you went into Hayfield or Edale or Castleton. You wouldn't see much of Bleaklow, even from Glossop, because it's rather tucked out of sight.

● Benny Rothman in interviews with Graham Atkinson for the *Socialist Worker* in 1978, and Jim Perrin for the *Climber & Rambler* magazine in 1990.

Right: 1931 Daily Worker article by Benny Rothman

GET READY FOR EASTER CAMP NOW

Manchester Have Learnt Last Year's Lesson

A CHEAP HOLIDAY

Summer's coming, and now is the time to get busy with arrangements for your Easter camp; it's not too soon, and there is plenty needs doing to ensure success.

Compared with other sports, camping isn't dear—3s. per head will sleep you really well, if you whack it out together and buy a strong bell tent. Apart from a groundsheet and a stove, there is nothing else you need buy, as you use blankets, towels, pots, pans, and other camping paraphernalia all the year round at home. So don't let the "expense" frighten you.

Manchester B.W.S.F. won't forget last year's Easter camp in a hurry. The arrangements were left until the last minute, and then the rush started. Borrowing cash for hiring tents. Scrounging tents and buckets and groundsheets. Wondering how we could lug the stuff down, and then the last minute job of pitching the tents.

The first night was the worst, and several members of the camp who had lain shivering and quivering all night, gingerly felt themselves in the morning to make sure that they hadn't died of cold.

But we did have a good time after that terrible "first night." The moral of this story is make your arrangements in good time.

The South Manchester B.W.S.F. have decided to go forward right away. The camping section is free to members with tents; and from those without we are asking an entrance fee of 1s. 6d.

Non-members of the club can join the camping section by payment of an entrance fee of 1s. for those with tents, and 3s. for those without, and then a small subscription of 3d. per month.

Kit is being collected and a suitable site is being procured, and we hope to have a real rousing Easter camp.

Workers who wish to try camping are advised not to suffer the miseries of the inexperienced by being outside the B.W.S.F. camping section. Get in touch right now with your local B.W.S.F. In Manchester the address is: Bernard Mothman, 15, Granton Street. Cheetham, Manchester.

Looking towards Kinder from the Ringstones Farm campsite

Previous protests

Benny Rothman earlier described how the idea for the Trespass originated after being turned off Bleaklow. He wrote about it in the third person in his published 1982 account, but in other interviews he appeared to have been present. The BWSF presented the mass trespass as their own idea and it is not clear whether Benny and his friends knew of previous trespasses and the work of older rambling organisations.

They were aware of the attempts to pass the Access to Mountains Act and the lack of progress but did they know of earlier protests? Seven years previously a hundred and fifty Manchester ramblers and members of Hyde and District Footpath Society began a series of protest walks to reopen the Benfield path which had been closed by farmers at Woodley. Just two years before the Kinder Trespass, six hundred people protested over the closure of an ancient right of way at Dutton near Blackburn.

There was also the biggest-ever land-rights dispute at Winter Hill in 1896 when over twenty thousand people demonstrated on two weekends over a blocked-off road. There were no prosecutions in any of these protests, but these and other incidents show there was commitment to trespass to the west of the Peak District just as there was in Sheffield.

Had the organisers of the Trespass heard of William Chadwick, the last of the old Manchester Chartists, who threatened in 1894 to walk over Kinder, even if he were to be imprisoned? However, a committee of the Peak District and Northern Counties Footpaths and Preservation Society formed a few days later, persuaded him that such action might ruin their attempts at peaceful negotiation over re-opening the Snake footpath. The Society was led by prominent businessmen and local officials from Manchester who would not have wanted confrontation with the law.

Benny Rothman during the hearing at the magistrates court in 1932 after the Trespass, quoted the example of action taken by ramblers to reopen the Doctor's Gate footpath which indicates the BWSF did have some knowledge of past protests.

There was a significant difference with the protest on Kinder from past mass trespasses. The organisers were not disputing the closure of an ancient right of way, but were challenging the right of landowners to prevent ramblers from having some access to one the wildest and most spectacular areas in the Peak District. It was a significant step in the campaign for the freedom to roam.

Hiking and camping in the 1930s*

SOL GADIAN - Kinder Trespasser

I had socialist friends at the factory where I worked in Manchester who were keen hikers and cyclists and took great delight in physical exercise. My whole way of life began to change. Instead of going to theatres and cinemas at weekends, I began to go for walks in the country. I became a keen hiker and bought all the necessary equipment. Four of us purchased a bell tent with floor boards, blankets, stove, pots and pans, and established ourselves at Ashes farm, Hayfield.

We joined the YMCA and began to do two or three nights' physical training each week. No longer was I to be seen in a neat tailored suit. Now I was wearing slacks, sports jacket and a khaki shirt opened at next-to-the-second button. I became so keen on the open-air life that during the spring and summer months I would leave work on a Friday evening, change into my rambling clothes, get the train to Hayfield and walk to the farm. With the help of my friends we would put up the tent for the weekend. From there we would walk over Kinder to Castleton, Edale and up Mount Famine.

Above and right: Harry Mendel & Sol Gadian

Heated political discussion

We would take chest expanders, boxing gloves and skipping ropes. When friends visited us, the camp site would become a hive of physical activity and tests of strength. In this way we spent the summer months, but now and again, we would get involved in heated political discussion.

Escape to the country

Hiking and cycling were the working youth's way to enjoy the countryside, the open-air life and exercise as an alternative and escape from social conditions around them. On a Saturday afternoon or Sunday morning, London Road (Piccadilly) Station would be crowded with young men and women going on cheap excursion trains to Marple, New Mills and Hayfield.

A few sandwiches and a pot of tea at one of the many tea-shops would see you through the day. An Easter, Whit Week, or a long weekend, could be managed on a few shillings. The return trains home would be crowded with singing ramblers and campers. It was even possible to take a 4d tram ride to Hyde from Manchester then walk to Marple.

After a year of camping at Ashes Farm, we decided to move and were accommodated by the farmer at Higher Bradshaw, Rowarth. We were given a plot of land surrounded by a high dry-stone wall next to the barn, and told that when we closed up for the weekend, it would not be necessary to drop the tent because the farmer would ensure its safety. We stayed at this farm for many years and became almost members of the family.

BWSF camp improvements

The experience of the Mass Trespass and the great interest in camping and rambling led to myself and Wolfie Winnick forming a rambling club. Within a few weeks we had recruited seventy members who paid 2d a week. We decided to call the club 'The Red Star Ramblers' and each member was issued with a small red five-pointed star cut from leather cloth. The stars were sewn onto rucksacks and berets. We affiliated to the Ramblers' Federation and sent two delegates to their meetings.

Throughout the summer and autumn we organised regular rambles, sometimes having as many as forty. We organised a weekend

camp at Higher Bradshaw Farm but as the facilities were not close enough, we found a new site at Rowarth (Ringstones Farm). During this period we maintained the BWSF camp here, spending as many weeks as possible there, and becoming known to many friends who would occasionally pay us a visit.

One weekend, the farmer suggested that he was prepared to build us a small wooden hut which would be more comfortable than the bell tent. That autumn and winter he built a two-roomed hut. One room had a rough wooden table with cupboards, shelves and a small stove in the corner. The other room had two, two-tier bunks and a small window for ventilation. The hut was a great improvement as compared to the room and facilities of our bell-tent, and we were only too pleased to increase our rent from 2s6d to 5s a week rent. More and more young lads and girls made our hut a meeting place for a day out, and often on a warm sunny weekend we would have about twelve visitors chatting politics, sun bathing, using the boxing gloves or going on short walks. They would end their day walking over to Marple Station or Bottom Hall and a tram home from Hyde.

The YCL ran many weekend youth camps at Rowarth, charging a few shillings for use of bell tents and cooking facilities. Later old army cooks were used to provide meals. As the popularity of the weekends grew, camps were organised at Edale, Little Hayfield and Abergele.

*Extract from Sol Gadian's memoir

Gadian family

The Trespass re-examined

For decades the people of Hayfield had grown used to the large influx of visitors into the village, mainly from the Manchester and Sheffield districts, at week-ends and bank holidays. At the 1932 Easter break before the Trespass, about two thousand people arrived by train from Manchester and large numbers by bus, along with many others from Sheffield. The trains were often so full that girls used to sit in the luggage racks. Numbers were swelled by the added attraction of an Easter fair in the village, along with many campers.

The Easter Sunday evening was wet, cold and windy, which drove some away, but an estimated ten thousand people passed through Hayfield en route to the Hope Valley over the holiday weekend. The track from Hayfield to Edale was so congested it was described as 'black with people' because of the restrictions on where they could roam. Another reporter described the overcrowded footpath as looking like a human caterpillar wound round the hill.

Thousands of ramblers from local federations acted as wardens in the Peak District because of past

Willow Publishing

Willow Publishing

RAMBLERS' SPIRITS UNDAMPED

Drenched but Happy

Heavy rain yesterday morning did not deter thousands of ramblers in Derbyshire who braved the elements, well equipped with capes and macintoshes. Many got drenched before dinner-time, but when the sun broke out in the afternoon they had forgotten their troubles. About a score of special trains were run to the Hope Valley, and carried about 10,000 people. Thousands more used the augmented 'bus services, and a large contingent tramped out from Sheffield.

The heavy rain overnight had made the moorland tracks rather treacherous.

Top: 1931 Punch cartoon illustrating the crowded countryside
Above: Hayfield postcard c1915
Right: Newspaper article Easter 1932

damage to walls, growing crops and farm buildings. There were also problems with litter and disturbance of bird and plantlife. Tighter bye-laws had been introduced, and this deterrent, along with the rambler patrols around Hayfield and Kinder, seemed to have improved the situation.

The week before the Trespass

But 1932 was to be different, for in addition to the usual hordes of visitors, the villagers heard there was to be a mass trespass on Kinder Scout which no doubt filled them with unease. The Sunday before the protest, leaflets were circulated around Hayfield and word was spread among ramblers. Leaflets were handed out around Greater Manchester, and one read: 'It is a crime where Lord Big-Bug and Lady Little-Bug do their big shoot. Come and join a fighting organisation'. The rally before the Trespass would begin at 2pm at Hayfield recreation ground.

Newspaper distortions

As Lancashire Secretary of the BWSF, Benny Rothman had been delegated to be interviewed by the newspapers. Benny explained the aim of the federation was to acquire better facilities and prevent the closure of footpaths. They would meet at Hayfield, before going to demonstrate on Kinder Scout with fifteen Lancashire and two Sheffield clubs of the federation participating. He hoped that unaffiliated clubs would support it, and it would lead to the formation of a federation of ramblers who were prepared to trespass wherever it seemed right for ramblers to go.

The basic facts were embellished by journalists, with the *Manchester Evening News* reporting that the BWSF was going to 'throw 200 or 300 shock troops into an attack upon Kinder'. Later in the trial of the trespassers, it was admitted this emotive phrase was the invention of the journalist Ted Castle, the news editor whom Benny Rothman went to see on the Monday before the Trespass. The newspaper followed this up with a letter in its correspondence column from 'an old rambler' attacking the proposed trespass, and a critical editorial entitled 'The right and wrong ways to achieve access to the mountains'.

TED CASTLE (1907-1979)

Castle, the reporter responsible for penning the phrase 'throwing shock troops upon Kinder', came to the *Manchester Evening News* in 1931 having previously worked at newspapers in Portsmouth, Southampton and Newcastle. He worked at the *Daily Mirror* in 1943 with a brief period in between as editor of *Picture Post*. During his time at the *Mirror* as assistant editor, he met his future wife Barbara who was then the

housing correspondent. Barbara Castle went on to become a formidable MP and government minister, and it was said that Ted was the only person who could tell her what to do!

Early in his career he was known as 'Red Ted' because of his firm support for the Labour Party and his enthusiastic singing of the Red Flag. He used to wear a wide-brimmed black hat and was often mistaken for the fascist leader, Oswald Mosley. He made one unsuccessful attempt to become an MP, but was for many years an alderman in local government. Castle became a Life Peer in 1974, then a Euro MP in 1975. He returned to the House of Lords and advised his wife on European politics.

Barbara Castle gave a message of support for the Trespass in the the 70th anniversary celebration programme. Barbara developed her love of walking in the Peak District and both she and Ted had been keen ramblers.

Hostile reaction

The *Evening Chronicle* carried an editorial against the Trespass, and continued with an article in the regular *Northern Window* column with the disturbing sub-heading *Mob Law on the Moors*. They also published a letter from the Manchester secretary of the Ramblers' Federation condemning the protest.

The two Manchester evening papers reflected the general view of the rambling world that a mass trespass would be a mistake. The membership of the BWSF was quite youthful whereas the established rambling clubs, comprised of older members, wanted to negotiate concessions with landowners. Unfortunately they were making no progress, but they feared a mass trespass would set them back even further if landowners were antagonised. They preferred to trespass individually or in small numbers and hoped to evade the keepers, or apply for permission to go onto the privately-owned moors. In this situation, land owners for many years had not felt under any real pressure to grant further rights to ramblers.

'Our grouse is grouse'

The rambling clubs advised caution but Benny and his friends were frustrated by the lack of progress and wanted to see if direct action would change the minds of the landowners. The day before the Trespass, a *Daily Worker* article read: 'Our grouse is grouse' is the slogan of the Lancashire ramblers, who are out for action to open up for worker-ramblers, the fine country now denied them by rich landowners, who are only concerned with preserving game for their own sport. Tomorrow's attack on parasitic privilege is being organised by the BWSF.'

The Derby newspapers were also against the protest with one correspondent writing: 'Such unconstitutional action is calculated only to make more difficult the negotiations now in progress by friendly overtures to secure all access that is required by all lovers of the countryside to spots which so far have been away from recognised paths'. Another letter suggested that campaigning should be left to the Peak District and Northern Counties Preservation Society.

CLAIMS TO FREE ACCESS

CAMPAIGN TO FORCE LANDOWNERS

CALL TO RALLY

SUNDAY'S ATTACK ON KINDER

Tired of unproductive protests and pleas, working class rambling clubs in Lancashire have decided upon direct action to enforce their claims for access to beauty spots in the country-side.

Sheffield reaction

In Sheffield there was a more cautious approach with the sympathetic *Independent*, although not publicly backing the Trespass, claiming the ramblers were not demanding the right to cross Kinder as and when they pleased but were highlighting that there were no public footpaths on this popular beauty spot.

The article writer went on to say he was not able to argue the rights and wrongs of it all, but there were likely to be strange scenes on Kinder the following Sunday, with about a hundred Sheffield ramblers expected to take part.

Sheffield and District Ramblers Federation did not give their official approval, with John Tate, its treasurer, stating he knew nothing of the proposed trespass, and did not want to be involved in sharing information about it.

Concern in Hayfield

Publicity about the Trespass, and the talk of mob rule and shock troops, predictably raised deep concerns in Hayfield, including the landowners and Derbyshire police force. The Trespass organisers tried to allay certain fears by promising to avoid the fields of smaller farms.

Although the people of Hayfield welcomed 'true ramblers', they were dismayed by a regular small influx of visitors over the last few years using foul language, with some being fined by New Mills magistrates. Rowdyism was particularly rife on Sundays with the singing of profane and obscene songs and ballads, and damage to gates and property being particular problems. The normal peaceful atmosphere of the village was shattered by the general Sunday morning babble with singing and the playing of banjo and ukeleles, and general horse-play. The high spirits were perhaps understandable after spending the week in grimy surroundings. There was also unfavourable comment about the short skirts and bright jumpers worn by female ramblers.

In view of the experience of unruly visitors and the threat of a 'great invasion' of ramblers, Hayfield villagers braced themselves and the police and landowners made their plans. Perhaps the landowners had reasons to be anxious but the villagers' fears were unnecessary - the 'townie' protesters weren't planning to cause disruption or damage - they wanted to demonstrate peacefully in favour of the countryside they loved being open to all. They certainly weren't 'a bunch of politically inspired hooligans' as labelled by a recent writer.

The day of the Trespass

Ramblers arriving at Hayfield station were handed a leaflet about the protest. Details were also chalked on the roads. Dave Nesbitt had been seen by the police selling the *Daily Worker*, shouting it was the only newspaper supporting the Trespass.

Benny and his friend and sparring partner, Wolfie Winnick, arrived early in Hayfield to make the final arrangements. By cycling there, they avoided the police at London Road station, Manchester who, it is claimed, were waiting to serve an injunction on Benny. They had called at his address several times during the previous days but, at that time, he lodged elsewhere to avoid being a burden on his family while he was unemployed. The police were also at Hayfield station hoping to detain him there.

Benny stated later, he had never travelled to Hayfield by train, as he could not afford the 3/2d fare. Benny and his friend stored their bikes at their regular haunt - the Stones Head tea room on Highgate, a favourite rendezvous of ramblers and also the home of John Simmonds, one of the Trespassers. This was on the upper floor of the cottages which had once been a Wesleyan school room.

Opposite page: Manchester Evening News article, Monday 18 April
Below: Stones Head tea room, Hayfield, where visitors gathered to be led to the BWSF camp at Rowarth

Keith Warrender

Trespass route surveyed

As Benny and Wolfie surveyed the possible routes to Kinder, they spotted groups of keepers already in position on the moors. They could see that the threat of a planned trespass was being taken seriously. There was likely to be confrontation and resistance, but there was no going back, the arrangements were in place. The situation must have seemed daunting but there was a steely determination to carry out their objective. On the way back to Hayfield they looked out for possible meeting places where they could give instructions to the crowd.

Recreation ground

They got back at about one o'clock to find the village teeming with ramblers as they began assembling at the pre-arranged meeting place, which was already ringed by police. An estimated third of the Derbyshire force were there, including the deputy chief constable, two superintendents, and reinforcements hidden away in the local cinema.

Also present were most of the local councillors who had taken steps earlier in the week to ensure that everyone knew that meetings were not permitted there, with copies of the byelaws liberally posted around the village. Herbert Bradshaw, Clerk of the Parish Council, was on hand to read out the byelaws if the ramblers attempted to make speeches. Playing games was also forbidden including leap frog

as some of the ramblers found out. It may have been known as a recreation ground but sport and exercise here were out of the question!

It was at the recreation ground that the decision was made on who was to to speak to the crowd. It's always been assumed that it was a last minute change at the next location, but in a description of the Trespass written by Rothman before his published account in 1982, he stated that after a quick consultation it was agreed it would be unwise for the original person to address the gathering due to his job, so it was decided that Benny should address the meeting.

The speaker

Who was the man whom Benny replaced? In his 1982 book, Benny gives a different version of events, and identified the man as Jack Clayton, 'one of the older members ... he was a very good speaker with an excellent knowledge of the history of the fight for access to the mountains ... a fine strapping chap and well-spoken but felt unable to speak at the meeting

Recreation ground

The land had been given to the parish by Francis Sumner of nearby Park Hall many years before, and in the past there were stipulations about its use, including the instructions males and females should stay apart, and that the site should not be used for bleaching cloth nor beating carpets. No obscene publications were to be sold there, nor the utterance of any profane talk or songs.

Hayfield recreation ground

Keith Warrender

The Trespassers set off

because it might have affected his job'. In an interview with Jim Perrin, Benny said Jack was 'a very able professional chap, quite a left-winger. But when we got to the quarry, he decided he didn't like the way it had been bounced on him and decided not to speak and asked 'Bunny', Benny's name in those days, to find a replacement. 'When you see there are a couple of hundred policemen and four hundred ramblers who'd turned up, I suppose it might make you a bit timid.' Jack later spoke at the 'victory' meeting at Ashop Head, but through not speaking at the quarry meeting, he avoided jail and went on to have a remarkable career, as recorded by his daughter later in this book.

The large police presence at the recreation ground concerned Benny and his fellow organisers because there was the possibility they would prevent the protest happening, and so they circulated a message for the crowd and those in nearby cafes and tea-rooms, to move off. Recently, it has been claimed that the police could have used their 'kettling' technique on the gathered ramblers, but as was later confirmed in court, the crowd had not broken the law at that point, so the police were unable to take any action.

The *Reporter* newspaper stated, without any evidence given, that most of the crowd were in opposition to it! I don't think that was true, the vast majority were there to play their part in the challenge to the private own-ership of the moors. They knew that this was far more than just a day out walking. There were certainly people present who were against the Trespass, such as John Anderson who had accidentally come across the protesters in the recreation ground, and William

Hanley and friends who came to witness the proceedings. There is also the account of Victor Wall who admitted he didn't take the protest as seriously as Rothman and his fellow organisers. But the presence of these people does not mean that most there were against the Trespass.

Water board site

The noisy throng of young ramblers marched out of Hayfield singing and came to a halt at a possible meeting site. This was Puddle Field just off Kinder Road, so named because it was the source of the puddling clay used to form the core of the Kinder Reservoir dam. Years before it had been the site of a print works, and before that cutlery production took place there which possibly pre-dated Sheffield.

It was not a good place for the ramblers to gather as it was water board property rented by a farmer and they were warned off by two officials stationed there. The ramblers had no wish to antagonise the water authority at this stage although the publicly-elected water boards were just as intransigent towards ramblers as the private landowners. So they moved on to another location noted by Benny and Wolfie.

Bowden Bridge Quarry

They had spotted an old quarry which made an ideal place for a meeting. This was Bowden Bridge Quarry which had been worked in 1910 for pitching stone used to face the Kinder Reservoir dam. The quarry was on land owned by the Calico Printers Association, opposite the former Kinder Print Works and mill pond. There used to be sidings here to transport stone in railway wagons to the earth bank of the dam, once the biggest of its kind in the world. The crowd was ushered onto the site to be given the all-important instructions about the planned trespass. The amphitheatre-like surroundings of the quarry and the acoustics made it ideal for speeches. Today it is a car park, with a plaque celebrating the actions of the Trespassers.

It is the name of Benny Rothman which is most associated with the Trespass, but it could have been so different. Benny was part of the organising committee, he had contacted the local newspapers and had co-planned the route of the Trespass. But he is perhaps best known for giving the speech in the quarry and issuing instructions on how the protesters were to follow the whistle blasts.

Keith Warrender

Benny Rothman at Bowden Bridge quarry 1982

Willow Publishing

Willow Publishing

Top: Bowden Bridge quarry (lower left) looking towards Kinder. Above: Trespassers assembled in the quarry

As I have previously stated, Benny was a last-minute stand-in for the scheduled speaker. If he had not bravely stood up and given an impromptu talk, maybe the protest wouldn't have gone ahead and five men would have been spared jail.

What happened next in the quarry was, in effect, a mini-Winnats rally, except this time there were no politicians present and most significantly, instead of fiery speeches and lobbying Parliament, there was going to be direct action. Benny, still wearing his cycling semi-plus-fours, scrambled onto a rock and after being introduced by fellow organiser Lance Helman, announced himself as the secretary of the Lancashire British Workers Sports Federation.

Inset: Plaque unveiled at the 50th Kinder Trespass anniversary. Above: The crowd listening to Benny Rothman

Keith Warrender

Willow Publishing

Benny's speech

Without any preparation, he gave a brief account of the Enclosure Acts stealing land from the people, and how the landowners had managed to thwart attempts for nearly fifty years to pass a Parliamentary bill which would give ramblers legal access to the mountains and moorlands. Benny said they could not wait any longer for change and so the Trespass would begin the campaign of access to mountains, hopefully in conjunction with other organisations.

He said it was only by action that ramblers could achieve their reasonable demands. Benny told them he wasn't sure whether they would succeed in getting on the moors because he thought there could be a hundred gamekeepers waiting for them. Benny dramatically said they had been warned that they may get lost and die of exposure on Kinder, so they had to keep together.

Watched also by the trilby-hatted water board officials and police, Benny made it clear that they were not hooligans nor did they intend to cause damage or injury - they simply wanted to demonstrate peacefully on the walk up to Kinder. He did warn, however, they were determined to achieve their objective and outlined the instructions to make it an orderly protest.

'General Rothman'

They were to follow a series of whistle blasts - one for stop, two for turn right and three blasts to advance in open formation. Someone in the crowd shouted out 'Where is the artillery?' These instructions earned Benny the nickname of 'General Rothman' later in court and the whistles described as 'military signals'. But those same critics would have been equally vociferous if the protest had proceeded in an unruly manner.

In the fairly boisterous atmosphere of the old quarry there was both cheering and heckling, and Benny, who was used to the rough and tumble of street politics, gave an impressive impromptu speech. At the end he received a huge round of applause, then climbed down from the rock and merged back into the crowd to avoid the authorities. They were now ready to confront the great landowning interests.

Willow Publishing

Benny (left) addressing the crowd, with Lance Helman (right)

Harry Rothman

The protesters move off after the quarry meeting

Moving on

Keeping in close formation to prevent the police from making any arrests, the large crowd of protesters made their way from the quarry followed by plain-clothes police, journalists, press photographers and officials and members of the Manchester Ramblers' Federation. The route took them past Stockport's Kinder Reservoir, with some singing *The Red Flag*, the *Internationale* and, according to police witnesses, chanting *Down with the landlords and up with the workers* and *Down with bobbies*. They also sang a Ewan MacColl trespass song which was an earlier version of his later more famous *Manchester Rambler*. George Sumner, one of the Trespassers, also recalled they joined in with the song *This piece of land is ours*. Benny Rothman, at this time, was towards the front of the group and shielded by other protesters. Uniformed police officers remained in Hayfield.

Right from the beginning, the number of protesters had been questioned - ranging from just two hundred to a thousand! A photograph showing the entire group leaving the quarry (see page 31 *The Battle For Kinder Scout*) confirms that four hundred would be a fair estimate. Never before had such a huge crowd been seen on the route to Kinder, which was lined with many spectators.

The group walked at quite a speed which the less experienced walkers found difficult to keep up with, including some of the police. As they reached

Sung on the Trespass

The Manchester Rambler
by Ewan MacColl sung to the tune
Road to the Isles.

We are young workers, who in search
of healthy sport,
Leave Manchester each weekend for a hike,
Though the best moorlands in Derbyshire
are closed to us,
We'll ramble anywhere we like.

For by Kinder, and by Bleaklow,
and all through the Goyt we'll go,
We'll scramble over mountain moor and fen,
And we'll fight against the trespass laws
for every ramblers' rights
And trespass over Kinder Scout again.
For the mass trespass is the only way for us
To gain access to the mountains once again.

This piece of land is ours

This piece of land is ours (repeat twice)
It's been in the family for ages now,
If you trespass on it you'll get into a row.

This piece of land is ours (repeat twice)
For the press and police will protect this piece,
For this piece of land is ours.

Nab Brow, they could see keepers in the distance below Sandy Heys, guarding any attempt to climb onto the Kinder plateau. Though it was a fine, bright day, the bare rocks on the plateau were veiled by a thin haze and looked forbidding. The group kept close together as they went over stiles so that no-one could be taken away by the authorities.

William Clough

From there the party, led by Lance Helman and Wolfie Winnick, began the steady ascent up William Clough. This was marked by an increase in the buzz and excitement among the ramblers. Most of them were experienced enough to know they would not die from exposure that day on Kinder but they had no idea how many keepers they were going to face.

William Clough was a public right of way, which thirty-five years before had been at the heart of an access controversy. For as long as could be remembered, Hayfield people had freely used this route on the way to the Snake Pass and Ashop Valley. Then in 1877,

four landowners, including the Duke of Devonshire, wanting to protect their shooting interests, closed the ancient path without warning. Despite the action being seemingly illegal it was approved by the Derbyshire Quarter sessions in 1880. This caused an uproar locally and resulted in the formation of the Peak District and Northern Footpaths Preservation Society. After many public meetings and consultations with landowners, agreement was secured to reopen the path in 1897. That was a decisive victory for access campaigners; the right to roam freely over Kinder was to take much longer!

During their recce up the clough earlier, Benny and Wolfie had noticed a spot where it was reasonably easy to scramble onto Sandy Heys moor towards Kinder. The moor was known to grouse shooters on the Park Hall Estate as the Kinder Drive. Benny and friends had decided against going to the top of the clough from which they might have been hemmed in by keepers. Their caution was well-founded because there were seven keepers waiting at the top.

Keith Warrender

William Clough, the old established path to the Snake Pass re-opened in 1897

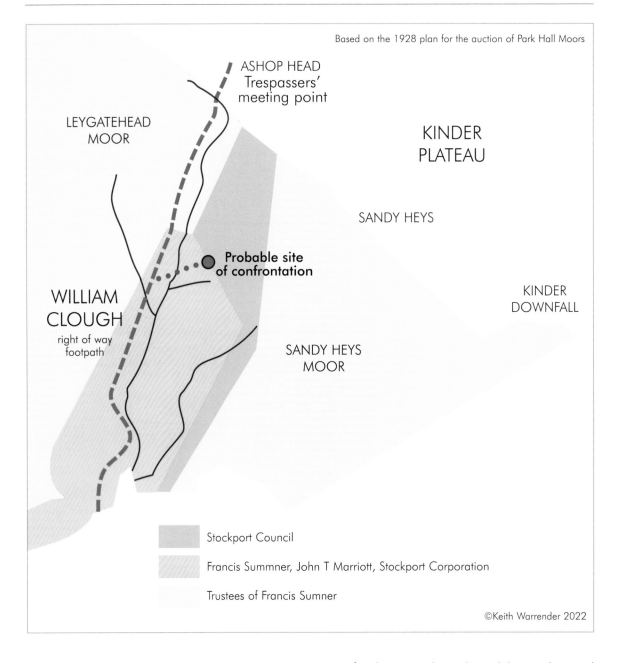

Based on the 1928 plan for the auction of Park Hall Moors

ASHOP HEAD
Trespassers'
meeting point

LEYGATEHEAD
MOOR

KINDER
PLATEAU

SANDY HEYS

● **Probable site
of confrontation**

WILLIAM
CLOUGH

KINDER
DOWNFALL

right of way
footpath

SANDY HEYS
MOOR

Stockport Council

Francis Summner, John T Marriott, Stockport Corporation

Trustees of Francis Sumner

©Keith Warrender 2022

Onto the moor

And so at 2.58pm, as noted by the *High Peak Reporter*, about half way up William Clough, Wolfie Winnick gave two blasts on his whistle for them to move onto the moor on the right of the brook, ushered on by stewards also known as 'whippers-in'. They were climbing out of the safety of the trench of the clough to meet the 'enemy' and were now officially trespassing on land, not belonging to the

Watts family as some have claimed, but jointly owned by the Park Hall Estate, Stockport Water Board and JT Marriott (see map). Sometimes the keepers are referred to as being from the Duke of Devonshire's estate or employed by James Watts, but the keepers and their associates who confronted the ramblers were from the Park Hall Estate, Water Board officials and local farmers. Watts's keepers were said to have observed the events taking place from afar, high above at Sandy Heys.

From this point events moved quickly, and in the chaos and confusion, accounts vary about certain details and numbers involved. I will try to give as balanced a description of events as possible, based on a number of eye-witness accounts. Between eighty and a hundred ramblers (some reports suggest fewer) then clambered up the bank to confront whatever lay before them. They were the first wave of walkers, journalists and plain clothes officers who faced the keepers on the skyline advancing towards them, waving their sticks and shouting at them to get back onto the footpath.

Keepers' fears

The keepers, especially the more elderly among them, must have viewed the situation with great apprehension. It was one thing confronting a handful of trespassers on the moors, it was another to be faced by a huge crowd. Would the young protesters turn violent? The keepers' sticks would offer little protection. Estimates vary of how many keepers there were, but they were heavily outnumbered. Benny recalled about twenty or thirty keepers while some reporters only saw between eight and twelve lined up four feet apart. The *Daily Express* stated that the ten regular keepers were being assisted by fifty men from Hayfield, including a local farmer, an estate worker and a Stockport Water Board official. It has been alleged that the keepers may have been slightly intoxicated but there is no confirmation of this.

Questionable numbers

Critics have tried to suggest that only a handful of activists took part in the confrontation, but this is contradicted by press and court accounts. It would seem there was a first wave who acted as an advance guard or 'spearhead' as it was described in one newspaper. Some claimed as few as forty went onto the moor. However, a head count on the press photograph of protesters surrounding the injured keeper indicates at least forty-five. There were likely to have been many more, out of camera shot, as well as those who swarmed to the top of the moor, or onto

Kinder. Other protesters joined them but it took some time for the whole of the group walking up the single track of the clough to reassemble on the moor.

The *Daily Express* correspondent reported that 'girl hikers pitted their weight against the moor guardians'. Throughout the protest, contrary to reports that women were kept in the rear in case violence broke out, they can be seen in one of the photographs. Sol Gadian, in his memories of the day, reported helping a girl onto the moor. The *Daily Herald* reported 'Youths and girls dashed up the side of William Clough'. As you will read later, in the lives of the trespassers, there were a number of feisty, committed young women present that day who would not have wanted to have been left out of the action and urged the others on.

500 HIKERS STORM A MOUNTAIN

SIX ARRESTS AFTER FIGHT WITH SIXTY GAMEKEEPERS

"Daily Express" Special Correspondent.

HAYFIELD (Derbyshire), Sunday.

GAMEKEEPERS guarding the heights of the Kinder Scout plateau, 2,000 feet above sea level, near here, to-day were severely handled and a number had to receive first-aid when they came into conflict with a party of 500 hikers, young men and girls, members of the Lancashire branch of the British Workers' Sports Federation, who had organised a mass trespass as a protest against the delay in passing through Parliament the Access to Mountains Bill.

Questionable Daily Express article 25 April 1932

There are varied accounts of how many surged up the moor. The *Daily Sketch* reported that 'Girl ramblers stood aghast at the scuffles, and many men and women did not cross the brook'. It is true that some people stayed back, including those who were looking after children and young teenagers. Nevertheless at the Derby trial, the prosecuting counsel stated that the crowd numbering two hundred rushed forward towards the keepers. The *Sheffield Telegraph* report of the incident dismissed the idea that most stayed back in the clough: 'Ramblers came pouring up the the slope in their hundreds and swarmed over the

Willow Publishing

keepers. Only a small number did not cross the stream in William Clough, the majority carried out their original intention.'

The *Yorkshire Post* reported: '...about fifty of the marchers jumped the stream and so onto the moor, an act of trespass. They were quickly followed by others. Above them, etched on the skyline were about half-a-dozen keepers armed with sticks, who stood and waited events. The reinforced ramblers spread along the side of the stream and then began their attack on the hill.'

AJP Taylor present?

Some who were just interested spectators, including John Anderson, made their way to the top of William Clough to watch the protest take place. It's often been incorrectly claimed that historian AJP Taylor was among the Trespassers. Although he records in his published diaries how he and other Manchester University colleagues regularly trespassed and hid from keepers on the forbidden moors, he also states that although he applauded the Kinder Trespass, he was not involved on that day.

Confrontation

Following three blasts on Wolfie's whistle, the Trespassers moved up the hill in open formation so that most of them would avoid the keepers. What happened next was later described in court by the police as 'the half-minute battle' and took place about a hundred and fifty yards off the William Clough footpath and over a distance of about twenty yards. The ramblers' group were said to have been two to three deep at this stage. Some found themselves involved in physical struggles while others continued uphill unopposed and completely unaware of any violence, including Benny Rothman, although he heard confused shouting to his right. It was the grouse-nesting season and one of the trespassers, Maurice Levine, who was a little older than the others, found a grouse sitting on its nest and watched over it to ensure it was not disturbed before organising others to keep watch while he continued to the top.

It seems there was a brief stand-off between the keepers and the protesters who politely asked them to stand aside. Possibly because he was provoked, a keeper made a grab at one of the ramblers which

Despite witnesses testifying in court that the keepers never raised their sticks, they are clearly seen using them against the protesters in this Leeds Mercury photograph. This photograph is also referred to on page 60.

Willow Publishing

prompted others to go to his rescue, and the struggle began. The protesters tried to seize the keepers' raised sticks and in the commotion two of the sticks were broken and returned to their owners. Tona Gillett grabbed a keeper to prevent him attacking ramblers with a pickaxe handle.

But others such as Wolfie Winnick were drawn into scuffles. He was not very tall but powerfully built and an amateur boxer at the YMCA. The photograph (right, in the light shirt)) shows him in the thick of the action where he received a blow to the head. Some keepers may have been pushed out of the way. A number of ramblers used their belts as weapons, and several involved in the scuffles overbalanced and rolled down the slope. The *Daily Express* reported that 'game keepers and youths struggled together pounding each other unmercifully'. Thankfully the keepers were not carrying guns, nor did they have their dogs with them.

Mystery man

There is another intriguing question in the photograph of Wolfie grappling with the keepers. A suited man is seen close to the action - was he a Water Board official, a reporter or even a detective? The identity of the man with the inappropriate clothing had puzzled me for years, however the mystery was solved as I gathered photographs from families of the Trespassers for this book. With this new source of information I was able to identify him as Sol Gadian, one of the protesters. But why was he wearing a suit and walking boots? For the explanation, read his account of the Trespass on page 75.

Injuries sustained by both sides

There were inevitable casualties, and the *Manchester Guardian* reported that many from Gorton and other areas would have been nursing bruises the next day. I'm unsure why he highlighted that particular district, because they were more likely to be from the Cheetham area of Manchester. There were a number of assaults on the Trespassers, with one of the protesters returning with a black eye. Some had been hit with the keepers' sticks, including at least one who was hit on the head. The composer Michael Tippett, friend of *Guardian* journalist David Ayerst, sustained

an injury to his hand from a stone and had to return to Hayfield. It is not clear who threw the stone - was it a spectator or a keeper? Fortunately the injury was not serious.

Other walkers were beaten up by keepers and their associates as they left the moors. It was also claimed that one of the acting keepers, a burly farmer, threw some of the attackers down the heather bank.

Willow Publishing

The assaults on the protesters weren't mentioned in press reports, unlike the injury to the temporary keeper, Edward Beever, which became a key incident in the trial of the ramblers. Beever, an employee of Stockport Waterworks, drafted in for the occasion, was one of the youngest amongst the keepers' group. His father, also named Edward, had been a game-keeper on the Park Hall estate. It is likely that forty-two year-old Edward jnr put up more of a spirited resistance than most, and was injured in the melee. There is no evidence that he had been intentionally assaulted, but the injury to the keeper brought the scuffling to a halt. A crowd gathered round him and someone fetched water from the stream. A photograph shows him being looked after by keepers or sympathetic spectators. Some reports state they were members of the Ramblers' Federation.

Once the ramblers were sure that the keeper had recovered sufficiently, they followed their fellow protesters to the top of the hill. Beever later claimed he had been hit in the stomach by Anderson's knee and sustained a sprained ankle as he rolled down the slope. However he had recovered sufficiently to walk two miles, escorted back down the hazardous William Clough and past Kinder Reservoir before being treated by a doctor and taken by ambulance to Stockport Infirmary.

He was discharged the same day, but sent back to hospital the following Monday and remained there for the next five days. It is not known whether his second stay in hospital was related to the Sunday incident. He claimed in court that he remembered little after being injured until he woke up in hospital, and it is quite possible he could have walked down to Hayfield in a dazed condition.

Arrest of Anderson

Plain clothes police followed the protesters onto the moor, and in their court witness statements claimed Jud Clyne, Harry Mendel, Tona Gillett and Dave Nesbitt took a leading part in the conflict, urging the others on. They were heard to shout 'They are only a lot of **** keepers, never mind them'. John Anderson was arrested at 3.30pm, after being seen supposedly striking a keeper and was being led back down as many of the Trespassers were still making their way up to Ashop Head, which indicated it took over half an hour for the large group to clamber onto the moor from William Clough.

'To the top!'

Some reports say the trespassers made their way to the top of the slope to gather at Ashop Head. The question is why they didn't proceed with their objective to climb onto Kinder. It was on the Trespassers' minds during the struggle with the keepers, as police witnesses later stated in court that Tona Gillett had shouted 'Come on, spread out. Never mind them. On to the top', pointing to Kinder Scout. Jud Clyne was heard to shout 'We are going to the top!'. The *Daily Express* stated '... the hikers, breathless after the fighting, tramped unimpeded over the plateau of Kinder'. The *Derby Evening Telegraph* reported after the injured keeper had been attended to, 'the ramblers continued to the forbidden area'.

The keepers:
- Horace Oldham, Water Board official knocked to the ground
- Edward Beever - injured
- (?) Neals - employed on the day
- Samuel Simpson, assistant keeper - farm labourer, knocked down or pushed
- Charles Gould, assistant keeper from Glossop
- Fred Simpson, farmer - allegedly threw some of the Trespassers on top of Beevers down the heathery bank, but may have also been pulled down
- John Frederick Gould, head keeper, Park Hall Cottage was pulled down

Police on duty:
James Main Garrow Deputy Chief Constable Derbyshire
Superintendent John McDonald, Chapel-en-le-Frith
Superintendent Ellis, Buxton
Inspector Clews brought Anderson into custody
D Sgt Brailsford
D Sgt Beaves
D Sgt Murphy
PC Mclean
PC William Hudson in plain clothes arrested Rothman and Nussbaum
DC Christian Buxton
Special Constable, Herbert Wardle

(Based on newspaper and court records)

Benny Rothman always claimed they had reached the plateau, but this was contradicted by witnesses such as Watts's head keeper John Watson who was stationed over half a mile away, and Trespasser Maurice Levine in a letter to the *Guardian* in 1982, who both claimed the protesters didn't complete the climb up Kinder. Maurice was at the back of the group after guarding the bird's nest. Perhaps it had taken enough effort getting a large group of people this far.

Rothman's stance that he had got onto the Kinder plateau was heavily criticised by Tom Stephenson and others. Even at the time of the Trespass 50th anniversary, Benny was still insisting they had reached the plateau, and, to the best of my knowledge, never deviated from it. In *Battle For Kinder Scout* published in 2012 I wrote that even if the protesters did not make it onto Kinder, they had made their point once they left the public footpath along William Clough and made their way onto the privately-owned moor. Others have expressed the same opinion - the trespassers had made their mark on countryside access history.

Did they get onto the plateau?

But this is not the end of the story - the Kinder Trespass is a subject which continues to reveal new things. I recently came across something which may make us think again. Maybe Benny was right after all! I've listened to the online memoirs of Walter Greenhalgh (read more about his life later in the book) who recalled how he and about twenty others, once they'd got past the keepers, scrambled onto the plateau to do a victory jig - perhaps Benny was in that group? I think Greenhalgh's recollections should be taken seriously.

It seems highly probable that a group of excited trespassers could have climbed Kinder while waiting for the rest of the group to make their way up the moor. There is another account which cannot be ignored. I've mentioned previously a description of the Trespass written by Benny Rothman prior to 1982. He was familiar with the geography of the area and in this account he is clear he went onto the Kinder plateau. He made the same assertion in a letter to *Rucksack* magazine, in summer 1980 where he wrote that the victory meeting was definitely on Kinder. He also showed his friend, footpath campaigner Don Lee, while out on a walk where he and others had climbed onto the lip of Kinder at Sandy Heys. The mystery is why they were not confronted by Watts' keepers.

Most of the protesters were fit, young walkers who regularly came to the Peak, and although it is a fairly vigorous climb up William Clough, they would have had little trouble in making the final steep ascent to the Kinder Plateau. However, if there had been a mass surge, they would have encountered opposition from sixteen keepers stationed nearby at Sandy Heys on the Watts estate who would have come along to guard that approach.

Kinder Scout, with the Kinder Downfall (right)

Looking down from Kinder towards the meeting place of the protesters at Ashop Head

It would have been much more dangerous to have been confronted there by keepers on its steep edges, than on Sandy Heys Moor, and there surely would have been more serious casualties on both sides. So, did the trespassers reach the top of Kinder and can we reconcile conflicting accounts? The evidence, based on eye-witness statements, is that the majority didn't but some of those who encountered no opposition including Walter Greenhalgh and Benny Rothman surged up the moor and onto Kinder to celebrate before rejoining the main party. No doubt they had expected the others to follow them onto Kinder - it had been their stated objective.

Late-comers on the horizon

The *Sheffield Daily Telegraph* report, which was an eye-witness account, states that the 'victory gathering' was held undisturbed at Ashop Head. But the group were alarmed to see a large number of people approaching on the Kinder skyline and wondered if this would be a further encounter with keepers or the police. Much to their relief, the approaching group was a party from Sheffield. They were also joined by another group from Sheffield who came via the Woodlands Valley.

Honours even?

The groups greeted each other, offered their congratulations on reaching the 'sacred territory' and talked about their experiences of getting there. The Sheffield contingent reported that all the stations en route had been thronged with police. Another group from Stockport had seen a similar thing. Benny again addressed the crowd, saying they had achieved the first part of their goal, but it was only the beginning. There were also speeches from Jack Clayton who should have given the speech at the quarry, and another by one of the Sheffield ramblers. There was a feeling of success, because the keepers and police had withdrawn, and relief that none of their number had been arrested, except Anderson who was an outsider not known to them.

It seemed that honours were even - the ramblers had carried out their objective, and the defenders had made their gesture. Both the keepers and some of the ramblers were nursing cuts and bruises. But would the celebrations of the protesters be short-lived? They realised there could be consequences for their actions, and a collection was made in case of a considered worst-case outcome of court fines.

The Sheffield contingents

Three parties from Sheffield joined the protest. A group of about fifty boarded the 8.45am Sheffield train at Hope, then walked over Rushup Edge to Edale and followed the track up Jacob's Ladder to Hayfield. The *Sheffield Telegraph* reporter who made the journey with them said they went in an orderly fashion, taking care to close gates and leave no litter. They arrived in Hayfield at around 2.00pm where they met up with the groups from Manchester.

Another group of thirty from Sheffield claimed to have had a trouble-free walk over Kinder from Edale and returned by the same route. They were the Spartacus Rambling Club led by Bill Keen, and were possibly seen by George Elliot (see page 79) as he descended Kinder near Jacob's Ladder. Elliot described how he was beaten up by two keepers, and then the group on the Edale Hayfield track swarmed past him up to the Kinder plateau. It was reported that from here the party witnessed the battle below with the keepers, and then went on to join the main group assembled at Ashop Head.

John Watson, head keeper of Watts's Kinder estate, along with sixteen other keepers was stationed at Sandy Heys overlooking the scene of the Trespass near Kinder Downfall, making sure that the Trespassers did not go onto James Watts's land. It is not clear what route Keen's party took, as Watts claimed no-one crossed Kinder that day. That could not be true, as we know that Elliot also made his way over the plateau. The question remains how Keen's group managed to avoid the keepers, both coming and returning? Bill Keen said that they walked over from Jacob's Ladder to the Downfall and didn't encounter any keepers. The best explanation is that Keen's group made their way further on to the plateau to avoid being seen. It could be that Watson and his fellow keepers were so engrossed in the trespass taking place below them, they were not aware of what was happening elsewhere.

There were others trespassing on Kinder that day. Albert Shirtcliffe from Sheffield went with friends onto Kinder where they joined another group from their home city. When they got to the western edge near Kinder Low they could see a big crowd below. It's not clear whether he was referring to the confrontation on the moor or walkers on the Hayfield Edale path. At the time he had not heard about the Mass Trespass. Could the group of walkers whom Albert and friends met up with, be the party led by Bill Keen? It also illustrates that Shirtcliffe and friends had also been missed by Watts's keepers.

A third group from Sheffield came via the Woodlands Valley to meet up at Ashop Head. They had been monitored by the keepers to make sure they kept to public footpaths.

Party split up

Benny Rothman was all for returning to Hayfield as a strong united body. It had been a principled demonstration, and he wanted them to go back by the same route as they came. They did not regard themselves as criminals nor was it to be viewed as a prank. They were proud of their actions and so they set off back to Hayfield. Besides, as one of the leaders, it would not have seemed right to desert his fellow protesters. They also thought the police would have less chance to pick people out of a big group.

Some of the ramblers had other ideas, and a number, including Lance Helman and Wolfie Winnick, made their way home by different routes. They were two of Benny Rothman's closest associates yet, because they feared the consequences of being caught, they left him and the others to face the authorities.

Lance Helman had come prepared, for he had brought in a rucksack flannel trousers, an old rain-coat and trilby which he changed into, then he and a number of ramblers made their way to Marple station via Doctor's Gate and Little Hayfield.

Lance got off the train at Ashburys before his usual stop of London Road in case the police were waiting for him. Wolfie's escape story is told later in the book. Perhaps if Benny had realised the police were waiting for them at Hayfield, he also might have considered taking a different route. However, he was a wanted man and may have found it difficult to evade the authorities. The police also feared that all the Trespassers would disperse in various directions over the moors, which would have made their job to arrest the leaders much more difficult.

Return to Hayfield

After the stop at Ashop Head for speeches and refreshments, the groups made their various ways back. The party who had come over Kinder returned to Edale by the same route. So while the main body of protesters had not gone onto Kinder, the Sheffield party trespassed over it twice in one day, and were not spotted by the keepers! The main group made their way back down William Clough in high spirits before the other Sheffield group turned off along the track towards Jacob's Ladder as they neared Hayfield on their way back home.

Arrests

The police may have withdrawn but they were still intent on making arrests within the Manchester contingent. They made a first attempt to make arrests but gave up and retreated. Unwittingly the protesters played into their hands, for as the group neared Hayfield, a police inspector asked them to walk in columns behind what the *Guardian* reporter called his 'baby car' - an Austin 7, with which they innocently complied. What a sight it must have been with

hundreds of protesters being led back into the village by a little car chugging ahead of them.

There were growing suspicions among the protesters that they were walking into a trap. By forming into columns they made it easier for the main culprits to be recognised. At a point where they were hemmed in by walls on either side of the road, a row of five police officers brought them to a halt while they and keepers moved along the ranks of walkers to identify who they considered to be the leaders. There was no resistance from the ramblers, nor did anyone try to escape. If they had been an unruly mob as suggested by police witnesses, it could have been a flashpoint.

Five arrests were made at 5.10pm and the rest of the group were allowed to make their way out of Hayfield. Benny Rothman and David Nussbaum were arrested by Constable William Hudson (see his account on page 77). Tona Gillett was arrested although he was not one of the leaders, nor a member of the BWSF, but stood out at 6ft 3ins.

The villagers were said to have looked on with satisfaction as arrests were made. They must have watched the arrested Trespassers being escorted into custody. Maybe news of what happened on the moor had filtered down to them. There's no doubt that the influx of several hundred noisy protesters must have seemed quite threatening. Possibly some of the keepers' and estate workers' families were amongst the onlookers.

However, many of the villagers would have mixed emotions because they made a living from ramblers, with their b&bs, pubs, tea rooms, farmhouse refreshments, shops and campsites. Those same ramblers on the protest would have been regular customers in the village. *Manchester Guardian* reporter David Ayerst, a staunch Anglican, noted that the trespassers arrived back in the village as the church bells rang for Evensong. For some of the villagers it would have seemed a triumph for law and order but they were not to know of the unfolding repercussions of the protest.

Willow Publishing

The protesters were led back into Hayfield by a car like this

Keith Warrender

Hayfield police station where the accused Trespassers were first detained, and is now a private dwelling.

Hayfield Police Station

The arrested ramblers were taken to the local police station on New Mills Road, where their details were taken. It is not entirely clear, but some of them may have been initially held in the old lockup known locally as 'The Dungeon' on Market Street. The arrested were: John Anderson, Jud Clyne, Harry Mendel, Tona Gillett, Dave Nussbaum and Benny Rothman.

Although Benny was identified as the speaker at the quarry, the police did not seem to recognise him as being the same person on whom they had wanted to serve an injunction. His photograph was said to have been circulated by the police, but there is no evidence of this.

Friends of the ramblers gathered outside the police station, hammering on the door, demanding their release. Sol Gadian, the man in the jacket on the Trespass, thought he could offer money to bail out his friends but the police began questioning him about who was on the Trespass and threatened to detain him too. With the situation becoming more heated, the police moved the ramblers from the rear entrance of the police station to the cells at New Mills police station where they spent the night while their identities were verified.

Benny later questioned why it took so long to establish names and addresses in the age of the telephone, although probably only the Gillett family would have had a home phone.

Even though arrests had been made, the remaining Trespassers had to pass through a cordon of police before they could leave the village. It was reported that police were present at the surrounding stations, and boarded trains, still asking questions.

For most of the ramblers it must have been an exciting, exhilarating day out with their friends, which also achieved the aim of bringing the issue of access to the countryside to a much wider audience. For those who had been arrested, they were not returning to the comfort of their homes, and their perceptions of the legal system would be changed for ever!

By nightfall, the protesters had finally dispersed and the village returned to its usual peacefulness, but the accused must have wondered with some apprehension what would happen to them. Even an energetic young man like Benny Rothman, must have been quite tired. Earlier he'd cycled from Manchester to Hayfield, walked twice from the village and up part of William Clough, probably clambered onto the plateau, given two impromptu speeches and been

New Mills town hall, location for the preliminary court hearings

Keith Warrender

Willow Publishing

RAMBLERS IN COURT.

SEQUEL TO MARCH ON KINDER SCOUT.

ALLEGED ATTACK ON KEEPER.

From Our Own Correspondent.
New Mills, Monday.

THE "mass trespass" on Kinder Scout yesterday afternoon had a sequel in court here to-day, when six ramblers were remanded to a special court on May 11, bail being allowed.

John Thomas Anderson, aged 21, cotton piecer, of The Quadrant, Cemetery-road, Droylsden, was charged with doing grievous bodily harm to Edward Beever, a special keeper.

Charges of unlawful assembly and breach of the peace were also preferred against Anderson and the following five defendants :—

Julius Clyne, aged 23, Elizabeth-street, Cheetham, Manchester;
Harry Mendel, aged 22, Townley-street, Cheetham;
Arthur Water Gillett, aged 19, a ......

involved in the stress and strain of organising the protest and being arrested. But alongside the fatigue there must have been a satisfaction that the day had gone well - there had been a good turn-out and they had managed to walk on the Kinder moors.

One critic suggested not as many came on the Trespass as Benny had hoped, but actually he had no idea just how many would support it. Many more attended the earlier Winter Hill protest but that was a dispute which attracted great local support. As the accused settled into their secure accommodation for the night at New Mills police station, appearances had been arranged for them the following day at the local courthouse. The momentous event was over, but not forgotten.

Magistrates' court hearings

The accused were brought before the magistrate at New Mills Town Hall, Spring Bank, for a preliminary investigation the following day, and charged with unlawful assembly and breach of the peace, with further charges to follow. Superintendent McDonald said the charges were the result of a mass trespass organised by a mob known as the British Workers' Sports Federation. There were no witnesses for the accused, whereas the police had their own witnesses, along with others from the Water Board and the local authority. The six ramblers were remanded on bail to the police court.

The Prosecutor at the next hearing on 11 May, Patrick Redmond Barry, brought smiles to the court reading out the BWSF's leaflet on Lord Big-Bug but warned the organisers of the Trespass were trying to hasten legislation. He accepted that there was 'no very great degree of violence used in the attack' but said that breaches such as this could not be tolerated otherwise the whole of law and order would come to an end. It was established that at least four keepers were pushed to the ground - but didn't record how many ramblers had been assaulted. It was claimed that the keepers didn't use their sticks, although ramblers said differently out of court, and press photographs suggested otherwise.

Herbert Wardle, the local ratings officer, testified he went to help the injured Beever and was struck with a leather belt and buckle by someone who wasn't present in court. Inspector Clews revealed he had received written complaints arising out of the ramblers' tussles with game keepers. It seemed to be over the keepers' raised sticks which the police witnesses never spotted, but Clews had not thought it necessary to bring the complaints to court. Presumably trying to show the Trespass's political links, it was mentioned that Gillett was carrying various Communist Party publications when he was searched at the police station. The defendants - Rothman, Clyne, Gillett, Mendel and Nesbitt had all been seen inciting the crowd to move forward up the moor towards Kinder.

The trial resumed on 26 May with only Tona Gillett legally represented. His counsel argued there was insufficient evidence to justify a committal on the charge of unlawful assembly. He said that if the Bench required evidence of Gillett's good character, they had only to call the head of Dalton Hall, Manchester University, or his mother who was a student at Oxford, who would both confirm he was a person of good character.

The other defendants pleaded 'Not Guilty' and Benny Rothman conducted his own defence because the BWSF Committee thought he should fight it on the basis of history and politics rather than law. He gave a long statement lasting over an hour about how the countryside had been closed to the people through the Enclosure Acts passed by the landowner members of Parliament.

He described how ramblers' action had resulted in the footpath at Doctor's Gate being reopened, and it was in this spirit that the Mass Trespass had taken place. Their peaceful demonstration was to gain support for the right of access to mountains. He submitted that the scuffle which occurred was not the fault of the ramblers and there had been a deliberate attempt to prevent them peacefully protesting.

Despite the only injury to a keeper being indirectly caused by Anderson who was not part of the Trespass, and other arguments in their defence, the accused were committed for trial at Derby on the charge of unlawful assembly.

John Anderson, at a separate court hearing on 1st June at New Mills, was charged with causing grievous bodily harm to the keeper Edward Beever. Anderson, representing himself, pointed out the inconsistencies of the police witness accounts. His case was also hampered by having no witnesses, and he was committed for trial with the others at Derbyshire Assizes on June 29th, which was later changed to 6th and 7th July.

Benny Rothman, in preparation for his defence at the Derby trial, discussed it with others and also read through some legal books at the library and, in his words, became a 'legal expert'.

Harry Rothman

John Anderson and Benny Rothman on friendlier terms with the police at the unveiling of the Trespasser plaque at the former New Mills police station 1994

The Trial re-examined

Police visit

Prior to the trial, the parents of the accused were visited by Detective Inspector King, as he supposedly gathered 'information in their son's favour'. Benny Rothman said that his mother and sisters found the visit and questioning quite frightening. Sol Gadian reported that detectives had visited his workplace asking questions about work-mate Harry Mendel's politics (See page 76). Parents also stated they received a questionnaire from the governor of Stangeways prison asking about their sons such as: 'Have you ever thought anything was wrong with his mind? If so, why and when?', 'Has he always been honest, sober and industrious and of general good character?', and 'What kind of companions did he mix with? How did he spend his spare time?'

The accused Trespassers arrived at Derby a few days before the trial, staying with sympathisers. They were so confident of their case, they held public meetings in the market. There weren't many listeners as they outlined the fight for countryside access. Their activity was also, as Benny admitted, absolutely illegal. They had been advised by some in Manchester who knew about legal matters that they could receive sentences of up to eighteen months for the Trespass.

Trial by Grand Jury?

Ted Rivers, writing in the *Progressive Rambler* journal in 1942, claimed he had researched the trial of the Trespassers and found that they had been tried by a grand jury of high-ranking military gentlemen. The idea was perpetuated by Professor Joad, one of the brightest minds of his era, and a supporter of the walker's right to access the countryside freely. In his 1934 book *'A Charter For Ramblers'* he wrote 'There never was a time when the love of nature was so widespread, when so many people had the habit of resorting to the country for exercise of the body, refreshment of mind and solace of spirit; and equally there was never a time when the country was so difficult to find'.

He spoke at the annual ramblers' rally at Winnats in 1932, famously saying that 'Sooner or later, the movement would have to consider taking the law into their hands'. At the 1935 Winnats rally he urged ramblers to become more militant. This would seem an encouragement to trespass but he later denied he had meant that in his 1946 book *The Untutored Townsman's Invasion of the Country*, where he said that access should be secured not through protest but by Act of Parliament.

He went on to say that the six accused ramblers at the Kinder Trespass were tried by a jury composed of two brigadier generals, three colonels, two majors, three captains and

The jury box, Derby Assizes

Working Class Movement Library

The judge's bench, Derby Assizes

eleven country gentlemen. We could imagine the Trespassers being viewed with little favour by a jury composed of retired military men and other land-and property-holders. They would surely be unsympathetic to ramblers whose aim was to have the right to walk over property like theirs!

For many, this has been the view of the jury in the trial ever since, and fits well with the narrative of the accused being found guilty by establishment and other land-owning interests. This misleading statement has been repeated many times but it is not the full story of what happened at Derby Assizes.

Petty jury

While it is true that the Grand Jury system was in existence at the time, the military gentlemen and their colleagues did not take part in the trial and were not the ones who passed final judgment on the accused. Benny Rothman and his fellow protesters were actually found guilty not directly by a Grand Jury but by a 'petty' or 'petit' jury, a group of twelve citizens. There is no information about who was on the petty jury nor how they were selected, but Joad should not have given his misleading statement.

The Grand Jury system, which originated in Norman times, had been introduced to prevent vindictive and

false accusations being brought to court. The role of the Grand Jury was essentially to assess whether there was a case to answer. They would examine the evidence before the case came to court and decide whether it should proceed, or pronounce 'No True Bill'. They were sworn in and presented with bills of indictment, which contained the charges presented to magistrates and sworn witness statements. They could also call upon prosecution witnesses. A judge advised them whether there was a *prima facie* case to answer. They met in private but crucially did not take statements from defence witnesses.

The Grand Jury usually consisted of twenty-three jurors, as was the case at Derby, although sometimes it was as few as twelve. They were selected from the higher echelons of society because they were deemed to be better-educated. Once the jurors had made their decision on a number of indictments they were discharged and the cases would proceed before a judge and petty jury in open court.

It's also interesting to note that in Justice Acton's summing up, he asked the jury not to be influenced by some of the defendants' 'strange-sounding' names ie Jewish. If the trial had been conducted in Manchester rather than rural Derbyshire the names may not have seemed so unusual. Some have read antisemitism into his comments, but I will give him the benefit of the doubt, that he was trying to be fair. Acton also called for the jury to ignore the 'somewhat extreme views of some of the defendants'. The judge went on to say 'It is the greatest pride of this country that a man gets a fair trial, no matter what his name, race, nationality or religion'. However there was a notable omission in the list - politics. The perceived threat from these activists was surely a significant factor in the minds of the judge and jury.

System abolished

The Grand Jury system came to an end in 1933 following over twenty years of questioning its efficiency and costs. Each case involved twenty-three citizens being away from their everyday business, and there was also the time and trouble of preparing evidence twice over, along with the questionable practice of relying on a jury which acted in secret and only heard the prosecution evidence.

So the Trespassers found themselves involved in a court process which was months away from abolition. The decision to end the services of the grand jury was not well received by some judges who regretted the end of the ancient practice while others welcomed it.

The Sentences

● Anderson - not guilty of grievous bodily harm but guilty of assaulting Beever - six months' imprisonment
● Rothman - four months in the Second Division
● Nussbaum - three months in the Second Division
● Clynes - two months in the Second Division
● Gillett - two months in the Second Division
● Mendel - discharged as evidence too slight

All the sentences were in the Second Division, which meant the convicted Trespassers were not supposed to mix with hardened or habitual criminals who may corrupt them. Prisoners in the Second Division were regarded as being people of good education who had not been previously convicted. It was recommended they were given work to do and to keep their cells clean. They could wear their own clothes and were supposed to receive letters and visits. Benny Rothman and Dave Nesbitt complained they did not receive post sent to them. Benny received his in a bundle when he was released. The meals

could not have been too bad, because, combined with the lack of physical activity, Benny put on weight while he was in prison at Leicester.

We don't know a great deal about prison life for the Trespassers, but there are some new details in Harry Rothman's article on Benny, and more in the article on David Nesbitt. Tona Gillett used his confinement to continue with his university studies.

Benny Rothman said that the accused got into immediate trouble in prison by jogging around the exercise yard. This was against the rules and regarded as disruptive and so his friends were dispersed to other prisons.

Reaction to the sentences

The rambling organisations, although not approving of the Kinder Trespass, were nevertheless surprised by the severity of the sentences and wrote in protest to the Liberal Home Secretary, Herbert Samuel.

Judge Acton

Sir Edward Acton was born in Stretford, Manchester in 1865, about five miles away from the Cheetham district of Manchester, the birth-place of some of the Trespassers.

Willow Publishing

His father, Henry Morell, was a leader writer for the *Manchester Guardian* and it is ironic that the father of the judge should be a *Manchester Guardian* man, because the newspaper had always been a firm supporter of greater access to the countryside.

The judge and Rothman and friends may have started out in fairly close proximity but their life experiences were worlds apart.

Willow Publishing

Leicester prison

They received the reply that the sentences had been reviewed and the Government saw no reason to reduce them. With little support for the accused in the local and national press, there was a letter in their favour in the *Manchester Guardian*.

It came from Giles Howson who did not agree with mass trespasses but thought that the actions of 'idealistic and energetic young men at a certain stage of their development' were no more lawless than an average student's rag which didn't end in imprisonment. He thought the sentences were out of all proportion to their actions.

Howson, educated at Manchester University, was a medical practitioner, a leading figure with the Society of Friends in his home town of Lancaster, and local historian. Despite the criticism and derision from some quarters, the Trespass was perhaps ahead of its time and more akin to the present-day protests of Greenpeace and Friends of the Earth.

Acton was educated at Uppingham public school Rutland, and Wadham College, Oxford. He was called to the Bar in 1891 and practised on the Northern Circuit until 1918. While a barrister he defended a German accused of treason during WW1. He was a lecturer in law at Manchester University, and while in the city, a leading member of the Playgoers' Club, and its president.

After presiding as a County Court judge for the Nottingham Circuit, he was promoted in 1920 to become a High Court judge. He was regarded as a success and set a precedent for the promotion of other County Court judges. That same year he was knighted by the King at Buckingham Palace.

Acton was reputedly a good lawyer, businesslike, sparing of words and amiable without being expansive. One court reporter in 1930 described him as having 'a quick way with him, while willing to give every latitude,

especially to young counsel and timid witnesses, but would stand no nonsense'. He was highly regarded within the profession as few of his decisions were overruled by the Court of Appeal.

After his retirement due to ill-health in 1934 he campaigned for the reduction in legal fees for ordinary people who could not afford to take matters to court. He also suggested driving tests for motorists long before they became compulsory.

Sir Edward died in 1945 aged eighty at Hambledon, Surrey. The *Birmingham Daily Post* described him as someone who attracted little attention and was not often in the press head-lines. Little did the correspondent know that Justice Acton would be for ever remembered as the judge who delivered what many have considered to have been severe sentences on the Trespassers and which helped to make the protest into a key event in the rambling world.

Trial Transcript

Derby Advertiser's report of the trial

July 8th 1932
DERBYSHIRE SUMMER ASSIZES
Riot Charges Sequel to Hayfield
Mass Trespass

Keeper rendered unconscious

An echo of the fracas which occurred at Hayfield on April 24 was heard at the Derby Assizes before Mr Justice Acton on Wednesday, when six youths were charged, 'with other persons unknown,' with being concerned in 'making a riot.'

The Red Flag

The charges arose out of what was called a 'mass trespass' organised by a sports federation in the Kinder Scout area when, it is alleged, a crowd of about two hundred people was given a series of military signals which they were instructed to obey. Evidence for the prosecution was that the ramblers were urged to carry on to the top and they came into conflict with a number of keepers, one of whom was grievously injured. There were shouts of 'Down with the landlords, up with the workers' and the 'Red Flag' was sung after the fracas by a section of the crowd. A police witness stated that a force of police was on duty in anticipation of violence.

The accused in the 'mass trespass' case were John Thomas Anderson, 21, a cotton piecer, who, in addition to being charged with 'riotously assembling to disturb the public', was also charged with maliciously inflicting grievous bodily harm on Edward Beever, Bernard Rothman, 21, a store-keeper; Julius Clynes, 22, machinist; Anthony

Walter Gillett, 19, student, Harry Mendel, 22, machinist and David Nussbaum, 19, labourer, who were indicted for being concerned in the riotous assembly. There were eight charges, to all of which pleas of not guilty were entered.

Mr Jenkyn and Mr Smallwood appeared for the prosecution, whilst Norman Winning represented Anderson and Gillett.

Mr Jenkyn, outlining the case against the accused, said that Rothman was the secretary of 'a kind of sports federation' and organised hikes about the country. For April 24, he organised what he called a 'mass trespass.' His intention was made public and a crowd of about two hundred people assembled at Hayfield. Nussbaum wrote on the roadway 'Mass trespass, meet on the rec', which, said counsel, he presumed meant the recreation

---

Norman Winning

Defence counsel, Winning, was called to the bar in 1919, and was known for his quiet, courteous yet determined manner. He practised on the Midland Circuit and was Chairman of Derbyshire Quarter sessions, and regarded as an expert on company law. During the last war his two sons both died in RAF flying accidents.

He was highly regarded within the profession and became a King's Counsel just months before tragically collapsing and dying on a train while travelling to London in 1946. He had been in ill-health for some time with heart problems.

ground. Rothman made a speech to the crowd, telling them what to do if they were opposed and arranging military signals to mean 'Advance,' 'Retreat' and the like.

The 'mass trespass' began and keepers were assaulted, one very grievously. There were shouts of 'Down with the landlords and the ruling classes' and 'Up with the workers'. Many people sang the *Red Flag* and there was an attempt, led by Rothman and Nussbaum, to overcome all resistance. Prior to the fracas Nussbaum was selling a paper called the *Daily Worker*, shouting out that it was the only paper which supported 'mass trespass.'

Inspector Clews described the scuffle between about one hundred and fifty ramblers and eight or ten keepers and stated that the leaders of the crowd shouted 'Down with them.' One of the keepers warned them to go back as they were trespassing.

Violence was expected

The witness was closely cross-examined by Rothman as to why there was a force of police at Hayfield that day and the Inspector replied that violence was expected.

Rothman: What made you think there would be violence?
Witness: Things I heard during the week.

Rothman: Do you know why officers from Derby were there?
Witness: For the same reason as myself, to try to preserve the peace.

Inspector Clews said that the ramblers were shouting and singing as they left the meeting.
Rothman: Cheerfully?
Witness: No, they seemed to be singing with a purpose.

In reply to a further question, the witness said that when he met the ramblers at Hayfield they were not violent but determined. He had no difficulty in stopping the crowd.

Mr Winning: You came to the conclusion that all the ramblers in the recreation ground were guilty of unlawful assembly?
Witness: Yes.

Mr Winning: Why didn't you arrest the lot?
Witness: Because they moved away.

Mr Winning: Why didn't you arrest them before they moved away?
Witness: I could not arrest them for doing nothing.

In reply to Mr Winning, the witness agreed that the only people who had useful weapons were the keepers, and violence only occurred when the crowd met them. There were about a score of police in reserve at a cinema at Hayfield and they were called out when the crowd was returning from the ascent of Kinder.

Cross-examined by Rothman, Herbert Wardle, a special constable, said that the crowd was hostile and 'undisciplined' after it left the recreation ground. Sergeant Brailsford said that in the quarry, Rothman said: 'No doubt we shall meet keepers and other forces, but we shall to able to overcome them,' and gave signs to be used for 'advance' and 'retreat'. When the crowd advanced, Nussbaum shouted: 'They are only a lot of xxxx keepers, never mind the sticks.'

Cross-examined by Rothman, the witness said that when he went to the assistance of Beever, the crowd stood back a little, and there was little hostility to the witness. Det constable Christian of Buxton, said he saw Anderson holding on to a keeper's stick as if he was trying to take it from him. He agreed, in reply to Mr Winning, that Anderson might have been defending himself from the keeper.

Evidence that Clynes shouted: 'Do you want any help; line up lads' when Inspector Clews came down with Anderson in custody, was given by Detective sergt Cleaves. About twenty ramblers gathered round Clynes, but when witness shouted 'Stop that,' they went up the hill. Coming down they were shouting 'Down with the landlords, up with the workers,' and some were singing the *Red Flag*.

Pc Hudson stated that in a speech Rothman announced himself as secretary of the British Workers' Sports Federation and said he would lead the mass trespass. Cross-examined by Rothman the witness said he also heard him ask the ramblers to follow the leaders in an orderly and disciplined manner.

The keeper who was stated to be badly injured, Edward Beever, said he tried 'gentle persuasion,' and Anderson grabbed his stick and, in the struggle for possession, the witness was knocked down and Anderson fell on top of him. The witness was kicked and lost consciousness.

John Frederick Gould, head-keeper, said he did not use his stick and did not see any of the keepers use theirs.

Five of the accused returned late after lunch, and when the court adjourned on Wednesday evening, the Judge said that with the exception of Gillett the accused would not receive any further indulgence and they would remain in custody until the conclusion of the trial.

Thursday hearing

When the hearing resumed on Thursday morning, several keepers were called and gave evidence as to the meeting addressed by Rothman and the subsequent trespass. This concluded the case for the Crown.

Rothman's defence

Rothman, who elected to make his defence from the dock instead of entering the witness box and being sworn, addressed the jury at length. On April 24th, he stated, some three hundred ramblers

Keeper Beever

gathered together to protest against the closure of certain moors in Derbyshire. Some sections of moorland were closed to ramblers who went out at the weekends to enjoy sunshine and a change of scene. Those ramblers found that only certain footpaths were open to them, footpaths which were so crowded that ramblers might as well stay at home in the towns. 'There is nothing unreasonable in our demands to see the uncultivated land in the Peak,' declared Rothman.

A Ramblers' Federation had been in existence for more than twenty-five years and had conducted campaigns and agitations on behalf of ramblers. The British Workers' Sports Federation, of which he was the Lancashire secretary, considered that the Ramblers' Federation was futile; that its policy would not gain access to mountains for ramblers. The fact that the Ramblers' Federation was supporting the Access to Mountains Bill actually prevented them from gaining access. April 24th marked the commencement of a campaign amongst the ramblers of the British Workers' Sports Federation to obtain access to mountains through their own action and by a policy of mass trespass. The intention of the ramblers was to walk across Kinder Scout and nothing else. There was a great drafting of police into Hayfield on the 24th; normally there were only two in the village. It seemed to be that the landowners brought pressure to bear on the police with the intention of frightening ramblers.

'The demonstration was peaceful from the start,' declared Rothman. 'When we saw we were not allowed to hold a meeting in the recreation ground we moved away.' The object of agreeing on military signs and advancing in 'open order' was to avoid trouble. They expected to meet keepers and it was their intention to walk round them. 'We were not a mob of hooligans. If we went with the intention of fighting how is it that only one keeper got hurt when there were so many ramblers?' He suggested that Beever's injuries might very well have been sustained if he was engaged with one single individual. That was in fact what happened, he declared.

Nussbaum, who also made his defence from the dock, said he was not a rambler and did not belong to the British Workers' Sports Federation. He went to Hayfield to sell the *Daily Worker* and that was all he did. Anderson, on oath, said he had nothing to do with the British Workers' Sports Federation; he went to Hayfield on April 24th out of curiosity. He denied that he caused Beever's injuries. Gillett, also on oath, admitted going to Hayfield with the intention of carrying out a mass trespass. There was no intention of violence. He did not see anyone knocked down.

Clynes, who did not leave the dock, stated that he only took part in a ramble. He did not shout anything. His Lordship said that with regard to Harry Mendel, the evidence was so slight that, with the consent of the prosecuting counsel, he asked the jury to find him not guilty. Mendel was accordingly discharged.

Summing up, his Lordship said he did not suppose that any other country allowed such freedom for demonstrations of various kinds and no one desired to interfere with that freedom. At the same time, the peace must be preserved. When the court resumed after lunch the judge continued his summing up for another hour.

He stated that he had only dealt with the case at such length because he considered it very necessary. At the conclusion of his review of the evidence, his lordship remarked that he knew the jury would not allow any opinion they might have with regard to the somewhat extreme views of some of the prisoners enter into the case. Nor would they allow themselves in any way to be prejudiced because some of the men had names which sounded perhaps strange to members of the jury.

Harry Mendel

'It is perhaps the greatest pride of this country,' he commented, 'that a man gets a fair trial no matter what his name, race, nationality or religion.'

The jury was absent for about fifty minutes and on their return found all five prisoners guilty of riot. Anderson was found not guilty of causing grievous bodily harm with intent to disable Beever, but was found guilty of assault. Rothman was found guilty of inciting to riot and assault, Nussbaum was found guilty of inciting unlawful trespass. Clynes was found guilty of inciting to riot and assault.

Inspector Clews gave evidence as to the characters of the men. Anderson and Rothman had good characters and no previous convictions. With the exception of a minor offence, Nussbaum had no previous convictions; and Gillett, a native of Oxford, was a Manchester University student. George Arthur Sutherland said Gillett was the best rugby player at his college at the University, and though he had caused some excitement by his views among the students, he had a good character.

Tona Gillett

His Lordship said: 'This sort of thing must be stopped. There is no other country in the world in which people can express their opinions so freely, but they must stop at breaking the King's peace and making tumultuous scenes of this type.'

Harry Rothman

Convicted Trespasser, Jud Clyne speaking at Jacob's Ladder with uniformed police in attendance

Jacob's Ladder meetings

A number of attempts were made to hold a rally at Jacob's Ladder in support of the five jailed trespassers. On Sunday 9 May, between two and three hundred people assembled there but the organisers, the recently-formed Ramblers' Rights Movement, a branch of the BWSF, remained silent, probably uneasy about the presence of police. The crowd waited patiently for two hours before the leaders asked them to disperse.

On Sunday 17 July, a meeting did take place at the same spot, and a resolution was passed demanding the prisoners' release. A petition to the Home Secretary was handed round stating that the charges made against the ramblers were unjust. None of the speakers gave their names perhaps because of the police presence. One woman said she had joined the movement because it was the only way in which ramblers would get their rights. There were speeches from representatives of the BWSF, then at the close of the meeting ramblers were asked to return to Hayfield as a group, singing as they went.

A smaller gathering of less than a hundred at the same location on 28 August welcomed Jud Clynes one of the recently-released jailed trespassers who claimed that his experience had only increased his determination tenfold to go on with the movement for better facilities for ramblers. The next speaker said they wanted not only access to mountains but also cheaper travel and refreshments, and be free from

Harry Rothman

> **BRITISH WORKER'S SPORTS FEDERATION.**
> **RAMBLER'S RIGHTS MOVEMENT**
>
> **Fellow Ramblers,**   1952
>
> The Shooting Season commences on August 12th and continues for a period of about 1 month and during this time some of the finest moorland in Derbyshire will be closed to thousands of ramblers.
>
> The R.R.M. has led the fight for access to mountain and moorland by the mass trespass over Kinder. We intend to organise the fight for better and cheaper facilities for meals, cheaper railway travel, and no petty restrictions on singing etc.
>
> The R.R.M. will hold a mass rally at the foot of Jacobs' Ladder on Sunday August 28th, where two of the arrested Ramblers (who will be released on Friday) will speak, also two worker Sportsman who have just returned from the Soviet Union will speak on Sport in the Soviet Union.
>
> **RALLY TO JACOBS' LADDER. AUGUST 28TH.**

restrictions on things such as singing. Joe Norman from Salford, another trespasser, told the crowd he had rambled in Russia where there were no notices and they were free to go where they wished. Tona Gillett, one of the jailed trespassers, was also present. Finally it was announced there would be a mass trespass from Sheffield on Froggatt Edge the following Sunday.

Alerted by this, a large presence of gamekeepers and police patrolled Froggatt Edge on 4th September. A party of six students who were attending a conference nearby, came to the Edge and were quickly surrounded by keepers and ordered off.

A representative of the Ramblers' Rights Movement later explained that the protest had been cancelled but there would be a mass trespass at Abbey Brook on Sunday 18th September. The official also claimed the Sheffield branch of the RRM had enrolled more than three hundred new members. Perhaps because of the robust response of the authorities, no further Ramblers' Rights protest meetings took place after a meeting at Longshaw on 16th October.

Winnats rally

It is often incorrectly said that there were record crowds in 1932 at the annual Winnats rally following the Trespass. Ten thousand people had been expected, but possibly due to poor weather the attendance dropped to between six and eight thousand that year. People came from at least six counties, in still substantial numbers, to the natural amphitheatre of the Winnats. The rallies began in 1926, organised by the Manchester Ramblers' Federation supported by the Sheffield ramblers and surrounding towns to promote the forthcoming Access to Mountains Bill. Sheffield Federation ramblers officially took over the running of the meetings in 1937.

The 1932 rally began at 2.30pm with chorus singing and marching songs, but the usual relaxed atmosphere of the meeting was disturbed by the arrival of the BWSF. Shortly before the speeches began, about two hundred marched up the gorge with a red banner distributing leaflets to the crowd. They grouped around the speakers' area where they harried the man leading the community singing, then began singing one of their own songs before being drowned out by the other ramblers.

From scattered points amongst the crowd, they heckled the speakers and chanted slogans. With Alderman CW Beardsley, former Lord Mayor of Sheffield, as the chairman, the speakers, Dr CEM Joad and Philip Oliver, Stephen Morton and Edwin Royce bore the heckling with good humour.

In his speech, Dr Joad said that people came to the countryside to escape the towns and cities of the north which were 'little hells of ugliness', but when they got there they found it barred and fenced off.

Willow Publishing

SUPPORT FOR RAMBLERS

In connection with the recent arrest of six Manchester ramblers, including B, Rothman, the British Workers' Sports Federation's Lancashire Group secretary, for the mass trespass on Kinder Scout, the London Group of the B.W.S.F. has embarked on a co-operative defence campaign.

At its last meeting, held to bid farewell to the B.W.S.F.'s London members of the delegation to the U.S.S.R., 15s. was collected as the first step.

Above: Daily Worker article
Left: Walkers returning from the Jacob's Ladder meeting. The Sheffield contact for the Ramblers' Rights Movement was Thomas MacDonald, a baker and confectioner at 53 Industry Street.

They were living in a civilisation where it was more important that rich people had facilities for slaughtering grouse than citizens having access to the wild places. The people who preserved the moors were not the old sporting gentry but rich businessmen and Americans who knew little about sport. Joad noted that Sunday cinema was coming, so why not Sunday rambles on the moors? A great deal was heard from the 'Come to Britain' movement - why not make Britain more interesting to visit by allowing freer access to its more beautiful and wild places?

Joad made a remark which would have caught the attention of the BWSF, saying 'Sooner or later the movement would have to consider taking the law into their own hands'. However, this stirring rhetoric was not what it seemed because Joad later clarified he was not referring to direct action such as trespassing.

At the end of the rally, the BWSF wanted to use the microphone but were refused as it belonged to the

Daily Express who also supplied the song sheets. They tried to conduct their own meeting but were jeered by the crowd. Their criticism of the Ramblers' Federation was of conspiring with the landowners and had 'talked, promised, crawled, done everything but call on ramblers to fight for themselves'. There was bitterness towards the Federation for not supporting the Trespass.

The behaviour and tactics of the BWSF at the Winnats meeting did nothing to close the gap between themselves and other rambling clubs. It could have been an occasion for solidarity, but their confrontational approach only alienated the established rambling organisations.

This reflected the BWSF's fundamental lack of respect for them, and the huge divide over the tactics of achieving the common goal of greater countryside access. Their hopes of recruiting people into the Ramblers' Rights Movement had failed.

The annual Winnats rallies attracted thousands of ramblers

Harry Rothman

The Abbey Brook Trespass, Sunday, September 18, 1932

By ALBERT RICHARDSON

After the Kinder dispute, they'd decided that they were going to hold a meeting in Sheffield to organise a protest at the activities of police and the keepers over the Kinder ramble.

There was a meeting organised in the Victoria Hall by the Ramblers' Federation, and they'd notified all the rambling clubs that this was going to happen. There were about twelve rambling clubs represented at this meeting, and we decided that we would make a mass trespass from Malin Bridge through the valley there, right over to Broomhead Moors and then to Abbey Brook.

When we met at Malin Bridge, the press didn't know anything about it, and we didn't know whether the police or the gamekeepers did, so we walked up the Loxley Valley and over to Abbey Brook.

When we got towards the shooting butts we saw the police on top of the hill, and as we approached the butts they all came down the hillside. I should say there were about thirty policemen at the time and about forty gamekeepers, and the gamekeepers had got pit props and the police had got dogs, and they approached us and told us we'd got to go back.

And a colleague called Hardy, of Shipton Street Settlement, was in charge of the ramble and he said: 'If you want to stop a trespass you must escort people onto the nearest major road. That's the ruling and the law.'

And the police wouldn't listen to it. They said: 'No, you've got to go back.' They said - they were persistent - that we must go back. And he said: 'Well, sit down a minute and let's talk

this out.' So we all sat down again. He says: 'Now, are you hungry?' So we all shouted "YES!", so he said, "Well then, get your rucksacks off, get your flasks out, and get your grub out, and get down, and we're stopping here while we've eaten it. We're not in any hurry."

And we followed what he said and all started eating, and the gamekeepers were getting annoyed, and they'd all got pit props, and they were getting very annoyed with it all, and the police were a bit upset, and one or two of the gamekeepers started doing a bit of pushing on one or two of the lads.

Well, the police stopped them and they told them they weren't having any of that. It got to be - you know - he was in charge, the police officer, and he said he'd got to see that everything's in order and 'We don't want that.'

But one of the keepers did push one of the Independent Labour Party lads, and straightaway he hit back at the gamekeeper, and hit him hard, and the police immediately grabbed them both and told them they had got to stop.

So, ultimately, we decided that we were walking back then. We'd go back, but we'd go at our own time and own pace and own way, and we made it as long as we could, and the policemen kept saying: 'You know, you could cut a bit and be reasonable.' And we said: 'This is what we intend doing and we're going to do it.'

● Albert Richardson became Lord Mayor of Sheffield in 1976. He and his wife, Elsie, were married July 1932 in a special Woodcraft Folk ceremony at a farm near Fox Lane in the Cordwell Valley, following the legal ceremony at Sheffield Register Office.

The 'raids' on Kinder Scout and Duke of Norfolk's Road

Extracts from the 1933 Sheffield Clarion Ramblers' handbook

Many affiliated ramblers and outsiders have said that the stiff sentences of two to six months upon the five young men for the Kinder Scout mass raid (and one assault) on April 24th last did not bring laurels to the other side. Many also regretted that the raiders' case was not straight-way put in the hands of a rising young barrister, and, according to some participants, the 'assaulting' was not all on one side - although the young man's fear, and the cost of six days' wages at the hearings and the Assizes trial were bars against the giving of evidence.

Ramblers also looked for, and missed, an intimation that the heavy detachment of police and officers had insisted upon an endeavour to prevent an offence, and addressed these young men and pointed out that, if trouble occurred, they would be prosecuted under a hidden form of law which few, if any, thought possible, and not for trespass and damage.

One press picture (*Leeds Mercury*) out of the press-snappers' gallery possibly should not have appeared. A small, altercating crowd was not aware of the camera man, and three men, with hooked and nob-sticks in the air, were ready to thump one or more (unseen) persons in the centre of the party. No one, from the picture, would suppose that these sticks were owned by the raiding members of the Ramblers' Rights' Movement. There may be other ways of procedure and tactics, but the punishment, on this occasion, did not fit the crime, and brought sympathy to

the punished, and the daily press wisely declined to comment upon, and 'feature,' the verdict.

It was also necessary to read no less than six press reports of the (September 18th) 'raid' on the 'Duke of Norfolk's Road' (Abbey Clough end) before learning that the members of the Ramblers' Rights Movement protested that they had been unnecessarily assaulted by the 'keepers' or 'beaters,' who, apparently, were not observed by the posse of policemen on this occasion.

GHB Ward

SHEFFIELD CLARION RAMBLERS
1933-34.
THIRTY-THIRD YEAR.
PRICE 1/3 - 192 PAGES.
A Rambler made is a man improved.

The Ruins of Cook's Study.
[Photo by W. Hy. Richardson.]

The man who never was lost never went very far.

LOXLEY BROS. LTD., SHEFFIELD

THE MASS TRESPASS ON KINDER, if it did nothing else, threw a little more illumination on the subject, and when Anderson, after being dismissed of the charge of grievous bodily harm, was sentenced to six months' imprisonment for assault (which may mean anything worse than the raising of the hand in a threatening attitude), the whole of the Federations of the country were aroused by what has been described as a savage sentence, and are now exerting every effort to obtain full support for the Bill. It will be noted there was no charge of trespass or damage preferred against any of the ramblers who took part in the Mass Trespass.

Frank Turton Hon Secretary,
Sheffield & District Ramblers Federation

The 'nominal' trespass

1933 Ramblers' Federation handbook

The year 1932 will not be remembered as a red letter year for the rambler. It has been a period of more than the usual froth and bubble, but out of the welter of society melodramas, bandit sagas, political legerdemain and emetical film-star poppycock, one gratifying fact can be recorded - the hiker's sun is setting.

It would have been interesting to observe how the 'powers' would have dealt with a large scale technical trespass. The trespass was, in fact, nominal, the demonstrators going a short distance on forbidden ground. Unfortunately, the organisers - the British Workers' Sports Federation - put in some poor staff work, and when their followers were faced by six keepers with sticks - which we may be sure were used - there was a nasty scuffle, and one keeper was so injured as to require some hospital treatment.

Only one of the men held in custody was charged with doing grievous bodily harm to the keeper. He was not an official of the BWSF, but came to see the 'sport', and unhappily for him the law will not recognise the difference between players and spectators in a riot. The others were charged with unlawful assembly and with a breach of the peace, as also was Anderson.

It should be pointed out that unusual publicity had been given to this 'mass trespass', and on the Sunday morning in question large numbers of police had been drafted to Hayfield and kept under cover. The demonstrators, however, were only prevented from holding a meeting on the recreation ground, no attempt was made to kill the 'riot', and the authorities grasped the opportunities offered by the bad tactics of the BWSF to proceed on more serious charges than mere trespass.

Maliciously causing grievous bodily harm is a felony and, therefore, triable at Assize. The committal to the Assize was a serious handicap to the prisoners, as it deprived them of their own witnesses, who were not prepared to lose the time and money involved in going to Derby. Anderson and his friends being working class folk had, therefore, little chance against the evidence of the injured keeper (who asserted that Anderson was one of his assailants, and his injury was caused to his knee in a struggle for a stick) and the mass of police evidence.

Public opinion expected the men to be punished, but was not prepared for the harsh sentences actually inflicted. There was at once a revulsion of feeling.

Edwin Royce, President of Manchester & District Ramblers' Federation

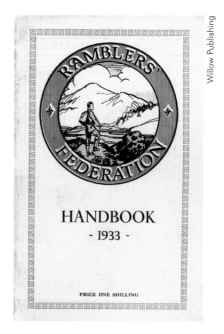

RAMBLERS' FEDERATION

HANDBOOK
- 1933 -

PRICE ONE SHILLING

Willow Publishing

John Anderson - the walk that led to jail

John Anderson (right) at the 1932 protest

Anderson born in 1911 in Droylsden, worked at a cotton mill in his early days, and enjoyed walking the moors at weekends. In 1939 he was living with his parents in Droylsden and employed as a bricklayer's labourer. Later he lived in the Bradford and Wythenshawe districts of Manchester.

He completely disagreed with the aims of the Trespass, but found himself embroiled in the protest. Anderson had been out walking and came across the gathering protesters at Hayfield recreation ground where he was photographed with them. As the group made their way towards Kinder, Sol Gadian, who was on the Trespass, wrote that Anderson made it very clear to those around him that he was against the protest, saying 'How would you like people tramping through your garden?'

Anderson left the main group to sit and watch the confrontation between the keepers and ramblers. He spotted a keeper being overwhelmed and ran over to help him. In the melee, he may have accidentally caught Beever in the stomach and this was misconstrued by the police who thought he was attacking the keeper and charged him with GBH. Anderson called on reporters to verify his comments about being against the Trespass, but they denied overhearing this.

He maintained his barrister (who also represented Gillett) was no good at the trial in Derby, and received the longest sentence of six months for assaulting the keeper. Like the other defendants, he had no witnesses. People on the Trespass have since confirmed that Anderson had not been in favour of protest and that he had not struck Beever.

The actions of the police that day soured his impression of them and after what they said in court he described them as 'trained liars'. Anderson met the injured keeper some time later who told him he had slipped and fallen down the hillside but the police told him to say he had been assaulted.

In 1981 Anderson wrote to me, aggrieved at being put in prison for a crime, he claimed, he didn't commit:

> 'I watched (the Trespass) for a short time and then I decided to go on my own way, but a few minutes later I was arrested and taken to the police station ... I am seventy years of age now, and have almost forgotten my troubles and I hope that in writing this letter I am not causing myself more trouble.'

Anderson does not mention that he had taken part in the scuffles - on the side of the keepers.

William Hanley of Droylsden wrote to the *Manchester Evening News* in 1982:

> I was one of a party of ramblers that was against the mass ramble. We thought it would lead to violence. After the meetings we went on ahead of the mass of protesters. John Anderson was on his own and came along with us. We sat on a slope leading from William Clough to Kinder Scout. Halfway up the slope there was a line of keepers about thirty yards apart. The police were in groups of four or five on the foot of the slope. We saw the crowd come along and then ascended the slope just before reaching us. There were a few scuffles and one keeper was beaten down.

> John Anderson who was with me immediately ran to his aid and was promptly arrested. Naturally he struggled against this. We protested to the police and were threatened with arrest. I did not see John Anderson again for thirty-five years until I came across him in the Friendship Inn, Droylsden. He asked me not to mention the mass ramble as he was the landlord.

The prison sentence continued to irk Anderson and in 1994 he wrote to the Home Office in protest against the miscarriage of justice, but to no avail. In 1995, the Derbyshire Constabulary stated that there were no surviving records of his arrest or imprisonment as they were routinely destroyed. It is very regrettable that the testimonies of Gadian and Hanley were not heard at the trial. Anderson had called another witness who didn't attend the magistrates' court at New Mills.

In 1994 Anderson was invited to the unveiling of the plaque at the former police station at New Mills where he and the others had been detained overnight. He interrupted the proceedings to repeat his belief that he was innocent of the charges made against him. He was applauded by everyone including the Chief Constable of the County. It meant a lot to Anderson but his family said he continued to talk about this great injustice to the end of his days.

After being landlord at the Friendship Inn, Edge Lane, in the 1960s and early 70s he retired with his wife Peggy to Cleveleys where he died in 2000 aged eighty-nine. Even in his latter years with his eyesight failing, he remained a keen walker and Kinder was the place he loved. Despite the traumatic events of the Trespass, which he never got over, his ashes were scattered on the Kinder plateau at his request.

John Anderson and family

 Derbyshire Constabulary
We Care

Keith Mans, M.P.,
House of Commons,
London.
SW1A 0AA.

Telephone (01773) 570100
Fax (01773) 572146
Tel. Ext. 2004
Direct Dial
Ask For Insp. Gee
Your Ref.
       HQX/CC/S(O/JB
Our Ref.

5th April, 1995.

Dear Mr. Mans,

     I write in response to your letter of the 22nd December, 1994, concerning the events surrounding the Kinder Trespass in 1933.

     Despite exhaustive enquiries, both locally and at national level, no records can be found, nor do they exist, in respect of Mr. Anderson's arrest and subsequent incarceration.

     I am sorry I cannot be more helpful.

          Yours sincerely,

          Inspector D. Gee
      Staff Officer to Chief Constable.

Forgotten for forty years?

It has been suggested that the Kinder Trespass had been quickly forgotten, and only 're-surfaced' in the 1980s. But is that true? As I reviewed its coverage in book, magazine and newspaper articles over the years, a different picture emerged.

The first decade after the Trespass

The year after the Trespass, the Manchester Ramblers' Federation and Clarion Ramblers didn't ignore it and included reports and comments on the protest in their year books. Contrary to one of the leading Trespasser's criticisms, both publications gave the protest good coverage, though not their full support. (See previous pages.)

The Trespass did find favour in other quarters. A 1933 article in the *Daily Herald* stated 'Already the mass trespass on Kinder Scout has shown that mountain and moorland cannot be closed to the people without a struggle...' Also during 1933, Frank Turton speaking at a Sheffield Ramblers' Federation meeting said '...it was their duty to go over forbidden paths at least once a year, and even mass trespasses had become necessary'. That year, there was even a 'Mass Trespass' dance at the Piccadilly Salon in Manchester organised by the Manchester Ramblers' Federation.

In 1934 Phil Barnes produced his landmark publication '*Trespassers Will Be Prosecuted*' which highlighted access problems and briefly covered the Kinder and Abbey Brook Trespasses. (See the section on Phil Barnes page 146.)

A letter to the *Sheffield Independent* in 1935 from the correspondent 'HALE-GON' recalled the Trespass and argued it was the time to continue with the tactic: 'For over twenty-five years

they have politely made this reasonable request (for public access to the moors and mountains) and it had not been granted. Surely it is about time they made themselves felt and adopted a more aggressive policy. It is up to everyone to fight for their rights and it is about time ramblers started fighting. That continual trespassing, and mass trespassing is often the only way of doing this and so breaking down the ridiculous resistance'. This was just one of a number of letters both for and against the Trespass published that year.

Newspaper articles in 1937 and 1938 by Tom Stephenson and Stephen Morton referred to the Trespass. Interestingly, the 1938 *Ramblers' Federation Handbook* included it in a chapter of significant events in the history of Kinder.

In 1939 it was certainly in the minds of landowners and the rambling organisations and there was talk of another mass trespass because of the ramblers' unhappiness over a clause of a fine for unintentional trespassing in the forthcoming Access to Mountains Bill which was denounced by ramblers as 'The Landowners' Protection Bill'! As Walter Tysoe, Hon Secretary of the Liverpool Ramblers' Association wrote in a letter to the *Guardian*: 'The 1939 Bill is worse than useless to the rambler; its value to the landowner is proved by the ease in which it is passing through the Lords and the Tory House of Commons.'

On the eighth anniversary of the Trespass, Ted Rivers in the *Progressive Rambler* magazine argued that the youth of this country were being conscripted, yet they were not considered worthy enough to walk upon the

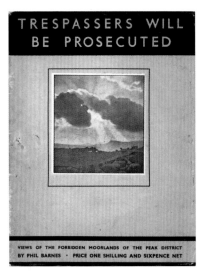

TRESPASSERS WILL BE PROSECUTED

VIEWS OF THE FORBIDDEN MOORLANDS OF THE PEAK DISTRICT
BY PHIL BARNES · PRICE ONE SHILLING AND SIXPENCE NET

Sandy Heys moor, below Kinder, where the confrontation with the keepers took place

land which was considered the sacred monopoly of those few rich persons who called upon them to fight for their country, freedom and democracy. He described the events of the Trespass and how the ramblers had swept to their objective, imbued with a spirit of freedom - a word that was being constantly brandished before their eyes!

The Trespass was also in the thoughts of ramblers' leaders and legislators. Tom Stephenson, in a memorandum to the Scott Committee set up to preserve rural amenities in 1941, reminded them of the mass trespasses of the 1930s which could be repeated in the new era, if there was no progress in countryside access. The Trespass had made its mark, and there was the implicit threat of further action if the authorities dithered. Despite his disapproval of the Trespass, Tom Stephenson nevertheless referred to it to press for change.

Journalists continued to remember the Trespass. A 1945 *Manchester Guardian* article about the proposed National Parks reported 'Many battles have been fought over (the wild moorlands) between members of the rambling fraternity and the representatives of privilege. The 'mass trespass' over Kinder Scout in 1932 will be recalled for example, when five impetuous trespassers received terms of imprisonment ranging up to six months'.

The *Yorkshire Post* carried an article on access to mountains in 1945 which referred to the 1930s incident. I've previously mentioned CEM Joad, a prominent campaigner for access to the moors and mountains, who in his book that year, '*The Untutored Townsmen's Invasion of the Country*' wrote about the Trespass but did not back it.

Under the heading 'This Land is Ours', in 1948 the *Manchester Evening News* outlined the Kinder Trespass story. It is clear from all these references that the Trespass had not been erased from the memory twenty years after the event - but what of the following years?

Books and articles in the 1950s and 1960s

Crichton Porteous in his book '*Peakland*' in 1954 included a chapter on the Trespass. It was not particularly favourable, and yet he chose to remind everyone about it. It was this piece of writing which first caught my attention on the subject and inspired me to find out more.

The Trespass story continued to be told in various newspaper articles in the 1950s and 60s. During the purchase of Kinder in the 1950s, newspaper articles described how in the 1930s 'pitched battles took place there with landowners who insisted that it was private and ramblers were trespassing'.

In 1964, the Ramblers' Association reported slow progress in the completion of the Pennine Way and ventured to suggest there would have to be 'another rising of the north' to make progress. Geoffrey Moorhouse, writing in the *Guardian* in 1965 about the opening of the Pennine Way, talked of the struggle for countryside access: 'It was fought for doggedly, sometimes literally when walkers and gamekeepers coincided on the same grouse moor; in the thirties five men went to prison after a demonstration against restricted access to Kinder Scout'.

In a 1967 article on the Coastal Way, the *Cornish Guardian* referred to earlier campaigns for access: 'veterans can recall mass trespasses, marches, battles with gamekeepers and the imprisonment of ramblers'

'martyrs'. Since those days, walking for pleasure has been in eclipse'.

A newspaper article in 1968 reported that Benny Rothman was to be one of the speakers at Crowden in the Ramblers' Association's campaign against the privatisation of three water authorities which could have endangered the public's right to roam over the hills and moorlands owned by them. It added Benny was jailed for his part in 'the famous mass trespass on Kinder Scout'.

A 1969 *Daily Mirror* article spoke of Britain's 500,000 ramblers who were 'up in arms over the miles of red tape barring them from much of the countryside' and concluded that 'Militant ramblers may consider mass demonstrations similar to those held in the 1930s when demonstrators went to jail for deliberately trespassing on private land on principle. It was this sort of action which culminated in the 1949 Countryside Act'. Yet again, mass trespass was an option still being considered by rambling organisations.

Mr Manchester's diary

A climber looks out from one of the curiously weathered rocks on Kinder Scout.

A day to remember

WORKS convener Bernard Rothman is busy helping with factory sit-ins, but today he is remembering another kind of protest that shook the North-West.

It was 40 years ago, on April 24, 1932, that a youthful Bernard decided to help thousands of young Manchester ramblers denied access to the wild moorland of the Peak District.

Over 600 people walked on to Kinder Scout to challenge the authority of the gamekeepers in a "mass trespass."

At the end of the day, five people, including Bernard, had been arrested on charges including a breach of the peace, riot, and riotous assembly. Bernard was jailed for four months, but the agitation that followed the sentence helped to bring about the first piece of legislation aimed at benefiting ramblers.

Mr Rothman, a

sprightly 60-year-old of Crofton Avenue, Timperley, remembers vividly the well-planned and orderly military-style march.

"We had all met at Hayfield, but there were so many police waiting for us, we moved away quickly and reassembled in a disused quarry at the bottom of Kinder. We blew our whistles and right-wheeled up the side of the hill in one long line.

"Looking down at us were about 10 keepers carrying heavy sticks. There were arguments, and some of the keepers used their sticks, but they were promptly disarmed."

Mr Rothman recalls that the party reached the top of Kinder, to come face to face with another party of ramblers from Sheffield. "It was a tremendous occasion and everybody was laughing and shouting."

When the party returned to Hayfield, five were arrested at random. It was pure luck that Mr Rothman, one of the organisers and secretary of the Bri-

tish Workers' Sports Federation, was singled out by the police.

He says : "I spent the first night in jail and there was a long delay until the trial in Derby I did four months, but I had made my point, I would do it again "

But for the sit-ins at Mr Rothman's factory, he would have celebrated the occasion himself by climbing Kinder with some of his five grandchildren.

Manchester Evening News article on the 40th anniversary of the Trespass. There was no anniversary celebration that year as Benny (or Bernard) was involved in a factory sit-in.

Gillett family

Trespassers Dave Nesbitt, Tona Gillett, Benny Rothman, Ewan MacColl and BBC producer Bob Toner gather at Hayfield for the making of the Look Stranger programme.

Interest rises further in the 1970s

Then in July 1970 the BBC Television's 'Look Stranger' series presented a reconstruction of the Trespass. Three of the jailed Trespassers, Benny Rothman, Tona Gillett and Dave Nesbitt, took part, along with Ewan MacColl. It is interesting that during the programme, visiting ramblers were asked if they had heard of the Trespass. I don't know how the responses were edited, but about half seemed to know something about it. I think it is little different today. I have given talks on the subject for many years, and have found that there is a variable degree of awareness of the Trespass amongst the public. 'Look Stranger' certainly brought the subject to life for a new generation of ramblers.

The protest also featured in a 1973 edition of the *Illustrated London News* in an article about national parks. Roly Smith, then a journalist in the Midlands in 1974, referred to the Trespass when reviewing 'The Kinder Caper' in John Hillaby's book 'Journey Through Britain'. Roly referred to the Trespass

in numerous newspaper and magazine articles over that period. Later that same year Chris Brasher in a *Guardian* article wrote about the success in gaining access to the River Spey in Scotland and compared it to 'the famous battle of Kinder Scout'.

On the 40th anniversary in 1972 of the Trespass Benny was involved in a factory 'sit-in', but he reminisced about the Trespass in a *Manchester Evening News* article describing it as 'a tremendous occasion when everyone was laughing and shouting'.

Another *Guardian* article in 1979 featured the dispute of climbers being forced to pay to use the Roaches and Five Clouds in the Peak National Park. Some were concerned it would lead to the prospect of another mass trespass similar to that on Kinder. Further coverage of the Trespass in both my own book 'High Peak Faces and Places' in 1978, and Howard Hill's 'Freedom To Roam' 1980 helped to keep the Trespass to the forefront. Also, I hardly need mention the ever-popular 'Manchester Rambler' song which has been a constant reminder of those troubled days. It has been a standard of folk musicians since the 1950s and popularised to a wider audience by the Spinners folk group. I think I heard the song for the first time at one of their Free Trade Hall concerts in the late 1960s. The song does not specifically mention the Trespass but it does take us back to the days of keepers and trespassing. The song is often heard as it has been recorded by many artists. There was also extensive coverage of the Trespass in an article by Dave Cook which first appeared in *Mountain* and repeated in *Marxism Today* in 1977. The *Daily Worker* also had an article in 1978.

Finally, there is another group who have never forgotten the Kinder Trespass - the families and friends of the Trespassers. I made contact with some of them as I researched this book, and they were pleased and proud that their stories would become known to a wider audience.

Some may have thought that the Trespass had been erased from memory, but after reviewing the many books, newspaper and magazine articles and television coverage over forty years, I have concluded that the Kinder Trespass was not forgotten and has held a special place in the thinking of many. But clearly the 1982 anniversary brought awareness of it to a new level. The evidence shows that the Trespass has always enjoyed regular coverage in the media.

Gillett family

Scenes from the 'Look Stranger' programme:
Right, Tresspassers in discussion with
former Water Board worker Horace Oldham (left)
Below, Re-enaction of the march towards Kinder

Gillett family

The Trespass - a turning point?

Those who took part in the 1932 Trespass could never have anticipated the impact the protest would have. Ninety years on, it is still talked about and celebrated. It is featured regularly on TV, in the press and on countless websites, as well as in numerous publications. Mike Harding wrote a play about it, its anniversaries are celebrated, the 'Spirit Of Kinder' event is normally held each year, and the Hayfield Kinder Trespass group was formed to publicise and inform about the event. In short, the Kinder Trespass has become a landmark in the campaign for countryside access.

50th Trespass anniversary at Bowden quarry

The Trespass was not the first, nor the biggest and not even the most violent, and yet this particular incident has captured the public imagination like no other. The trial and the resulting jail sentences caused it to receive extensive coverage so that the story, over the years, has become familiar to many.

Controversial

But it was a protest mired in controversy. The established rambling clubs and other organisations strongly disassociated themselves from it because of its political undertones, and those involved in discussions with the landowners thought it had hampered progress. Even in more recent times it has had its critics.

Tom Stephenson is to many, including myself, a hero in the walking world, because he along with others campaigned for many years to help bring about a successful outcome for ramblers with the opening of the Peak National Park, the Pennine Way and the momentous 2000 CRoW Act. He was at the very heart of the negotiations with other ramblers' leaders and members of government. His book 'Forbidden Land', described the difficult route to success with many years of discussions, internal arguments, setbacks and sometimes despair.

Stephenson described the Kinder Trespass as the most dramatic incident in the access to mountains campaign, yet thought it contributed little. He could not bring himself to endorse the Trespass, even though he was a self-confessed trespasser. Writing in the *Daily Herald* in 1937, he described how he explored Kinder but managed to avoid confrontation with keepers. He wrote 'Some day we will have that Pennine Way and be able to sit by Kinder Downfall and chat in friendship with the game-keeper'. The following year in an article headed *'Trespassing Without Apology'* he described his experience of walking on forbidden Bleaklow. But even Stephenson rejected the criticism that the Trespass had set back any hopes of access for twenty years, because at that time he realised there was little hope of the Access to Mountains Bill being passed.

Stephenson's gripe with the Trespass seems to have been over certain details of the protest. He was right to say that most of the protesters did not reach the Kinder Plateau - they got only as far as Ashop Head, although my recent research suggests that some of the Trespassers made their way onto Kinder to celebrate.

Another problem for Stephenson was the estimate of the number of Trespassers. Press reports varied from a few hundred to a thousand. Rothman accepted his earlier report of numbers was excessive and agreed on a more accurate figure of four hundred in his book. Benny invited Tom to write the foreword for the 1982 book on the Trespass but he declined. The differences between the two were equally over politics as well as historical facts. Stephenson's affiliations were with the Labour Party rather than the radical left. There was perhaps another fundamental reason for his rejection of the Trespass, which I will explain later.

Discussions with the BWSF

Benny Rothman admitted later that they should have co-operated with other rambling organisations, but it is difficult to see how it could have worked. However an attempt was made to work together because it was reported at the Manchester and District Ramblers' Federation meeting in September 1933 that discussions had recently taken place with the BWSF, but they did not come to an agreement. The BWSF believed the rambling federations had compromised with the landowners, but the rambling community were not in favour of law-breaking mass trespasses. Possibly if the two sides had got together with regular large demonstrations around England, the landowners might have been pressed to make concessions. As Howard Hill wrote in his book 'Freedom to Roam': 'It was not militancy that had failed, but lack of it'.

Stephenson was dismissive of the BWSF, stating they had no previous interest in the access problem and played no further part in the campaign. But the BWSF could not sustain a long-term campaign of confrontation with the authorities in isolation. The jail sentences had been a shock, and it is understandable the accused were in no hurry to be imprisoned again - they had families and jobs to think of. The Young Communist League turned their attention

to a more pressing cause, with many, including some of the Trespassers, going to fight and die in the war against fascism in Spain. Other former Trespassers, with the growing threat of fascism in this country, took part in protests at Oswald Mosley meetings and marches. With the outbreak of the Second World War, progress on moorland access came to a halt, although lobbying of MPs continued. As I concluded earlier, the Trespass had not been forgotten, but had it been in vain?

The impact of the Trespass

Tom Stephenson believed the Trespass did not contribute in any way to the passing of the 1949 National Parks Act. While no-one can reasonably claim that the Trespass brought about immediate change, we should note some of the reaction to it.

In the second annual conference of British ramblers' federations at Derwent Hall in the October following the Trespass, there was a recognition that new tactics were required. It was reported 'The access to mountains question caused much concern because of the recent drastic actions taken in the mass trespass cases which is resulting in the virile younger ramblers combining together to get something practical done instead of the endless shelving of the Access to Mountains Bill. Attempts to get the Bill through Parliament have been going on for forty years.'

Sheffield Ramblers' leader, Stephen Morton, who was not initially a supporter of the Trespass but perhaps unwittingly revealed its impact, wrote in 1933 'I believe that we were all roused by the result of the trial following the mass trespass, and even those among us who were not in sympathy with such methods have realised that the dice has been somewhat unfairly loaded and have rallied round upon this question. The erstwhile apathetic south has declared that it now supports us and every Ramblers' Federation supports our case for Access to Mountains.'

In a 1937 Sheffield Independent article, Morton wrote 'Following upon the Hayfield Mass Trespass a great change of public feeling was noticed and the landowners and their agents began to feel that perhaps after all they had gone a little too far, and so they put out feelers in the proper quarters *and a conference at the Victoria Station Hotel, Sheffield in 1934 resulted. The ramblers' movement sent a representative deputation of experienced middle-aged men who were prepared to concede many points if the other side would do so. For the granting of five permissive ways principally along edge routes in Derbyshire the landowners could have undermined the agitation for Access to Mountains for a generation, but they could not concede even this small point.'*

Stephen Morton

Change in public opinion

So Morton had concluded the Trespass had brought about a fresh surge of enthusiasm for the access campaign, and it had also caused ramblers in Southern England and every Ramblers' Federation to unite behind the case for the parliamentary Act. Crucially the Trespass resulted in a shift in public opinion towards access and the landowners felt forced into being seen to be doing something by holding a meeting with ramblers' representatives, even if it still resulted in no agreement. The Trespass, dismissed as a 'political stunt' by some, had actually produced a positive effect.

Morton later went further on the impact of the Trespass. In a letter written to Benny Rothman towards

the end of his life he wryly wrote 'the Trespass had become the most valuable piece of history for our own cause'. He still thought it was 'mired in myth' but accepted that 'the Trespassers were the more important historical figures, and those who had struggled on to success could only marvel'. The last part of the statement was written in a degree of regret, and it should be acknowledged that while we will always remember and celebrate the Trespass, it was the ramblers' leaders who crucially steered agreement with the landowners. Towards the end of his life, Morton wrote 'That is not to say that they (the Trespassers) weren't right and, with hindsight, that it might have been better if we had taken it up and organised it', although he went on to admit that the Sheffield and Manchester ramblers' federations would not have supported it.

This brings us back to Tom Stephenson who continued to criticise the Trespass, and the crux of his rejection of its impact. He could not accept that the one-off Trespass should be viewed by so many as a symbol of the campaign for access, and seemingly to overshadow the years of hard work done by him and others to establish walkers' rights. It may seem unjust, but public perception is everything and there is no reason why an accurately-presented Trespass account cannot be placed alongside the

Derwent Hall, venue for the 1932 annual conference of the Ramblers' Federation. The 17th century hall was demolished in 1944 to make way for the construction of Derwent Reservoir completed in 1945.

Harry Rothman

Benny with John Beadle (left), chairman of the Peak Park Planning Board, and Alan Mattingly (right), Secretary of The Ramblers

undoubted achievements of the access pioneers. Stephen Morton had been faced with the same dilemma and eventually came to terms with it.

Benny Rothman, did not as some have thought, suddenly re-appear on the scene at the time of the 50th anniversary of the Trespass - he had been campaigning on environmental, rambling and access issues since at least the 1950s. His papers and documents can be seen at the Working Class Movement Library in Salford.

New recognition

Another criticism of the Trespass is that its significance has been over-exaggerated by the organisers of the various anniversaries and that the facts of the protest have been distorted. It is true that at the time of the 1982 anniversary, either the Ramblers or the Trespassers were 'brought in from the cold' - depending on your point of view! The two sides had viewed each other with suspicion for many years but here they came together. Suddenly, the 1932 Trespass had become mainstream, with a recognition of its role in the path to greater countryside access. Alan Mattingly of the Ramblers' Association said: *'The famous Kinder Trespass has become a symbol of the long campaign for access to the moors and mountains of Britain. Because of the publicity and public sympathy which was attached to those who suffered imprisonment following the event, the Trespass stands*

out as one of the best-remembered episodes in that campaign.'

Mattingly was right to highlight its symbolic importance but no-one should think that success was achieved simply by the protest. The 1949 National Parks Act and the Countryside and Rights of Way Act in 2000 were the result of years of patient and often difficult negotiation with the landowners, alongside friendly governments driving the process. Benny Rothman, in a description of the Trespass written some time before 1982 gave a fair summary of events: '...in its own small way the Mass Trespass was one of those little flareups in the general fight for Access to mountains which we didn't inaugurate, which we were not alone in fighting, although of course we felt at the time that we were leading it, as people do, youngsters especially ...'

At Trespass anniversaries and *Spirit of Kinder* events there is little time to fully acknowledge the part played by past ramblers' leaders to bring about change, but no-one should underestimate their role. It is pleasing to see that in recent years the work and life of GHB Ward has been given more prominence, and I hope the contribution of Phil Barnes, Stephen Morton, and Edwin Royce among others will also come more to the fore. I pay tribute to some of these people later in this book. Far from spreading myths, the organisers of these events, the speakers, and this

Keith Warrender

Mike Harding and the Chapel-en-le-Frith Male Voice choir sing the 'Manchester Rambler' at the 80th Trespass anniversary

Keith Warrender

The next generation: the 2016 Spirit of Kinder event at Hayfield with Jan Gillett (right) son of jailed Trespasser Tona Gillett

writer are attempting to bring accuracy, clarity, balance and new research to the subject.

False claims

Regrettably, we cannot control what others may claim about the Trespass. For example I once read in a newspaper article that Ewan MacColl was the leader of the Trespass! One of the people who was directly involved in the negotiations for access to the National Park wrote to the *Guardian* in 1985, stating that the Trespass took place in 1931, and that the Ramblers' Association had paid the fines of the 'deluded unemployed youngsters'. Surprisingly, for someone closely involved in discussions with landowners, he had got all his 'facts' wrong - the Trespass was a year later, the ramblers were jailed not fined and the Ramblers' Association was formed in 1935! Benny Rothman, as you might expect, responded robustly to these claims, stating it was the Trespass which brought about a surge of interest and paved the way for the 1949 National Parks Act.

The situation is not made easier by ridiculous claims such as those made by the lead singer of a northern rock group. In an interview given in the late 1980s, he stated 'The first time (Benny Rothman) went on the land, all these Lords whipped him to the ground. The next week he came back with six thousand people and held firm, and that led to the setting up of the National Trust'. Another false claim was that GHB Ward had organised the Trespass even though he had no part in it.

Direct action

Lord Hattersley described the Trespass as 'the most successful direct action in British history'. This is echoed by countryside activist Howard Hill who wrote in 1980: 'One lesson which shines like a beacon through all the long years of struggle for access is the vital importance of public demonstration. It was this which saved the London Commons; over a period of forty years it won many notable victories in the Peak, secured access to Barden Moor in West Yorkshire, and partial access to Bowland in Lancashire. Drawing upon the lessons of the past it is within our power to make the dreams of James Bryce, GHB Ward, Edwin Royce and Tom Stephenson become a living reality'. The Trespass therefore did have an impact on public opinion and the wider rambling world, and continues to be a significant event in the ongoing campaign to protect and secure more access to the countryside.

Keith Warrender

Members of the Hayfield Kinder Trespass group unveiling the Trespass Trail information board in the old station car park 2017

Trespass day memories

Inside story

SOL GADIAN

My Young Communist League friends told me that a mass walk of ramblers was being organised as a demonstration of opposition to the enclosure of the moors. During the week prior to the demonstration I found out I had other commitments at the weekend but promised to be there and asked a friend to take my walking boots.

I arrived in Hayfield not dressed for walking over the moors, and ran from the station to the recreation ground which was deserted apart from a small group of men in conversation. I asked which way had the people gone and was given a sullen look and told the marchers had gone towards the Snake Path about a quarter of an hour previously.

I caught up with them beyond Kinder Reservoir. As they streamed up the path in ones and twos they made a tremendous sight - far more than I expected. Nearly all were in agreement with the Trespass, although I saw an occasional frown from some who I later found out were detectives walking among the ramblers. As I passed group after group I voiced my agreement with the march and the pleasure at seeing it so well supported.

I walked some time with a lad [John Anderson] who wore a khaki shirt and shorts. He expressed some doubts about the march and thought it was wrong to trespass on other people's property. He said to me 'How would you like someone going through your garden?' I told him I did not think that wild country, hundreds of miles square was someone's garden and that humans had a greater right to walk on it than a few men shooting grouse. I left him and continued to look for my friend. I soon caught up with him, and quickly changed my light shoes for the heavy rambling boots he was carrying for me.

When we got to William Clough at the foot of Kinder, I heard a sharp whistle from a leader at the front. This was a pre-arranged signal because the long file of ramblers came to a halt. There was another short blast and we turned right to the steep slope of the hill. I then saw on the skyline what appeared to be keepers standing swinging their sticks waiting for the trespassers to come up the hill.

I noticed a young woman I knew scrambling up the slope and I reached out to give her a hand. As we neared the top of the moor, the keepers came down the hill to meet us swinging their sticks wildly. The steepness of the hillside made it difficult for them to keep their balance, and as the ramblers avoided the vicious swinging sticks they overbalanced and rolled down the hill. Other keepers tried to grapple with the ramblers but were easily pushed to one side. Heavily outnumbered, they soon gave up the struggle and the trespassers assembled at the top of the hill.

The 'battle' was over in a few minutes, everyone was jubilant. The protesters then turned back in a disciplined column down the clough and on to the Snake Path to Hayfield. The happy hikers were singing as they came to the outskirts of the village, but we had not fully appreciated the enormity of our effort on the sacred right of private property, nor the fury of the landed gentry who saw their precious shooting rights challenged by a group of ordinary working-class ramblers.

As the march neared Hayfield, a police inspector and about five constables stepped into the road, and with a raised arm brought the demonstration to a halt. A few of the lads were for pushing past the police and continuing into the village, when a whisper went through the ranks, 'It's a trap!'

One of the marchers had gone ahead and came back with the news that dozens of Derbyshire policemen were waiting for us to break through and were ready to wade in with truncheons drawn against our group, which contained a high percentage of women and girls.

As the column stood, detectives picked out a number of lads who they thought to be the leaders. Then the ramblers were allowed to disperse and soon only a few of the protesters were left. I had lost my two camping mates on the climb and loitered around waiting to see whether they would meet me as arranged.

Half an hour later, the woman who I had helped up the slope came over and said that my friends Harry Mendel and Jud Clynes had been arrested and were now in the local police station. Not having had any practical experience of dealing with the law, I thought that I could enquire as to whom had been arrested and, if necessary, offer a substantial amount as bail for their release. Innocently, I went to the police station and they asked who I wanted to bail out. Immediately I was subject to a barrage of questions as to what I knew about the other ramblers. I became cautious as they began to describe people who I knew not to be in custody. When I asked who they had arrested, they became aggressive and pushed me away saying if I wasn't out of their sight in two minutes I would also be 'inside'. I stayed in the village until early evening and then took a lonely train home.

The following day, the Daily Express showed a photograph of my friend Wolfie Winnick grappling with a keeper, and I then realised why I had been repeatedly asked at Hayfield police station whether I knew someone wearing a high-necked pullover. They were referring to Wolfie. Fortunately I had answered 'I did not think so'.

My workmate Harry Mendel was one of the six arrested and he was released with the others on bail, and came back to work, giving me the full story. It was only then I realized that only house-holders could get bail for anyone.

One afternoon, a few weeks before the trial at Derby, my employer wanted a word with me about Harry Mendel. He said there were two detectives in his office enquiring about him and wanting to know if he was a member of the Young Communist League. I asked my boss to give a good account of him, and of course he was a very good worker. As far as his membership of the YCL was concerned, I pleaded ignorance.

The employer must have spoken well of him, because he was the only one acquitted out of the six. Also, Harry was a small chap, barely five feet tall, and I could not imagine any keeper or policemen charging him with assault. The lad who protested his innocence received the heaviest sentence of six months, one of the reasons being he was carrying an offensive weapon in his belt - a Bowie knife.

Wolfie had not been arrested because, on the way back to Hayfield, he stayed at the rear of the column of walkers and then jumped over a wall and made his way back by a different route. He spent the night with a friend because he thought it inadvisable to go home. The following day his fears were proved correct because his photograph was in the newspapers and enquiries had been made at the YMCA to check if he was the one the police were looking for. This was because I had let slip at Hayfield police station that I had friends there. In the evening Wolfie came round to see me. He thought he should stay out of sight for a while, but he had no money because he was unemployed. I gave him five pounds and he went to stay in London with his brother Maurice and found work there for a few months. I did not see him again for almost twelve months, and by then the Trespass had been forgotten in those changing times.

One of the effects of the visit by the detectives to the factory where I worked, was my indignation that a person's innocence or guilt was determined not by his actions, but whether he was a member of a political party. When my employer said to me, 'By the way are you a member of the YCL?' I unintentionally replied 'Yes', while still having reservations about becoming a member. That weekend I received a week's notice for something very trivial - breaking too many needles. There was an immediate protest by the other workers and the notice was withdrawn.

The Kinder Scout Riot

INSPECTOR WILLIAM HUDSON

On Sunday, 24th April, 1932, there was an occurrence in Derbyshire which had a lasting impact upon the nation's laws and attitudes concerning public access to the moorland and mountains. I was heavily involved in this event which has become widely known as the Kinder Scout Riot.

Preparations for a 'Mass Rally' to be staged at Hayfield in the Peak District had been well publicised and it was expected that large groups of ramblers would gather together to form a huge assembly whose declared aim was to trespass en-masse onto and over the Kinder Scout Peak which was private land patrolled by the usual gamekeepers and bailiffs.

On Saturday, 23rd April, I was instructed by the Assistant Chief Constable to accompany him in his car, in plain clothes, the following morning. [Hudson worked at the Police Headquarters in the Chief Constable's office at Derby.] We duly arrived at the village of Hayfield where we joined up with a large contingent of Derbyshire Police.

The village was eventually swarming with mostly young men and women, a large proportion wearing ramblers' attire and rucksacks. At around two o'clock they made their way towards the old quarry, where they assembled for their meeting. Two men who seemed obviously to be the leaders or organizers stood on a protruding rock in the quarry and addressed the crowd of ramblers. The main speaker, a young man in his twenties, urged the ramblers to proceed with determination to win through in the face of whatever obstacles they may meet. After a rousing speech he concluded, his arms held high, with what appeared to be their clarion call: 'Access to the Mountains'.

The crowd moved off in a reasonably calm manner through the entrance to the moorland. The police made no attempt to follow, but remained in the quarry area with the exception of a few plain clothes men (of whom I was one) who watched the progress of the ramblers. A line of gamekeepers and bailiffs confronted the ramblers near the summit in an attempt to turn them back, but they were attacked and overcome by the ramblers who now continued their progress to the peak.

From our viewpoint, we were concerned that the ramblers might decide to continue onward instead of returning to Hayfield as we had good reason to believe they would. After a little while, however, they reappeared on the horizon and began the descent towards Hayfield. We reported to the Assistant Chief Constable who outlined the Police strategy which was to stop the procession of ramblers after they entered the stone-walled lane where they would be trapped. We were instructed to arrest any men who we were able to identify as being the leaders of the unlawful assembly at the quarry.

I had made a careful mental note of the identity of the main speaker and his close companion when leaving the quarry. My task now was to pick them out from amongst some three hundred ramblers. Luck seemed to be on my side as I searched through such a large crowd and eventually recognised the two men. I arrested both men and handed them over to uniformed constables. Three other men were arrested with the assistance of gamekeepers who had witnessed the assault by the ramblers and could identify the main culprits. It seemed natural that I should feel rather proud to be the one to arrest the two principal offenders and I received compliments from the Chief Constable and others.

The prisoners were charged by me with being involved and taking part in an unlawful assembly. They gave their names as Bernard Rothman and David Nussbaum. It was soon realised that Rothman was the man who had been sought, unsuccessfully, by the police for some days in an attempt to serve him with an injunction forbidding the assembly and the trespass. At later dates I was taken to visit the prisoners in custody when I charged Rothman and Nussbaum with taking part in a riot, and Rothman with also the more serious offence of Promoting a Riot.

This was probably the first and only occasion of a case of riot in Derbyshire and provides an example of the change of attitudes. Nowadays such an occurrence would warrant relatively little attention and publicity, but in those days it was profound. It did, however, serve its purpose and led to the freedom now enjoyed by ramblers such as could never have been envisaged before the riot.

● I'm very grateful to William Hudson's daughter for sending this account and giving permission for it to be used. Many years ago I received a letter from Hudson's wife offering to give his view of events. To my later regret I didn't take up the kind offer, but kept the letter with the contact details. Recently I managed to trace his daughter, and was delighted when she sent her father's memories of the Trespass which were included in his memoirs compiled by his grandson in Australia.

There are a number of points to note regarding Hudson's account of events. He identified Benny Rothman and his 'close companion' Dave Nussbaum to be arrested. However, if Benny had a 'close companion' in the quarry, it would more likely have been Wolfie Winnick or Lance Helman who both absconded after the Trespass.

The second thing is William Hudson's acceptance that the Trespass had an influence on the campaign for access to the countryside. His account was written for the benefit of his family, and he had no way of knowing this section of his memoir would later be read by such a wide audience. On the day of the Trespass he was doing his duty, but in this account he fully accepted that the Trespass 'had a lasting impact upon the nation's laws and attitudes concerning public access to the moorland and mountains.' Interestingly, he thought that a similar event today would not have attracted as much publicity. Hudson was a constable at the time of the Trespass but later rose to the rank of Inspector.

Sadly, there are no surviving official police records of the Trespass as items are routinely destroyed after a certain amount of time. KW

Inspiring sight

ELI HAGUE

If I forget anything else, nothing will ever eradicate from my mind that famous Sunday, April 24th 1932. It is with humble pride that I recall that I was one of those who joined in the great Mass Trespass that fine day. From Hayfield the small army of around 500 surged up William Clough to the Sandy Heys Moor, singing as they went. It was an inspiring sight.

Seen clearly against the sky, ranged on the crest of Kinder's steep slope was a line of gamekeepers armed with sticks ready to repel our advance. At a briefing, given by Mr Rothman, our instructions had been simple. The intention was not to fight but merely to walk around the keepers. At a long blast from a whistle we crossed the stream and dashed up the steep slope. The paid guardians wielded their heavy sticks but they were no match for us.

Outnumbered, the defenders were quickly subdued. One keeper was injured; at first it was thought he had suffered a broken thigh but it later transpired that the only damage was a twisted ankle which came about when he and a certain Mr Anderson were struggling for possession of the keeper's stick ... the demonstration struck a significant blow in the battle which eventually resulted in the formation of the National Parks.

Extract from 'Streets away from Paradise' published by Neil Richardson 1987

Streets away
from Paradise

Reminiscences of a
Stalybridge Lad

Eli Hague   £3.50

Caught up in the Trespass

GEORGE BEATTIE ELLIOT

To say I was a witness is a rather lugubrious statement, because my involvement in the affair was purely accidental, but I may have triggered other people's behaviour on that day, rather more than I realised at the time.

I was eighteen years of age, and I had 'slept" (no sleeping bag) the previous evening in a cave at Laddow Rocks. Consequently, it must have been shortly after dawn that I made my way down to the Longdendale Valley, then crossed Bleaklow, and onto Kinder, and set a course to bring me out at the Edale Cross side, as I was en-route to the Goyt Valley area. I was quite unaware that an organised Mass Trespass was intended for that day.

I do not remember having noticed anything unusual as it sloped down from the Kinder plateau, and further down the ground levels, and cuts off your forward downward view, so it was not until I had covered this stretch and was overlooking the remaining slope to Edale Cross that I saw the line of gamekeepers with their backs to me, who were facing a large crowd with a spread of people all along the Hayfield-Edale track. No doubt, some of the people spotted me as I made no attempt to conceal myself.

However, I naturally sensed that the Cross area was a trouble spot, so I discreetly altered my course to slant down towards the stream which runs past the bottom of Jacob's ladder. All went well until, at the same time as I caught sight of the track again, my way was baulked - as I saw the backs of two more gamekeepers.

I altered course again. All might have gone well, except for some of the people on the track who saw me and sent up a rousing cheer. I waved, but as I was coming 'off' the moorland, I made no attempt to avoid the two gamekeepers, who were now alerted, and who moved towards me as I approached them. I expected to be grabbed, but not rough-handled, to the extent that I lashed out, and they in turn punched me to the ground.

I am rather hazy as to what happened next, but recollect some solicitous hikers attending to me, and a lot of shouting and cheering, and people swarming past all over the place. The two keepers had gone, and I was most embarrassed, as my helpers made it clear that they approved of my 'action', whereas I was not at all certain as to what I was supposed to have done? Except defend myself.

George Beattie Elliot was born on the outskirts of Stalybridge, Cheshire. As a young man, he spent most of his time exploring the local moors and crags of the area. After acquiring a motorbike, he visited the Lake District where he developed a deep love of climbing and walking and became a member of the Fell and Rock Climbing Club.

George was a staunch socialist and was an aircraft designer by profession and eventually became employed at British Aerospace at Warton and remained there until his retirement in 1980.

He was also very interested in archaeology, especially the Stone Age period, and became an expert on cup and ring markings and megaliths. He gave many lectures on the subject during his retirement. George's final ambition was to live long enough to see the end of the Conservative government. He got his wish and died in July 1998.
BOB ELLIOT

● The crowd of people seen by George Elliot on the Hayfield to Edale path was most likely to have been the Spartacus Rambling Club led by Bill Keen who were on their way to meet the main group of Trespassers.

They had taken the train to Edale and were making for Kinder via Jacob's Ladder. After the meeting with the Hayfield contingent at Ashop Head, they made their way back to Edale. It is unclear why Watts's gamekeepers stationed near Kinder Downfall did not see them. KW

Apparently they had come to my help - which in turn may have sparked off a rush in this area to get past the gamekeepers. As for myself, still half-dazed, I went on my way - the exact opposite direction to where everybody else was going! Indeed, it was only the subsequent press publicity about the people arrested on that day, that really gave me a better idea of what had taken place.

It was very noticeable, after this day, that attitudes hardened, and even on our rock-climbing activities; where formerly our relationships with the local gamekeepers had been good, we were now increasingly interfered with at Laddow Rocks, Dovestones Quarry, Raven Stones and other places.

Ironically, in '39 when it was thought necessary to organise night patrols on our moorlands - to spot enemy parachutists - an appeal went out for people who knew their way around such places - and gamekeepers and the former trespassers were working together. It was during this period that I learned that some of the gamekeepers had quite enjoyed our little game of trying to outwit each other, providing no violence or damage had taken place.

Again, during the 'thirties' with its mass unemployment problem, they were dependent on holding their jobs, and just had to carry out the instructions of their employers. I am still able to wander around the mountains and moorlands of our country, and on the very rare occasions I am stopped by a game-keeper or warden, they are very kind, and appear to be more concerned for my safety than anything else.

John Beatty

Arial view over Jacob's Ladder and the track towards Edale Cross

Harry Rothman

Trespass vets at the 60th anniversary celebration: L-R Benny Rothman, Jimmy Jones, Walter Leigh,
Bella Costello, Len Wood, Arthur Schofield, not known, George Sumner, Harvey Jackson.

The Trespassers

Here is the largest collection of Trespasser stories ever assembled.
The deeds of Rothman, MacColl and Tippett are well recorded.
Now meet the future speedway ace, soccer pro, talented musician
and TV science presenter. Another was a reluctant guard of Mahatma
Gandhi and two were Greenham Common ladies.

There was a strong political element among many of these idealistic
young men and women. But all shared an enduring passion for
walking in Peakland.

My research has led as far as Australia and New Zealand and it has
unearthed new information about the Trespass. Many thanks
to everyone who helped, and if there's anything further to add,
I should be delighted to hear from you.

The Spanish Civil War was fought from 1936 to 1939. Insurgent nationalists, led by General Franco, overthrew the republican government. During the conflict Spain became an ideological battleground for fascists and socialists from all countries. Nine known Trespassers were among 526 volunteers from Britain and Ireland who died. TW

Alec Armstrong (1909-1937)

Born in Hulme, Alec was a roofer in the building trade, although most of the time he was unemployed. He was a keen rambler and climber, and would spend days alone on the moors or in the forests, sleeping rough and living off the land. He caught grouse and trout, and trapped rabbits. Once he returned to meet up with friends saying he had been 'exploiting the exploiters' and removed from his rucksack what he described as 'a gift from our masters'. He had raided a shooting cabin laden with food and drink for the following day's shoot, and had taken bottles of claret, smoked ham, venison pate and a game pie. As he handed round the stolen booty he claimed he was 'redistributing the wealth!'

Armstrong was a close friend of Jimmy Miller (Ewan MacColl) and a member of the Theatre of Action company run by Miller and wife Joan Littlewood. It was known as an 'agiprop' theatre group - a combination of the words 'agitation' and 'propaganda' originating from Soviet Russia. The satirical street theatre presentations reflected their political views.

Armstrong fought in Spain and went in the same boots he used when rambling in Derbyshire. He was killed in 1937, and a memorial meeting was held at the Coliseum Cinema, Ardwick Green for him, Clem Beckett and seven others who died in Spain. Dame Sybil Thorndyke gave a speech saying she was proud to join in this great celebration of heroes.

Bill Banks (1909-1938)

An outdoors enthusiast for camping and the outdoors, he was from Eccles and a member of the AEU and the CP. He was killed at Ebro, Spain.

Clem Beckett (1906-1937)

Clem was born at Scouthead near Oldham, and after first working at Platt Brothers' engineering works he became an apprentice blacksmith but left following victimisation over his trade union activities. Throughout his teens he had a great interest in motorbikes. When he was eighteen he attended a meeting at the Temperance Hall in Oldham which led him to join the YCL, and later the BWSF where he later became a vice-president. He and Benny Rothman used to go to the London national BWSF committee meetings on his big Brough 1000 bike. In the late 1920s he was a dirt-track rider and rode many races in Europe and Turkey. He was fearless and sometimes known as 'the brave young blacksmith from Oldham'.

In 1930 he started the *Wall of Death* shows, riding around a circular walled enclosure at great speed. He took the show around Britain and Europe for a year. This earned him the name of 'Daredevil Beckett'. To add to the tension, there was a lion-cub waiting to pounce, below the riders in the enclosure. Clem's niece remembered the lion, which was kept in his garage

Beckett family

between shows. Clem also took her for rides on his bike until her mother told him to stop and threatened him with a large knife. He also took her, more safely, in an open-topped car which helped to cure her travel sickness. She also recalls he always had a cigarette dangling from his mouth.

Beckett joined the speedway team at London's White City where he helped to set up the Dirt-track Riders' Association to protect the young inexperienced riders who were suffering death or serious injury as well as the financial exploitation all riders suffered. His revelations about the sport earned him a one-season ban. He became

The restored 1928 Rudge Whitworth which Beckett rode in the 1920s and early 30s

one of the star riders of Belle Vue Aces, Manchester, before helping to form the Sheffield Tigers at the new Owlerton Stadium in 1929 where he was a big star, as the sport gained great national popularity. He took a tour party to the Soviet Union in 1932 and stayed there four months giving demonstrations of his riding skills.

On his return he bought a shop on Oldham Road, Manchester, where he sold bikes made from spare parts. He volunteered to fight in the Spanish Civil War and collected money for five ambulances which he helped to drive there. In February 1937 he took part in the battle of Jarama in which the British battalion found themselves under heavy bombardment. Beckett and his friend, poet and novelist Christopher Caulwell, volunteered to cover the retreating forces with a Chatto machine gun but tragically lost their lives, after the gun jammed.

Earlier Beckett had written to his wife that he would never have been satisfied if he had not assisted in the conflict because of his hatred of fascism. Nearly two thirds of the battalion lost their lives on what became known as 'Suicide Hill' during the battle which went on for three days. Beckett's body was never brought back to England. Margaret, Clem's niece, also recalled that at his home in Oldham, his accordion and violin were kept behind the living room door - ready for his return home.

A memorial meeting was held in May 1937 at the Coliseum Cinema, Ardwick Green for nine men who had given their lives in the Civil War. Beckett's widow, Lida a Dane, he had met on one of his tours, said 'My husband like hundreds of others, went to Spain and faced death, not because he was reckless with life, but because he loved life and believed that people can live freely and happily only if they take power into their own hands'. It is thought ten men from Oldham went to fight in Spain, but only four returned alive.

The play *Dare Devil Rides to Jarama* by Neil Gore about the lives of Clem Beckett and Christopher Caulwell and performed by Townsend Theatre Productions in 2016-17 was commissioned by the International Brigade Memorial Trust.

The Oldham Museum collection contains Beckett's leather helmet, photographs of him and a 1980s relief memorial to the local men who fought in Spain.

Ernest Beesley (1902-1986)

Ernest was born at Gorton, and by 1939 he was a cloth inspector living in George Street, Manchester. He described himself as always a rebel, and was involved in campaigns such as the unemployment movement in the 1920s and The People's March For Jobs which passed through Manchester to London, and the No More War Movement in the 1930s. He also helped to set up the Levenshulme CND.

Beesley realised they were breaking the law on the Trespass, but for years they had tried to get access by peaceful means. He believed that every great reform in this country had been achieved through breaking the law, right from the 1381 Peasant's Revolt.

He wrote: *'On the day of the Trespass, the trains from London Road were crowded. We set off for Kinder where a party of gamekeepers armed with sticks tried to turn us back, and hand to hand skirmishes broke out. However, we persisted and the mass trespass took place. Afterwards we set off back to Hayfield in great spirits singing 'Tipperary' and other popular songs. We were met by a cordon of police and gamekeepers and six of the ramblers were arrested. Our efforts were rewarded nineteen years later when the Peak District became the first British National Park in 1951 - giving everyone the right to walk in peace in this wonderful countryside. The democratic right of access to many of today's beauty spots we enjoy today was bitterly fought for, and in some cases dearly paid for.'*

Bill Benson (1914-1968)

From Oldham, and involved with the National Unemployed Workers Movement. He was a member of the CP, the Electrical Trades Union and the Workers' Arts Club. He contested Eccles Council for the Labour Party and died in 1968.

George, Ciceley & Florence Boatte

They were the children of Charles, a calico printing warehouse packer from Tipperary. Their mother Annie came from Grimsby. They were all born and grew up in Cheetham Hill.

GEORGE BOATTE (1904-1948) became a solicitor, and in 1938 spoke at the Left Book Club at the Burlington Cafe, Manchester, along with Harold Lever, where the subject was *Justice For England - imperfections in British law*. In 1940 he gave a speech for the National Council of Civil Liberties at Nelson, and also that year, represented defendants accused of presenting a play at the Free Trade Hall, Manchester before it had been approved by the Censor. The half-hour play *Spectacle*, depicted five scenes from the Russian Revolution and was organised by the Manchester branch of the Russia Today Society. The following year he represented six engineering apprentices involved in a trade dispute. In 1946 he moved office to Corporation Street, now the site of the

Lloyd family

Jess and George Boatte

Manchester Arndale, and also that year married saxophonist Jessie Filler at St Asaph. Two years later he became concerned over the health of his wife who was admitted to hospital with cancer. The worry broke his health and he was found dead in his office on Corporation Street with gas poisoning. Jessie died three months later, age 36, at Withington Hospital.

Jack and Florence Franklin

Lloyd family

FLORENCE BOATTE (1906-1988) trained as a teacher in Manchester and taught in Cleethorpes in 1928. From there she went to a teaching post in Grimsby in 1929 and became involved in local politics with the Labour Party. She met her future husband, Jack Franklin there, and in 1955 she was elected to the borough council and then in 1974 she switched to the newly-formed Humberside county council.

Florence was Mayor of Grimsby in 1972 and her husband Jack had held the office in 1957. She made history in 1986 when she was granted the Freedom of the Borough, ten years after her husband received the honour. The Franklins had championed the opening of Grimsby College of Education which had been initially nicknamed 'Franklin's Folly' but became very successful and known today as Franklin Sixth Form College.

Lloyd family

CICELEY BOATTE (LLOYD) (1915-1988) Before having children, Ciceley worked as a bookkeeper and secretary for several Manchester businesses. She later returned to work first of all in the charity sector and then for many years as Buildings Officer for the Salford Roman Catholic Diocese. Ciceley became politically active in her teens, encouraged by her older brother and sister, George and Florence. Throughout her life she backed campaigns for rights and justice, from supporting the Republican cause in the Spanish Civil War, to being an active volunteer for several charities and to joining the women protesting at Greenham Common in 1983. Sir Tony Lloyd MP is her son and a supporter of the right to roam campaign.

Ciceley and Florence Boatte

Martin Bobker (1911-1983)

By BARBARA WHITLEY

Martin Bobker was described by the *Jewish Telegraph* at the time of his death as one of the most outstanding 'secular' leaders of Manchester Jewry. He was best known as a Socialist, Jewish defence fighter and a fierce opponent of anti-semitism. During the early 1930s he was very active in the fight against Oswald Mosley's Blackshirts who roamed the streets spreading their hatred. On one occasion when they were marching officially in Manchester protected by the police, fights broke out between the fascists and anti-fascists and Martin was involved in a fight for which he was arrested and spent a night in jail. It was very important for young Jewish men at that time to be able to protect themselves and many kept themselves fit and disciplined by attending the Jewish Lads' Brigade, the YMCA and taking boxing lessons. These experiences laid the basis for his future involvement in politics.

Bobker family

Martin Bobker

The deprivation he suffered in his early years undoubtedly led to his desire to become a teacher. He was the fifth child of six born in a very small house in Salford. His father died when he was six years old leaving his mother to support her family alone. They were very poor and often went hungry and although the Jewish charities helped, it did not prevent the shame and embarrassment he suffered when the children were asked in front of the whole class at the Jewish school if they needed any shoes or clothes. Martin had to wear the cast-offs of his older brothers. He won a scholarship to Salford Grammar, but when his mother died there was no one to look after him, so he had to leave school at 14 to take care of himself. Later he found work as a garment maker and he joined the Garment Makers' Union in which he played a prominent role.

During his war-time service he passed his matriculation enabling him to take an emergency teacher training course at Freckleton College near Blackpool. Initially he taught at the Jews' School and then he taught at Cheetwood Primary School and became the headteacher in 1963. He never forgot his experiences as a young child and made sure that the children in his care were given the support and encouragement they needed. His work in primary education was greatly appreciated by fellow professionals and the children.

His political activities were all concerned with promoting a fairer, more equal society. He was a member of AJEX (Association of Jewish Ex-servicemen) and later became vice president. Through Martin, AJEX organised an annual oratory contest to celebrate the life of Mordechai Anielewicz, a young Jew who organised an uprising in the Warsaw Ghetto and who died in the battle. It was important to Martin that such examples of bravery in the fight against Nazis were publicised. Martin was AJEX delegate to the Jewish Communal Council in Manchester where various organisations were represented. His contributions were described as 'fortissimo and passionate'. A very appropriate way to describe him!

Below: Martin Bobker (right) with Labour leader and later Chancellor Hugh Gaitskell (front left)

Martin was a member of the Labour Party for many years and held a number of posts including vice-chairman of the former Prestwich and Middleton Constituency Party. His socialist principles underpinned his many other community activities. A particular concern in the 60s and 70s was the resurgence of organisations with extreme right-wing racist policies. He was a member of the Anti-Nazi League working in areas of Manchester which were home to many Afro-Caribbean people.

He was also a prominent member of Manchester Council for Community Relations which represented the many ethnic communities in the city and, for a short time, served as its chairman. The council was called upon by the government in 1981 at the time of the Moss Side riots to help bring about a peaceful end to the unrest.

George Brown (1906-1937)

George's parents were immigrants from Kilkenny who settled in
Collyhurst. His father Francis was a blacksmith, shoeing horses for the
railway company. George was the last in the family to be born in Ireland,
near Ballynail in 1906. He had various jobs in Gorton and Trafford Park,
followed by Manchester Corporation Highways Department and as a
building-site labourer.

He attended the weekly debating forum at Queen's Park Hall where
he gained confidence by taking part in the lively atmosphere. At the time
of the 1926 General Strike, he joined the Communist Party and was a good
all-round sportsman enjoying boxing, swimming, fishing and walking.

Brown was one of about 160 activists from Britain who attended the
International Lenin School between 1926 and 1937, which trained men
and women for leadership positions within the CP. (See also Jud Clyne,
Arthur Newsom and Nellie Wallace). The courses lasted from three years
to nine months, and Brown was a student in Moscow from 1931 to 1932.

George Brown

When he stood for Openshaw in the municipal elections in 1934, his agent
was fellow activist Evelyn Taylor whom he later married before going
to Spain. During the the Thirties' unemployment struggles he was greatly
involved in mobilising membership in trade union activities. He became
a well-known figure in the Manchester Labour Movement, and many
benefited from his advice and activity during industrial disputes.

He went to fight in Spain in 1937 and was wounded within a month.
He was appointed as a Political Commissar but insisted on joining the
troops on the battle-front where he was injured at Brunete in the attack
on Madrid. As he lay disabled, retreating fascists shot him dead.

There was a memorial meeting for him at Manchester's Co-operative
Hall, Downing Street, and Mr FW Harrison of Manchester Trades Council
expressed his council's esteem for Brown, who had proved his sincerity
in the hardest way of all. A plaque was unveiled in his memory in 2008
at his birthplace by Jack Jones, union leader and President of the
International Brigade Trust. Since then, there has been an annual weekend
held in his honour.

Hilda Brown (1901-1998)

Hilda was born in Flixton, the daughter of a shipping clerk at a textile
merchants. By 1911 they were living in Urmston. Hilda gave an address
at the Manchester College of Technology in 1933 on *The Position of Men and
Women in the Soviet Union*, organised by the Society For Cultural Relations
with Russia and the Ethical Society, a forerunner of the British humanism
movement. By 1939 she was a shorthand typist for a textile company,
and single, living in Urmston with her mother. In 1940 she was on the
executive committee of Manchester Trades and Labour Council.

Jack and Florrie Clayton

By JANE O'NEILL

My parents met on the top of Scafell Pike. My father, then a newly-qualified, recently-widowed chartered accountant, had walked there with his dog, and my mother had come up with a gang of friends from Manchester, among whom were Jimmy Miller and Joan Littlewood. My mother was a rebel, and a member of the Communist Party in her youth. The eldest of fourteen children, several of whom died in the 1918 Spanish Flu epidemic, she came from a family with very little money, but shared, with her father and mine, a lifelong love of music, books and walking. Anyway, they talked for hours on the top of Scafell, walked down the mountain together, and were never parted afterwards, until his death in 1982. They married in Manchester in 1930.

Clayton family

Jack and Florrie Clayton

My mother was once arrested, but never charged. She stood up in the Strangers' Gallery in the Commons and shouted 'rubbish', encouraging everybody else to join in. I can't remember what the debate was. Several of them (she was with friends) were arrested and there is, or was, a jail of some sort in the House of Commons, so they stuck them in there, but not for very long I don't think. Probably happy to just chuck them out. She was a feisty lady, all 5'1" of her.

Jack was born in 1904 in Prestwich. His father, also known by the same name, at the age of 18 went on a gold rush to Canada with his cousin. Wisely they made a great deal of money by selling equipment and clothes to the speculators, and when he came home he bought three butchers' shops, two garages and a house with his earnings.

Jack and Florrie walked and climbed all over Europe, going to the Alps whenever they could. Every weekend they would flee Manchester for the Lakes, with a tent and rucksack, sometimes with friends, but often just together. They knew the countryside backwards, and loved it deeply. I don't think there was a hill in the Pennines they hadn't climbed.

My father was long acknowledged as having played a large part in the introduction of PAYE. He also did a lot of work in the nationalisation of coal, and helped William Beveridge with the finances involved in the setting up of the NHS. He remained in touch with Beveridge until Beveridge's death.

Brought up in Cheadle Hulme, he was the youngest of four brothers. He was, probably, a mathematical genius. His headmaster suggested he go into accounting, but, in those days, one was articled, and paid the principals for teaching, which his widowed mother couldn't afford, his father having sadly died when he was fourteen. His headmaster wrote to the firm McLintocks, and said if you don't take this kid on free, you're nuts. So they did. He is mentioned in the book on 20th Century Accountants by Michael Mumford. He was very proud of the fact that he was the first non-practising accountant to be invited onto the Council of the Institute of Chartered Accountants in England and Wales, on which he served for many years.

He left the profession early, and went into industry, starting, I think, in Mowlems, the builders, where he was head of finance. He and my mother moved south, as his work was based in London, from Bury, where my sister Ann was born. First I think, to Esher, and moving in 1945 to Cheam, where they stayed for the rest of their lives. Mowlems did a great deal of government building work during the war, but in the late 40s he joined Rediffusion where he was managing director and chairman for many years, and later responsible for setting up all the finances for Associated Rediffusion, one of the first commercial TV channels, of which he was joint managing director.

Jack Clayton

Rediffusion owned a lot of useful things, Keith Prowse and Wembley Stadium, to name just a couple. We had tickets to anything we wanted. We had lunch with the Queen at Wembley and watched one of the cup finals in the Royal Box. Unlike now, curtesying and bowing was compulsory if one wanted to be presented, and my mother, sticking, as ever, to her principles, said she wasn't curtesying to anyone, and neither were her children, so we sat opposite the royals at lunch, and behind them at the match. I think my father would probably have managed a bit of a bow to be able to sit next to the Queen, and have a chat, which, as chairman, he should have, but he would never offend my mother. Associated Rediffusion put him into a charmed world.

Jack Clayton

He was very popular as an after-dinner speaker, having a wicked sense of humour, and a seemingly endless collection of quotes. As well as being a keen walker and climber, he was a great sportsman. In his youth he was a talented tennis player, and holder of many championships. He was also a scratch golfer at Walton Heath Golf Club, and had a handicap of seven when he died in 1982.

Fly fishing was one of his great passions, and we had a holiday home in Bolton by-Bowland, then moved to Skirden Hall. Later he bought Beckfoot Hall, in Kirkby Stephen. The house had the river Eden at the bottom of the garden, even better fishing, and a golf club in the village, so my father was in heaven.

Beckfoot Hall, holiday home of the Claytons

John Cleary (1903-1992)

By MAUREEN BURROWS, Sheffield 2012

My father took part in the Trespass and was a member of the Clarion Ramblers Club. He loved walking, especially in the Derbyshire hills, and believed that the countryside should be open to all, not just the landowners! He thought that ramblers respected the countryside and did not cause any damage. Some time ago the *Sheffield Star* printed an article on the Trespass and on a photo you could see my father with other ramblers on the moor. He loved walking until the end of his life and could never understand why people drove cars when they could have been on their feet walking. He was known locally as the man who was always walking. He was a painter and decorator and when work was hard to find, he went round the country for about four years painting theatres and cinemas. John's other interests were history and art.

Jud (Joe) Clynes (1909-1995)

Clynes family

Jud Clynes army photo 1943

Born in Manchester, his father Morris came from Russia and his mother Miriam from Poland. His father was in the tailoring business. Jud was influenced by his mother's and father's political views, and joined the YCL in the late 1920s, and was followed into the organisation by four sisters. He was a close friend of Sol Gadian and Harry Mendel.

When he was arrested after the Trespass he was twenty-three, and a clothing machinist living in Cheetham. After his release from prison, he addressed a crowd at the foot of Jacob's Ladder, Derbyshire, organised by the Ramblers' Rights Movement. He said *'If they think they have smashed my spirit, they have made a mistake. It has increased my determination tenfold to go on with the movement for better facilities for ramblers and for a mass trespass because it is only by direct action that we shall ever get access to the mountains'*.

He attended the International Lenin School in Moscow from 1932-4, and on his return campaigned against fascism. He was jailed for four months in 1935 after hitting a policeman during an open-air meeting of Mosley's followers. The previous year, his father and sister Leah, then seventeen, were fined for disorderly behaviour following a Mosley meeting at the Free Trade Hall during which crowds were shouting 'Down with the Blackshirts!'.

He married Blanche Krebs in 1949, and they helped organise solidarity meetings, distribute propaganda, collect food, clothes and funds for the cause of Republican Spain. Two of Jud's sisters married Spanish Republican refugees. During WWII Jud was an anti-aircraft gunner and wounded in North Africa. He had malaria three times, but recovered to take part in the Allied invasion of Italy. He and his family enjoyed rambles around Hayfield and Glossop. Jud continued to be active in the unions and in the CP. They opened a health food shop in around 1957 just off Cheetham Hill Road, which reflected his own lifestyle.

In 1963 they emigrated to Australia to live a healthier outdoor life. They started out in Melbourne, then moved to Perth and finally to Sydney in the Bondi district, attracted by the sunshine and the beach. Jud, who called himself Joseph in Australia, worked as a clothing machinist. He worked with Greek and Italian immigrants and was instrumental in getting the factory unionised.

After retirement, Joe and Blanche were active in the pensioner movement and the local public tenants' association which fought to maintain a bus route for pensioners, and also dealt with everyday problems facing tenants. He loved to talk politics with people, engaging in lengthy discussions and arguments. He had to prove his point, even if that meant doing some more research and then coming back for a second round! Joe died unexpectedly at the age of 86, and the *Manchester Rambler* was sung at his funeral.

Jud Clynes outside the factory where he worked.

Jud Clynes (right) arguing the pensioners' case with an Australian state official in 1990.

Max Clynes (1913-1987)

Max, the brother of Jud, was fined 30s in 1934 for disorderly behaviour during a demonstration organised by the Manchester Youth Anti-War Committee. He and eight others were arrested among a crowd of three hundred who were trying to lay a wreath at the Cenotaph, which read 'To the young victims of the Capitalist War, 1914-1918, from the youth of 1934 who are supporting the Youth Congress at Sheffield on August 4 and 5, determined that there shall be no more war'. The Cenotaph had been barricaded up for a royal visit and a group with Clynes holding the wreath aloft moved on to Devonshire Street, where there were scuffles and they were detained by the police. At the time, Clynes was 21 and listed as a machinist at Broughton Street, Cheetham.

He married Angela Cockshoot in 1936, and three years afterwards was living at Lowthorpe Street next to Manchester City's former Maine Road stadium. Max was a machinist in the clothing industry, ran a grocer's shop in Hulme, and then a garage on Chorlton Road. He was a popular character and always had a repertoire of one-line jokes and ad-libs.

Max Clynes

Harold Colley (1909-1984)

Born in Levenshulme, he married in 1938 Eva Wiseman who had been the secretary of the Manchester League of Youth. She was a speaker at an 'All-Manchester Rally organised by the Labour Party's Unity Committee in Ardwick in 1937. In 1939 they were living at Lindley Road, Fallowfield, with Harold listed as a railway clerk. Eva died in 1965, and Harold lived at that address until his death at the Royal Hallamshire Hospital, Sheffield in 1984.

Bella Costello (1915-1999)

Costello family

She was born Bella Lerner in Bethnal Green, London, the daughter of Jewish immigrants from Moldova. Her father was a tailor. She was known as 'Bil', and even when young held communist views. Bella won a scholarship to grammar school but did not go on to university. Years later, in a tribute to her late husband, she said that he was her university.

She went to Cambridge to help out with her brother's family and while there she met her future husband, who was at Trinity College. Bella married New Zealand-born, Cambridge-educated diplomat, soldier and academic 'Paddy' Costello in 1935. Their communist beliefs led to allegations that they were Soviet spies. He was working in New Zealand as a diplomat but the British authorities forced him to return to Britain, where he became head of Slavonic Studies at Manchester University. Paddy and Bella were said to have entertained many Soviet guests, and had links with members of the Soviet government but it was never proved they had any involvement with Russian Intelligence, and neither was charged.

In his book *The Sixth Man 2008*, James McNeish asserts that the accusations had been based on false information. The release of MI5 papers in the National Archive did not provide any conclusive proof that Costello had acted as a spy. Paddy had been a diplomat in Moscow and Paris. While in Moscow, Bella learnt Russian rather than playing bridge with other diplomats' wives.

In 1967 Bella translated the play *The Easy Path,* a satire on free love by Valentin Kataev, which was performed at the University Theatre as part of a festival of the arts of the Russian Revolution. Two years later she translated *Marriage: an Absolutely Incredible Incident in Two Acts* by Gogol. Bella wrote a letter to *The Guardian* in 1969 objecting to expensive plastic surgery for older women, encouraging them to try to live naturally and not to try to compete with younger women

In 1985 she translated *The Murder of Rasputin: A First-Hand Account from the Diary of One of Rasputin's Murderers* by VM Purishkevich. Bella also did some acting at the University Theatre and the 69 Theatre Company in Manchester. She lived in Didsbury and attended the 1982 and 1992 Trespass anniversaries.

She remained strong in her political views and was remembered as a kind and generous person. She used to knit jumpers for the family at Christmas and, even in later life, cycled to the shops.

Joe Davies (1907-1981)
By JOHN DAVIES

Joe was born in Crumpsall, Manchester, one of nine children of a Yiddish-speaking refugee immigrant family called Michaelashatsky (later changed to Davies). Desperate to escape being smothered by his 'Jewish Momma' he had a good education and became an atheist, communist, actor, scientist and rigorous rational thinker.

He was passionate about geology and archaeology, as well as folklore and folksong, an interest he shared with his friend Jimmy Miller (Ewan MacColl). They were both keen ramblers and politically active and together they took part in the Trespass.

MacColl described Joe in his autobiography as '... *short, bird-like, and agile. Bob Goodman and I were fast walkers - but Joe was faster. He could negotiate rocks like a mountain goat, could read a map quicker than anyone I have ever known and could run up the side of Derbyshire stone walls like a cat. He walked with a fast, springy step, only altering his pace to take a short run at a wall or to go leaping down the rocky shoulder of a hill. And all the time he would be talking about rocks and fossils, about Einstein and relativity, about sex and religion, about languages.*

'*He had a knack with languages. He knew German and French, more than a smattering of Italian and Russian, and could read Arabic. When we first met him he was teaching himself Gaelic. He loved to sing, too, and knew the words of three or four Gilbert and Sullivan operettas, a truly enormous number of Schubert lieder and numerous Kennedy-Fraser-type Hebridean songs. His sense of pitch was less than perfect.*

'*Though Joe considered himself to be a Marxist and was in complete agreement with the Communist Party's general line, he never actually joined the party. His reasons for not doing so lay in his personality. He had a wide range of interests and he found it impossible to apply himself exclusively to any single one of them.*'

Joe worked for an oil company in the Persian Gulf in the 1930s and in 1940 married Dorothy in Lancaster, where their two sons were born. They later moved to Liverpool and then Bradford.

In the 1970s, having moved to Scotland, he learnt Gaelic and toured remote crofts of the Outer Hebrides, talking to native-speakers and recording their songs. Never one to pay much attention to mundane surroundings, he was killed by a car while crossing the road in Glasgow.

Davies family

Middle: Joe Davies in the Persian Gulf
Below: Joe and Dorothy with their first grandchild in 1971

Davies family

93

Max Druck (1917-1994)

Born with a Lithuanian Jewish father, Max grew up in the Strangeways district of Manchester and later joined the YCL where he was branch secretary. He went on to become the full-time organiser of the Lancashire YCL and was involved in demonstrations against Mosley's 'Blackshirts'. In 1939, he was listed as a rainproof garment cutter. In the 1940s and 50s he worked as the Manchester and Salford CP organiser and was a regular speaker at meetings, although he became disillusioned with the party leadership in later years. He had always loved countryside walking and later went with his own family to the Peak.

He served with the Manchester Regiment during WWII and was posted to India and Burma for four years, and afterwards suffered with bouts of malaria. During the war, much to his irritation, he was ordered to guard Mahatma Gandhi. In a letter to home, Druck wrote he shouldn't have been wasting valuable time guarding a man whose main crime was to want independence for India, when he should have been fighting the Japanese.

After he returned to his old job, then resigning his CP role, he retrained as a women's clothing designer and continued with it until retirement in 1984. His interests were cultivating roses and dahlias after moving to a larger house, and attending Hallé and Manchester Camerata concerts.

Druck family

Max Druck

In 1948 Max married Nancy whom he met at a CP conference and named their only child after Paul Robeson, the American singer who was blacklisted during the McCarthy era. After retirement, Druck remained an activist and campaigner, speaking out against increased bus fares, defending local hospitals and pensioners' rights, and agitating for changes in community care funding.

He collapsed and died while giving a speech for the pensioners' movement in 1994. It was clear by the large number of people who attended his funeral that he had touched many lives and was hugely respected and loved.

Max Druck

Sidney Fink (1914-1938)

Born in Salford, he lived in Fenny Street, Higher Broughton, in the 1930s. He was in the YCL, a member of the Workers' Arts Club at Higher Broughton, and worked in the printing trade. He volunteered to fight in Spain and was killed at Aragon in March 1938.

Nat (Nathan) Frayman (1912-1989)

Nat was born in Prestwich and had two brothers and one sister. Their father, Jacob, was a walking-and umbrella-stick varnisher born in Ukraine in Tsarist Russia. The surname was probably Fraiman - meaning 'Freeman', then changed to Frayman by an immigration officer. The family moved around before settling in a larger house in Higher Broughton by 1939.

Nat narrowly escaped death as a child when he ran into Bury New Road chasing a bouncing ball and didn't notice an oncoming tram. Fortunately, the quick-witted driver dropped his 'cow-catcher' which scooped Nat up from under the front of the tram. He used to earn half a crown for cycling round the district collecting money owed to his uncle. He attended Salford Secondary School which later became a grammar school.

He joined the Young Communist League where he became an effective debater, and spoke at a Free Trade Hall meeting which included the eminent Labour Party politician Sir Stafford Cripps, in the campaign by opposition parties to drive the Conservative Party out of office.

In 1938 as representative of Labour League of Youth, he was part of a campaign amongst the leaders of Manchester youth organisations for democracy and peace in Spain. That same year the same organisations met with the Lord Mayor to discuss what role under-19s could play in national defence.

By 1939 Nat was a book-keeper, living with his parents in Salford. Also that year he was a member of the National Advisory Committee of the Labour League of Youth which sent a letter to the National Executive of the Labour Party protesting against the removal of Sir Stafford Cripps from the party.

Nat Frayman

Fraymann family

During WWII he was a staff sergeant, decommissioning weapons in Italy. The work involved the use of chemicals and gave him severe headaches. Friends at a party gave him a beer and the headache stopped. Drinking beer had the same effect on a later headache. He reported this to his commanders who were dismissive of it. Later HQ officially endorsed the use of beer to reverse the effects of chemicals.

After the War, he campaigned for the People's Parliaments, and

Nat Frayman

trained as a teacher, becoming active in the National Union of Teachers. For many years he taught during the day then coached children in the evening to get into grammar school. He taught at Halton Bank Secondary School in Pendleton, King David Secondary School and a primary school on Singleton Road, Salford.

In 1959 he took his family to join the first CND march from Aldermaston to London and remained an active supporter of the campaign. By 1960 he had a Morris Minor and enjoyed taking the family to the places where he had once rambled. Ewan MacColl and Peggy Seeger were family friends. After retirement, he helped to start the Anti-Nazi League in Manchester, became a member of the newly-launched CND, and was also active in the Labour Party. His brother Jo became the London editor of the New York Times.

Fraymann family

Nat Frayman (writing) with school children

Sol Gadian (1907-1982)

Sol was born in Prestwich. His parents, Jewish immigrants from Lithuania, lived at first in Stockport, then moved to the Strangeways district. Sol's father was a master tailor specialising in ladies' costumes and was very successful. He used to work in a room containing just a table and sewing machine.

Sol can be seen in the photograph with the keepers at the Trespass (page 39). He is not in hiker's clothing after arriving late due to another commitment and is seen here amongst the action wearing a suit with collar and tie. His friend, Harry Mendel, brought his walking boots for him. Throughout his life he loved the countryside and was a keen rambler and cyclist. By 1939 he was a raincoat clothing machinist, and a member of the Cheetham branch of the Communist Party, speaking at a meeting at the Shakespeare Cinema about the Defence of the British People, with the growing threat of fascism under Hitler and Mussolini.

During the last war he served in the Royal Artillery then was invalided out with a medical condition which remained with him for the rest of his life. He was a full-time communist organiser in Manchester but following disagreement returned to his job as a clothing machinist in the 1960s, before retiring in 1972. He remained very active in trade union activities and received the TUC's Tolpuddle medal for his endeavours.

Sol had a wide range of musical tastes including jazz and blues, classical music, and opera in his later years. He was a Manchester City season-ticket holder, and his hobbies included the *Guardian* crossword and watching classic films, his favourite being Gary Cooper in *High Noon*.

Sol, a popular and much-respected figure in political and trade union circles, had lived in Manchester all his life. His friends remembered his sharp, analytical mind that would not accept any authoritative statement without first probing into it.

(See his account of the Trespass page 75)

Above and top: Sol Gadian

Gadian family

Tona Gillett (1912-1992)

He was born Anthony Walter Gillett, in Oxford, and lived in the Richmond district for over forty years. His family were Quakers and possibly his Non-Conformist background contributed to his radical views. Arthur, his father, a bank director, liked to roam the countryside without paying much attention to the trespass laws. Margaret, his mother, was from the Clark's shoes family. Tona was rightly proud of his great-grandfather, the MP John Bright, who famously opposed the Corn Laws, and later the Crimean War. Bright also supported the North in the American Civil War.

During the trial, a witness said Gillett was the best rugby player at Manchester University's Dalton Hall, and although he had caused some controversy with his views among the other students, he was known as a good character. The prosecuting counsel, knowing of Gillett's religious background, asked sarcastically if he quaked during the confrontation with the keepers. Gillett replied he did not, nor was he ashamed of his actions. He was found guilty of riotous assembly and sentenced to two months' imprisonment. The judge commented that he was at a loss why a person of his ability should have been involved in this 'disgraceful scene'.

Gillett family

Tona Gillett

While in prison he continued with his studies and then went on to St John's College, Cambridge University, who didn't regard his conviction as an obstacle to entering the college. Tona had excellent references, including one from South Africa's prime minister Jan Smuts, and completed his engineering degree at Cambridge. AJP Taylor, in his autobiography *A Personal History* 1983, wrongly claimed the Trespass had been organised by students. Tona was the only student jailed and he was certainly not one of its organisers. Taylor also wrote that the student organisers had been threatened with expulsion by the university until there was a students' protest meeting, but there is no evidence of Tona having been expelled.

Tona married Diana Maltby in 1935 and by 1939 they were living in Avon Dassett, Warwickshire and they had three children. After divorcing in 1950 he married Jean Turner in Cambridge the following year and they had two further children. His children describe him as a kind and gentle person who talked very little about himself or his own life. During WWII he was a member of the Home Guard at Billingham.

While he worked at the engineering company British Thompson-Houston and ICI, the family were living in Avon Dassett, Morecambe and Stockton on Tees. He was deputy manager of Kingston Power Station in the 1950s and later chairman of companies in Battersea and Essex.

His early communist views modified and he became a keen member of his local Labour Party and CND. Politics were constantly discussed in the family, and he was an avid Guardian reader. He was bemused by how interest grew in the Trespass over the years, and took part in a re-enactment of the protest for the BBCs *Look Stranger* series. Fellow trespassers, Ewan MacColl, Dave Nesbitt and Benny Rothman were also involved. Tona's son Tim went along and found himself used as a gamekeeper during filming.

Tona Gillett, to the right of the policeman nearest the camera, on protest march

Harold Glencross (1910-1973)

Harold was born in Birmingham, but his father later had a job at Ford's, Trafford Park, painting the red and gold line on their cars. Harold grew up in Salford and was a keen walker and friends with Benny Rothman and his associates. His daughter recalls how later they used to set off on Sundays from Central Station to go into the Peak District.

His first job was as a goods checker and he worked in the arches underneath London Road Station. He was promoted to carter taking goods by horse and cart around the area now known as Chinatown. He used to cycle to work at 5am and saw many rats on the city streets. Following the bombing during the Blitz, horse-drawn vehicles were withdrawn and he got an HGV licence to drive a Scammell Karrier Cob.

As he worked on the railways, which was classed as a reserved occupation, Harold was not called up to fight during WWII. During that time he campaigned for the formation of the NHS. He had hoped to become a doctor but his lowly circumstances prevented that, but he joined the St John's Ambulance Brigade in his teens and later acted as the first-aid officer at London Road Station, where he also served as a night-time fire watcher. Throughout his life, he was renowned for his smart appearance, even as a carter.

During the war, he was called from the station to a woman trapped between two trams near London Road Fire Station. The police wanted to drag her off the tracks but Harold told them to stop and made a temporary stretcher out of two brushes to stabilise her before the ambulance arrived. The woman made a good recovery and he was commended for his efforts by doctors at Manchester Royal Hospital who said he had probably saved her life.

He had been a member of the Labour Party since he was a teenager and became a councillor in 1945-6 which included service on the Manchester and Salford Planning Committee. His home resembled a Citizens' Advice Bureau with many people coming to him for help. He was known as a person who was always helpful and willing to listen. Politicians Frank Allaun and Charlie Royle were regular visitors. Between 1950 and the early 1970s Glencross was a JP and also a Governor at Salford Grammar School.

Harold was involved in the early Manchester industrial tribunals, a forerunner of ACAS. As North West branch secretary of the NUR, he helped people made redundant by the Beeching cuts in the 1960s. Later he was the NUR Secretary for goods and cartage in the UK. He was a regular attender at union conferences, and campaigned for the 1944 Education Act.

Harold and family moved to Bredbury, Stockport in 1970, close to the hills he loved, until his death. There was a massive turnout at his funeral for the man who was at ease in all levels of society and greatly respected.

Glencross family

Salford City Municipal Election
Saturday, November 1st, 1947

WEASTE WARD

VOTE FOR COUNCILLOR
H. GLENCROSS
OFFICIAL LABOUR CANDIDATE

Top: Harold Glencross
Above: 1947 local election leaflet

Bob Goodman (1912-1937)

A welterweight boxer from the Adelphi Club, Salford, who was said to have had twenty-two professional fights between 1929 and 1934. He was a close friend of Ewan MacColl who described him in his autobiography *Journeyman*, as having *'black hair, eyes that were almost black, and a sallow complexion which at first sight suggested he was liverish. It was misleading for he was in the pink of condition - tall, lean and very quick on his feet. His nose had been broken and flattened in a fight, for he was a boxer whose father had been grooming him for the ring ever since he could remember.'*

Goodman worked in a rubber-stamp moulding shop overlooking the Shudehill book market where he familiarised himself in his spare time with some of the great works of literature. He went with MacColl to the Young Communist meetings then on to the Clarion Players rehearsals. Tuesday evenings were spent at Hallé concerts at the Free Trade Hall where they stood at the back under the balcony for eight pence. He later became part of Millers' Workers' Theatre group, along with Martin Bobker. They both enjoyed walking weekends in the Peak with their actor-friend Joe Davies.

Bob Goodman died while fighting for the International Brigade at the battle of Jamara in 1937. A memorial meeting was held for him and three others at the Co-operative Hall on Downing Street, Manchester.

Wilfred Green (1911-2005)

Wilfred came from Pontefract, joining a Leeds rambling club as a teenager and enjoyed walking both in groups and alone. Most Sundays he would be out walking in Derbyshire but often came across public rights of way which had been closed off, or keepers barring his way. He used to argue with the keepers then report back about the blocked footpaths.

He learnt of the forthcoming Trespass through handbills which were being handed round at Hayfield. Wilfred remembered the scuffles with the keepers but didn't notice any police action or arrests. He was proud to have taken part but had some regret that the establishment of the right to roam had ended the thrill he used to have of challenging or evading the keepers. He had climbed all the highest mountains in Britain as well as those in Bavaria where he used to stay in hostels. During the last war he took part in the D-Day landings. Later, he and his wife Phyllis ran a menswear shop in Spalding.

Walter Greenhalgh (1914-1998)

Walter's father was a self-employed clog-maker, and Walter would often wear clogs in later years. Walter joined the Miles Platting YCL, and was later involved in the Youth Peace Council in Manchester and the trade union movement.

He worked as a decorator but in his leisure time he was a keen hiker and remembered being chased off Kinder, and also attending Winnats ramblers' rallies. Among his memories of the Trespass, he significantly recalled that about twenty of the protesters, once they had got past the line of keepers, went on to the Kinder plateau to celebrate. The majority of the Trespassers congregated lower down at Ashop Head.

At the age of twenty-four, he served with the International Brigade in Spain between 1936 and 1938 as one of its earliest recruits. As a machine gunner he was wounded in action in 1937 at Laz Rosas. He edited *Our Fight* newspaper and was later promoted to captain. During that time he learned Spanish and French which helped him during his service in WWII. After his return from Spain he organised aid for dependants of the brigade.

Walter served in the British Army as a wireless operator with the Royal Signals from 1939 to 1944, then in the Army Personnel Department in Belgium and finally the Control Commission for Germany in Munster in 1945. He got into trouble for speaking out against unfairnesses in the service, and was court-marshalled for not wearing a beret.

After the war he ran an engineering company, then a scrap-metal business, and started a property company which is still running today. In later life he was involved with the Labour Party and became a councillor for Brent for about four years, eventually becoming deputy leader of the council in the late 1960s. His family remember he was friendly with a number of Labour MPs who came to their home. He always had an enquiring mind and began learning Chinese in his later years.

Greenhalgh family

Below left: Walter Greenhalgh speaking at a Labour Party conference

Below right: Walter received Spanish nationality for his involvment in the civil war

Greenhalgh family

Greenhalgh family

De conformidad con el Real Decreto 39/1996, de 19 de enero, dictado como consecuencia del acuerdo unánime del Parlamento español de fecha 10 de noviembre de 1995, obtendrá la nacionalidad española, una vez cumplidos los requisitos exigidos, la cual será efectiva tras la inscripción en el Registro Civil correspondiente.

Madrid, 4 de noviembre de 1996

EL DIRECTOR GENERAL,

Luis Mª Cabello de los Cobos y Mancha

Sr. D. Walter GREENHALGH

Eli Hague (1913-1999)

By PATRICIA HAGUE BLAKE

Eli Hague

Read Eli Hague's account of the Trespass page 78

Hear his talks online about his life, for the East Midlands Oral History Archive, recorded in 1988.

Author of *Streets Away From Paradise - Reminiscences of a Stalybridge Lad*, 1987 and *All This and No Milk - a taste of life in the Holbeach Marches*, 1994, both published by Neil Richardson

Eli was born in Stalybridge and used to go camping at Ashes Farm, close to Jacob's Ladder. He was made redundant as a machine shop apprentice and at the age of thirteen he hiked from Stalybridge to Spalding, Lincolnshire, and I do not know how he fed himself or where he slept as the journey took days. I only remember him saying that he gave a farmer the shock of his life as he crawled out of a haystack one morning. During his work he met a young man who insisted he take my dad home to meet his mother. She immediately took him under her wing, as did the rest of the family, I would come to know them as Grandma and Grandad.

He then came to Coalville to work at Pegsons, where I think they were making gun barrels for tanks, and during this time he met and married my mother, Lillian. He moved on to the South Colliery to work as Chief Wheelwright during the war, and at the same time working an allotment and the back garden Digging For Victory. On the few occasions he was able to go back and visit my Grandma and Grandad in Spalding, he cycled! He always loved cycling, right from boyhood, and was very fit.

Throughout his life he was a staunch Labour supporter, and loathed Thatcher. He taught me about Milton and freedom of speech. He was a natural 'explorer' and found an old pit near us where an old Newcomen engine was rusting away! He also discovered an old railway incline, but back then nobody was in the least interested and it would be many years before other people took over and brought them to light. He and a friend used to mend radio sets - and later TV sets - with old valves etc. which he and his old friend managed to save and scrounge. This was done at no charge to those, mainly elderly, who benefited. He was an excellent carpenter and made all the cupboards in the house.

At the age of nine I was already reading books on the history of medicine because my dad had said he would have liked to be a doctor. He also taught me about rocket engines and at eleven I was the only kid who knew how a nuclear reactor worked and what clouds were. He loved cricket, playing for the local colliery, and tried to teach my elder sister and me how to play. I used to watch the test matches with him and the Sunday one-day games, too. The same applied to tennis.

He was quite accomplished at drawing, he loved marquetry and made a beautiful fire screen. He played crown green bowls, had a fine tenor voice and a love of music, classical and popular. Books were a must, he read avidly and passed this on to me. He coached my eldest through A level maths, so she could go to university. She is now a GP and I am sorry he did not live to see that, he would have been so proud.

His last job was lecturing at Coalville Technical College where he taught mining engineering and was an inspired lecturer and (as far as I am aware) the only teacher there who received Christmas presents from the lads he taught! He also lectured on mines' safety and there were many who would never forget his lecture on Aberfan. Long after his retirement, men would approach him in the street and shake his hand, and thank him for '..getting me where I am today.'

George Haigh (1915-2019)

George Haigh interviewed at the 2012 Trespass Anniversary, Edale

Born in Reddish, Stockport and possibly the oldest surviving Trespasser when he died at the age of one hundred and three.

He was sixteen at the time of the Trespass, and getting out into the countryside at weekends was important to him, even though he was limited by football commitments. Haigh was a supporter of the right to ramble, and proud of being part of the Mass Trespass. On the day of the Trespass, he and his friends were warned off by older ramblers who tried to keep him away from trouble, but he took an alternative route towards Kinder and avoided the confrontation. When he was interviewed during the Trespass 80th anniversary celebrations, he remembered dodging gamekeepers. If they caught him they sent him back, but as soon as he was out of sight he would do a detour and resume the walk. A number of the keepers had guns which was quite frightening.

Haigh worked at a bleaching factory but from 1931 was playing for Manchester City's A team. During the twice-weekly training sessions he became a good friend of goalkeeper Frank Swift. He was distraught when Swift, then working as a journalist, died in the Munich air disaster.

Haigh signed for Stockport County in 1935 and played twice for the first team. He made his playing debut at centre-half in 1936, and unfortunately scored an own goal. He earned £5.10s a week and got an extra £2 if they won and £1 for a draw. The outbreak of war effectively ended his professional career, and he joined the RAF as a physical training instructor based in Morecambe, where he trained new recruits and parachutists, but was still playing football at weekends. He was selected for armed services teams as well as Morecambe FC and played against the Manchester City goalkeeper, Bert Trautmann. Sometimes he had the arduous task of marking Stanley Matthews after joining Rochdale in 1942. Later he was player-manager with Rossendale United. Another talent was billiards, and he was the Manchester champion for three successive years.

George later ran a tobacconist's and sweet shop with his wife on Ashton Old Road. He suffered from macular degeneration towards the end of his life and was also involved with the Blind Veterans' Association. He enjoyed a close connection with Stockport County and in 2017, officially opened their museum. His family said he was a quiet man, with a great dry sense of humour who was known all around the world for his achievements. In his later years he moved to be near his daughter in Oxfordshire, and died the day before the 2019 Spirit of Kinder event at Castleton.

Lance Helman (1912-1982)

Lance was born in Manchester. His Russian father, a ladies' tailor, was a member of the Arbeiter Freud Group - a Jewish anarchist organisation and the Foreign Jews' Protection Committee, a group which supported Russian Jews threatened with deportation to Russia if they did not enlist in the British Army. Lance's mother, also Russian, was a dressmaker and secretary of the the Free Thinking Organisation in 1904.

Both parents were members of the Bundist group in Russia, a cultural movement influenced by the playwrights Ibsen and Shaw. Their children were named after characters in Ibsen's plays. In 1911 the family were living at Cheetham with two daughters, a boarder and domestic servant. Their home was the venue for the Clarion Players, who were joined by Jimmy Miller (Ewan MacColl) in 1929.

Lance introduced Rothman at the Bowden Bridge quarry trespass meeting, and made his own way home after the Trespass, taking a different route from the main group. He spoke at the meeting in the July of 1932 at the foot of Jacob's Ladder, appealing for donations for the jailed Trespassers as Secretary of the Ramblers' Rights Movement. The year after the Trespass, he organised the BWSF camp at Rowarth. In 1939 both Lance and his wife Elizabeth were mantle and costume machinists.

During the last war he worked for the Auxiliary Fire Service and then the National Fire Service where he was in action in various cities. After the war he worked in his stepfather's handbag business and later took it over. It was named OH Cantor after his half-brother Oliver Horace, and they manufactured bags mainly for markets. It was situated at Waterloo Road, Hightown.

Top: On Auxiliary Fire Service duty
Above: Bag producer
Right: (centre) On labour march

Lance moved to Cheadle in 1965 and took up an interest sea fishing in later life. He also enjoyed taking his family out on walks.

After his death in 1982 he was cremated with his last copy of the *Daily Worker* in his coffin. His ashes were scattered on the lower slopes of Kinder on a cold, windy day.

Helman family

Helman family

Harvey Jackson (1914-2000)

He was an eighteen-year-old apprentice living in Stalybridge at the time of the Trespass. He and friends were regular Sunday walkers and decided to join the main group on Kinder by walking over Chunal to Mill Hill. They met up with the marchers then went with them into Hayfield but when they saw some of the protesters being arrested they decided to head back up William Clough and over to Chunal. Here they were confronted by keepers and hired assistants and beaten up.

Three years later, Harvey had an interview to join the police in which he stated his love of hillwalking. The interviewing officer replied 'We do not like hill walkers in Derbyshire!' Harvey recognised him as being the Assistant Chief Constable who had been in charge on the day of the Trespass. Nevertheless, Harvey became a serving officer followed by his son Peter, who also joined the Mountain Rescue Service and was a part-time National Park Ranger.

Harvey Jackson

Abe Jacobs (1909-1991)

Born in Manchester, Abe was the son of Maurice, a waterproof garment-maker. He was probably in the YCL and married to Edith Capelovitch in 1936. By 1939 he was a cabinet maker at Northgreaves St, Manchester, but later became a market trader and lived at Prestwich.

In 1982 he wrote to the local newspaper protesting over the comments of the Hayfield parish council chairman, who refused the invitation to officially open the 50th anniversary celebrations of the Trespass at Hayfield. Robin Capstick, a descendant of a Kinder gamekeeper Stanley Capstick, said that the Trespass had played no great part in the battle for access, and controversially compared the Trespass to the recent riots around the country.

Harvey Jackson

Jacobs wrote: *'How dare Mr Robin Capstick become a judge of the band of the poor, but decent honest citizens, whose only pleasure was to walk the moors at weekend, without being threatened by the landowners' lackeys, who were working for 30s a week and all they could poach?*

How dare he compare us to the Brixton, Toxteth and Moss Side rioters! We came to Hayfield on a peaceful demonstration in 1932, and found Hayfield full of foolish-looking hikers in all kinds of strange garb, who turned out to be the police. We were demonstrating against landowners who invited their friends for a week's grouse shoot, and for the rest of the year kept those moors idle.'

Eric and Louise Jessop

They remembered renting a cottage in the 1930s with a group at Ashes Farm, Kinder and scrambling up Kinder Downfall and somehow avoiding the keepers. They recalled their old friends George Westfield, Monty Rosenfield and Jack and Flo Clayton.

(side text:) Jackson family

Jimmy Jones (1917-2003)

Jimmy's father was the first Communist candidate in the Bradford area of Manchester, and used to give speeches at Stevenson Square in the centre of Manchester - the City's 'Speaker's Corner', while Jimmy sat and listened on the fringe of the crowd in a cart. In about 1932, Jimmy played rugby for the works team of Ferguson Palin at Openshaw, one of the earliest Rugby League teams in Manchester. He had hoped to study pharmacy but had been turned down because his father was a labourer. Jimmy was later apprenticed at Ferguson Palin in the pattern shop.

He camped every weekend with friend Benny Rothman, who used to be known as 'Bunny' - because as Jimmy said, he was small and round.

Bill Keen (left) and Jimmy Jones at the 70th Anniversary Trespass celebration

He was fifteen at the time and had little memory of the Trespass, and did not recall contact with the keepers. He thought he could identify himself in some of the newspaper photographs. He volunteered to fight in the Spanish Civil War but he was too young.

Jimmy continued to campaign for ramblers' rights throughout his life. He lived in Northenden, and in his retirement years when I visited him, he showed me the trophies and medals he'd won playing darts and bowls. Jimmy, a great-grandfather of fourteen, told me he had also joined the local campaign to ban mobile phone masts from the neighbourhood. At the age of 86, he was tragically fatally injured while crossing the road near his home in 2003.

Bill Keen (1911-2002)

Bill was born at Hague Lane, Sheffield. Alfred, his father, was listed as a joiner tool grinder. By 1939 Bill was lodging with the Fretwell family in Sheffield, and working as a file stripper. Later he became an insurance company agent and lived in Totley.

He was a committed countryside access campaigner, and a member of the Spartacus Rambling Club, formed in 1932. Bill took part in the Trespass, leading a group from Sheffield over Kinder to meet up with the main party at Ashop Head, and then returned the same way to Edale. He was also involved in the Abbey Brook Trespass a few months later, and was a member of Sheffield Access to Moorland (SCAM).

Fred Killick (1916-1937)

He was from Southport, listed as a clerk, and died in fighting at Jarama in February 1937. Killick, along with fellow Trespassers Clem Beckett and Alec Armstrong, was commemorated at a memorial meeting in May 1937 at the Coliseum Cinema, Ardwick Green, along with six others from the city who gave their lives fighting in the Spanish Civil War.

Walter Leigh (1913-2004)

Walter, born in Dukinfield, worked in the Midlands for thirty years as a furnace repairman before returning to the Manchester region in about 1977. By the 1980s he still enjoyed walking on the moors when his son and grandson visited from Coventry.

Walter was not a member of the BWSF, but joined in with the protest because he agreed with their aims. He said the Trespass had been orderly: 'You can read what you want, but they were all obeying instructions from whistles. I went through easily - there were no keepers, though I looked over to my right and saw a couple of keepers waving their sticks.' Although he had not heard about the Trespass beforehand, he was convinced their action had been worthwhile.

Maurice Levine (1907-2000)

Born in Cheetham, he was one of a family of eleven children. His parents came from Lithuania. After becoming unemployed, he emigrated to Australia in 1928, then returned to the UK in 1931 after the Wall Street Crash, where he joined the CP. Maurice worked as a garment cutter at the Co-op clothing factory in Broughton before he left with five others to fight with the International Brigade in Spain in 1936. They were among the first hundred Britons to join the war. He fought at Lopera, Jarama and Brunete where he was wounded. A letter from George Brown, 1937 states:
'Maurice got wounded a few days ago. He volunteered for a patrol to go over towards the enemy lines on reconnaissance, and was unfortunate enough to get a bullet through the arm although not serious. He will back with us in a few days. I think Maurice is one of the most courageous men in our battalion which has already displayed its supreme courage to the world, and I may say with all fairness that our comrades from the Manchester and Salford area are second to none.'

Maurice Levine

Maurice wrote about his experiences in Spain in *Cheetham to Cordova, a Manchester Man of the Thirties* published in 1984, and online for the Imperial War Museum Oral Histories. He married Joan Murphy in 1939 and after being demobbed he worked at a small Cheetham Hill clothing factory. After working for several employers, he and his brother Sam started a successful clothing manufacturing business in 1949 and continued there until retiring in 1967. He remained politically active, and in the 1960s was involved in demonstrations during the Cuban Crisis. Maurice and his wife moved from Altrincham to Gloucestershire where he campaigned against the threatened privatisation of the Forest of Dean.

Edward Levy (1913-2000)

Edward was born and grew up in Levenshulme. He learned the violin at school and joined the Gorton Philharmonic in the 20s but also enjoyed playing dance-band music. He went on to become the longest-serving member of the orchestra, playing with them for about sixty-five years. He had been invited to join the Hallé Orchestra but declined because he thought it would have prevented him from walking in the Peak District. He played in all the major theatres in Greater Manchester in amateur musical productions.

Edward lived close to the railway station and was easily able to get a train to Hayfield. He was a keen rambler and often had to dodge the gamekeepers who carried guns, although when he got back to Hayfield, ramblers often enjoyed a drink in the pub with keepers. He had a life-long love of walking, going out even on Christmas Day.

On the day of the Trespass he was late getting there because he had a rehearsal with the Gorton Philharmonic. He missed the meeting at the quarry and by the time he got onto the moor, the confrontation with the keepers was over. Nevertheless he was proud to have taken part in the Trespass. Edward was manager of a furniture shop in Levenshulme when he appeared before a Conscientious Objectors Tribunal in 1940 and said he was objecting because of his socialist views.

Nell Logan (1910-2001)

Logan family

Her maiden name was Wallace, and she was born in Pendlebury, the daughter of a miner. She was an active member of YCL and since the age of fourteen had walked eight miles into Manchester to collect *The Young Worker* newspaper to sell at Pendlebury. In 1930, after taking part in two successful strikes, Nell was selected by the Co-operative Movement to go to Moscow for nine months as a student at the International Lenin School. The experience left her disillusioned and she said the lectures went over her head. She joined Jimmy Miller's (Ewan MacColl) group in about 1931 which met in the cellar of the Workers' Arts Group and Miller's kitchen.

Nell Logan

At her first job as a weaver she started a wall newspaper. Her anger over poverty motivated her, and she became known as an agitator. Her brother Thomas had to change his surname when he applied for jobs, because of her reputation. She enjoyed rambling on the moors above Bolton and in Derbyshire from the age of fifteen. On the Peak District moors she got talking to young Sheffield Communists and discussed politics. She wanted to go off to the Spanish Civil war with her friends but was the family breadwinner after her father died. Nell brought her younger sister Ivy to the Trespass.

She married John Logan, cousin of Ewan MacColl, in Manchester in 1934, and they moved to Bristol where John had an engineering job at the Bristol Aircraft factory. They were both conscientious objectors. They came to

*Above and below: Nell
and her husband John*

Corsham in 1942, living at first in prefabs built for BAC workers.
He worked in the underground Spring Quarry which, during the War,
was used for ammunition and art storage.

After the war John went to Worcester training college and in 1948 became
a teacher at Chippenham, then deputy head in Bradford upon Avon and
in 1959, headmaster of Biddestone School - the year of his death. They
were involved in the 1950s Aldermaston Ban the Bomb marches, through
friends at Bath Academy of Art and the Quaker movement.

The women's protest at Greenham Common began in the early 1980s,
and at the age of seventy-three in 1983, Nell was among
a group of thirty who climbed over the fence at the air-
base. The sprightly granny received a two-week prison
sentence, during which time she refused food for nine
days because they would not provide her with vegetarian
food and fresh fruit. Before she was sentenced, she told
the magistrate 'I am shocked. All my life I have struggled
to keep the peace. I will always keep the peace so long
as I'm doing the right thing for mankind'.

Afterwards she went with a group of Greenham women
on a tour in America speaking about peace. She
continued to protest over the US bombers flying to Libya
in 1985, and then the Gulf War. Locals knew her as 'the
woman who never stopped marching' and as 'the woman
with history'. They were used to seeing her walk down the
high street with 'Green' slogans attached to her front and
back. When she came back to celebrate the 60th anniversary of the Trespass, she said 'It'll be a fine old day. There's
still much to be angry about'. In 1986, a documentary film
Greenham Granny about her lifelong commitment to peace
and socialism, won a World Peace Council prize.

Issey Luft

Israel (Issy) Luft (1913-1985)

Born in Manchester, and his father, Nathan, was a Romanian cloth cap maker. In 1911 the family were living in Bury New Road, Cheetham. His father died when Issy was six and their once-prosperous business declined.

Luft was a good boxer, and trained at the Miles Platting Boxing Club. He was a member of Cheetham YCL then resigned to become secretary of Crumpsall CP where he was the representative on Manchester's Spanish Civil War Medical Committee.

Both he and Eileen Staunton, his future wife, were regular ramblers in the Peak and went on the Trespass. They first met at a YCL discussion group and she had been impressed that he was among a group of anti-fascists who helped to save her when she got isolated amongst the brawling crowds at an Oswald Mosley meeting at Belle Vue. At another Mosley meeting at the Free Trade Hall, Issy had a black Alsation dog which he trained to growl and, unsurprisingly, had little trouble with the black-shirts. Martin Bobker was regarded as the toughest member of the group and he was seen at one meeting with a fascist under each arm.

In 1939 Issy was listed as a raincoat and waterproof clothes worker. During the Spanish Civil War he helped to organise medical aid, and sold the *Daily Worker* newspaper along Cheetham Hill Road. He served with the Royal Artillery as a dual-national then transferred to the Pioneer Corps in Scotland. The accommodation was poor and he suffered with asthma and bronchitis for the rest of his life. His later job as a clothing cutter didn't help because he was also allergic to the dust which came off cloth.

He was secretary of the Manchester Federal Council of Tenants in 1968 when he led a protest against rent rises in a council meeting. Luft threw leaflets down from the gallery to the applause of Labour members. Other women shouted out 'We will not pay, we will not pay'. Luft was escorted out by the police and said afterwards the new rents would cause hardship. He led a deputation to London to meet local MP Paul Rose, and was also active in CND. Issy's other interests included opera which could reduce him to tears, the works of Charles Dickens, and Lancashire dialect authors such as Edwin Waugh and Samuel Laycock.

George Willis Marshall (1904-1992)

Ann Beedham

George Willis Marshall

Born in Sheffield, George spent as much time as he could out walking with his friends. He recorded his walks in his journals, adding sketches and poems, and taking many photographs. His lovingly-compiled records of his days out can be seen in *Days of Sunshine and Rain* by Ann Beedham. He walked with GHB Ward and the Clarion Ramblers in the 1920s and 30s, but on the day of Trespass in which he took part, he simply wrote in his journal 'No ramble'. George and friends featured in the notorious wanted notice issued by landowner Watts, but as it was only circulated around Manchester they were never identified. Willis was a friend of aspiring escapologist Rendal Douglas, a confidant of Houdini after he visited Sheffield. Because of later health problems, Douglas became a model-maker and opened the Douglas Museum House of Wonders at Castleton.

The year after the Trespass, Willis left to work at a silver works in Birmingham, but he and his wife travelled back most weekends to walk in their beloved Peak District. He died in 1992 age, eighty-eight, still fondly remembering his favourite 'Manchester Rambler' song and all those glorious days of sunshine and rain.

Walter Martin (1911-1985)

Born in Manchester, the son of Wilhelm who was an assistant manager of German descent at a yarn merchants. By 1939 he and his parents were living in Westholme Lane, Withington, and he was listed as an accounting machine salesman. Later he came Head of Business Studies at a Manchester college. He attended the 50th Trespass anniversary and at the time of his death, his residence was Cromford Court, Withy Grove.

Harry Mendel (1909-1998)

One of the Trespass organisers, Harry was born in Stockport to parents of Russian Polish descent. He married Nellie Bradley in 1935, and by 1939 he was listed as a raincoat machinist, living at Reddish. Harry had the nickname 'union man' because he managed to get unions started at various 'sweatshop' businesses. He was small, wiry, full of energy and vitality, and friendly to everyone.

He used to organise big Christmas parties for the employees' children, and was an entertainer. He knew all Marriott Edgar's monologues off by heart, and did magic tricks. Mendel was thought to have been a friend of Edgar. Harry had thick bushy eyebrows which he used to move up and down for the entertainment of children.

He was Wolfie Winnick's sparring partner, and around the age of twenty-two surprisingly grew two inches. Harry was good at maths, and he and Wolfe's wife, Ann, used to solve complicated maths puzzles. A war-time shrapnel injury caused ongoing problems after the Land Rover he was driving was blown up, although he never talked about his war-time experiences.

After his retirement, Harry and his wife spent six months exploring New Zealand and Australia in a campervan. They emigrated to New Zealand in the 1960s and from there they moved to Australia. Harry remained active into his latter years in Australia, rising at six am for walks and going to the beach for a swim. *The Manchester Rambler* was sung at his funeral and his daughter read out her tribute to him (see overleaf)

Mendel family

Harry Mendel

MAKING THE BEST OF IT

'You've got to learn to make the best of things and smile.'
Our Dad would say. But children never listen do they?
We'd sulk and fret and moan when slings and arrows loomed
And paint the precious hours in gloom all day.

But at making the best of things, our Dad was an expert.
He'd take you up a mountain to find the blue glory in a peaty pool.
He'd show you the magic of maps, the mystery of dry stone walls.
The proper way to ride a bike.
The secrets of staying dry in a tent, the joy of tea from the primus,
Of cooking on a wood fire.

And he made the best of us:
Tailoring our small garments,
Topping up our diet with home grown fruit and veg.
Teaching us to question everything,
Telling our achievements with that big, shy, smile

And gatherings were the best if Dad was there to lead the cheer
With songs and games, with monologues and joi de vivre.
If there are angels, then likely
He's teaching them THE MUSIC MAN.

And once he made the best of living in a dirty city
Escaping to the mountains at weekends,
And making the best of it for others
Leading cycle rides and rambles, organising camps,
Risking prison to fight for rights of way to the best of it.

Making the best of things, he led a big life did our small Dad,
Pushing to the limits a war damaged body.
Pushing out for a swim in the wintry Irish Sea.
Pushing on in the garden in punishing Australian sun.
Pushing away to Tasmania, in a camping van, pushing 90 years.

And now he's pushed off.
And it's up to us
To smile ... and make the best of it.

JUNE COOPER -
A tribute to her father Harry Mendel, November 1998

Mendel family

Top: Harry Mendel
Above: Harry and Wolfie Winnick

Charlotte Merrington (1907-1993)

Charlotte Olive was the daughter of John Henry Merrington, who worked as a textile finisher in Manchester. She inherited his love of organ music and played frequently. She was the niece of William Massey, writer of hymns in the Methodist Hymnal. Charlotte loved walking and there is a family photograph of her with a walking group in the 1920s.

She went to teacher training college then married Joseph Warm, the son of a Jewish immigrant, in 1940 at St Asaph. They moved to his place of work in Northamptonshire where they had two children. During the Second World War, because Joseph was the son of a Pole but defined as Russian, owing to Russian jurisdiction over Poland, he was not allowed to fight, and the family moved to Longsight in about 1942, where he set up his own hat and cap manufacturing business. Later they moved to Birch Vale near Hayfield where their third child was born, then Highgate Hall and finally Walk Mill Lane.

When Joseph died shortly before Christmas 1949, Charlotte closed the business and began her teaching career. She taught at New Mills and Whaley Bridge before returning to Northamptonshire where she was head of mathematics at a secondary school. She was a gifted teacher and continued working beyond retirement age and gained a degree from the Open University at the age of seventy. She returned to Chinley where she played the organ at a number of local churches.

Merrington family

Merrington family

Above top: Olive, Devon 1928

Above: Olive aged 70 after gaining her BSc in 1977

Left: Olive's walking group 1925 (back row 3rd from left)

Jimmy Miller (Ewan MacColl)
(1915-1989)

The world-famous singer, songwriter, actor and activist was born in Broughton, Salford. His Scottish parents William and Betsy were both ardent socialists and also talented storytellers and singers. A lodger first introduced him to Communism, which led him to join the YCL and the Clarion Players theatre group. At the time of the Trespass he was a member of the Red Megaphones radical theatre group, and he also helped to write, publish and distribute factory newspapers. At the age of about seventeen he was the publicity officer for the Trespass and would have been responsible for the handbills and posters advertising the protest, seen around Greater Manchester and at Hayfield, as well as notifying the press with hand-written letters.

He had been introduced to rambling by an old school friend, although according to his third wife, Peggy Seeger, his boots were painful and he initially hated it, but grew to like walking. Peggy also remembered it was on the moors where they used to court in the 1950s. One day as Miller and his friend sat in a Hayfield tea-room, they got talking with Bob Goodman from Salford. He and MacColl became good friends and they spent most weekends away from grimy Salford walking in the Peak District. With practice they found they could cover many miles each day, and MacColl developed a great understanding and love for the terrain and the wild-life. Later they walked and climbed in other parts of the country. MacColl's song *The Manchester Rambler* was written after the Trespass and has become synonymous with it. He wrote two other songs about access protest, but it is *The Manchester Rambler* which is best remembered.

Peggy Seeger and Ewan MacColl

MacColl's activities in Salford came to the attention of the security services at this time and he and his first wife, Joan Littlewood, were subsequently tracked for more than twenty years. They and their friends were closely monitored at their house in Hyde and forced out of jobs with the BBC. However, when Ewan MacColl's security files were released in 2006, they revealed nothing untoward and stated he had exceptional ability as a singer and organiser. During the last war he was described as popular with his fellow soldiers, and a member of the Regimental Concert Party. MacColl hated military life and went AWOL, spending the rest of the War in hiding at a house with friends in Urmston. He re-emerged in 1945 with the new name of Ewan MacColl after a little-known 19th century Gaelic poet. After the war he was arrested for desertion but was discharged from the army on medical grounds.

In 2007 he was reunited with some of the jailed Trespassers in the BBCs *Look Stranger* in which he provided the voice-over in a reconstruction of the protest. In his autobiography *Journeyman* published just after his death in 1989, he mentions his old friends from the 1930s - Bob Goodman, Nat Frayman, Alec Armstrong, Martin (Myer) Bobker, George Sumner, and Nellie Wallace who were all on the Trespass. His ashes were scattered on Bleaklow.

Morris family

Harold Morris

Harold Morris (1913-2007)

Born in Manchester, Harold was the youngest of a large family. He was employed at the Hans Renold engineering company in Burnage working on munitions. Harold, a quiet man, enjoyed walking, cycling, and bowls in later life.

Hilda Mott (1913-1994)

By FREDA CURNOW

My mother, Hilda, was born in Ardwick and was the third child of Eliza and Edward Williamson. With her mother conscripted for war work, as a porter at the local railway station, Hilda and her two brothers were looked after by their grandmother with four other grandsons. Being the only girl, among so many boy cousins, it was little wonder that Hilda was quite a 'tom-boy' who later enjoyed rambling, cycling and camping.

Mott family

Hilda Mott

She was also extremely bright and excelled at her schoolwork - and when at the age of twelve she was put in charge of the younger children in her school, as well as running the school bank which involved taking the money and account books to the local bank.

At fourteen she had sat and passed the scholarship to the local grammar school. Despite this and passing another exam which would have provided her with her uniform and books, her father vetoed the idea as he felt that education was wasted on girls and that it was the boys who needed it. Despite the head of the local Education Department visiting her parents at home, to argue her case, she left school at fourteen with no formal qualifications. Her father later managed to find the wherewithal to have his two sons take up apprenticeships!

Meanwhile Hilda found work as a tailor's cutter for a local firm near Belle Vue Zoo. Even though she had to curtail her studies to start work she later attended night school classes in English Literature, Poetry, History, Current Affairs and even learned some basic French.

She was also very sporty and after her brother had bought her a gents' bike for her fifteenth birthday, she became a keen cyclist, later joining a local club named 'the Grecians'. She also enjoyed hiking and camping as well as ice-and roller skating and joined a local rambling club.

She married Bill Mott in 1940 in Openshaw, then with the outbreak of war, as my father was in a 'reserved occupation' they left Manchester and moved to Bristol where he worked on Spitfires, Brabazons and finally, Concorde at Bristol Aircraft Corporation. In 1982 my parents moved from Bristol to be nearer us in Cornwall.

My mother often talked about the Trespass, and I would be taken to Derbyshire as a young child when visiting relatives in Manchester, where I would be regaled with tales of how proud she had been to have played her part in bringing it to fruition. So, she was really delighted and surprised when, on the morning of the 50th anniversary of the Trespass in 1982, not only did she receive a letter from Benny Rothman but also two ladies from the local rambling club knocked at her door and presented her with a commemorative book and a beautiful bouquet of flowers.

In her latter years she had several serious falls which led to her entering a nursing home, which was on the cliff tops, overlooking the sea at Mullion, Cornwall. She was to die there, two weeks later, thus fulfiling a prophecy, given to her by a complete stranger in a tea-shop in Penzance some thirty- odd years previously, before she had ever been to Cornwall, telling her that although she now lived in a town she would die, on a windy, stormy night, within sight and sound of the sea.

Hilda Mott

We booked a short holiday in Buxton to scatter the ashes of my mother and father at the base of Kinder. We came across a quarry that had been designated as a picnic area, and, the first thing that caught our eye was the memorial plaque commemorating the meeting place of the original Trespassers. We then made our way towards Kinder where we found a lovely spot overlooking the reservoir, and, after a short prayer, we buried the ashes, along with two small red roses (representing Lancashire) and a miniature stick of rock - my mother's favourite sweet!

Dave Nesbitt (1912-1972)

He was born David Nussbaum in Cheetham, and ran away from home in his early teens because of a difficult relationship with his father Solomon. He ended up in the Gorbals, Glasgow, where he was looked after by a family of showmen and it was they who gave him the Scottish name of Nesbitt.

In the 1932 trial court record he was listed as a labourer aged nineteen at Red Bank, Cheetham. He was found guilty of inciting unlawful trespass and sentenced to three months in prison. According to a *Daily Worker* article, 21 September 1932, Dave complained about his harsh treatment while in Wandsworth Prison. He was interviewed by the governor following a demonstration by some of the London BWSF outside the prison. The other prisoners were singing the *Red Flag* and shouting slogans. Nesbitt wrote a letter requesting the visit of Comrade George Sinfield, the national secretary of the BWSF but this had been intercepted by the governor, Commander Foster and he was hauled before him. Foster said 'What do you mean by telling lies about this prison?' Nesbitt replied that he didn't understand what he meant. 'Well listen to this' said Foster, and he read out Nesbitt's letter. 'Is that the truth?' he then asked. [The contents of the letter were not reported]. Nesbitt said it was and Foster instructed the prison officer in attendance to suppress the letter to Sinfield and to stop all letters and visits until after his release.

George Sinfield, National Secretary of the BWSF

Nesbitt had been told he would be treated like an ordinary prisoner but he believed they were trying to break him because he had defied the laws of public property. He had learned before they stopped his letters that there had been a BWSF demonstration in Glasgow against the closure of Milngavie Park, a popular area for ramblers, and also of the Sheffield Ramblers' Rights Movement's organised demonstration on the Broomhead Moors. After his return to Manchester, he married Deborah Simensky in 1935.

During the war Dave fought in Italy and while doing his service, he was ordered to attend a course on photography where the instructor said 'There are big hills, little hills ..' and David chipped in '...and jellied eels'. For his quip he spent some time in the 'guest house'. Dave experienced anti-Semitism in the Army and changed his name back to Nesbitt.

Dave Nesbitt

He became a 'showman' seller making a good living touring the markets of the Lancashire coastal towns. Later he owned a bingo hall and then a launderette. He was said to be kind and generous with friends and family, and when he went on holiday to Israel many years later with his family he met up with people whom he had managed to get out of Italy to Palestine on a boat during the war.

He became disillusioned with communism during a three-month trip to Eastern Europe, after what he witnessed in Russia away from the main tourist sites. He found poverty and shops with empty shelves - not the utopian dream he thought it was. After everything he thought he knew about Russia and Israel had been turned upside down, it made him distrust authority and he became a firm supporter of Israel within the communist party. In 1970 he took part in the BBC *Look Stranger* reconstruction of the Trespass and led a robust discussion with an ex-Water Board employee Horace Oldham who was involved in the Trespass.

Dave Nesbitt (centre) with friends in Italy

Arthur Newsome

Arthur Newsome (1912-1937)

Newsome or Newsum was one of the founding members of Sheffield's Spartacus Rambling Club in 1932 which was named after the leader of a slave revolt in Rome. This was originally a YCL club but was renamed with the intention of having trespass rambles to highlight the problems of land access. The Spartacus group joined the Manchester contingent for the Trespass.

George Revill, another founder member of Spartacus and participant in the Trespass, said 'We wanted to use the club to win youth for socialism. Our aim was to get people to appreciate the countryside and fight for better access. We hoped they would join the YCL but we weren't prepared to bludgeon them. Our principal object was to build up a strong rambling club yet get people into a socialist way of thinking.'

One of Arthur's earliest jobs was in a rolling mill, then later as a labourer on the construction of a pea-packing factory. He was a leading figure for the YLC in Sheffield and became its secretary. During 1932 he attended an unemployed demonstration and a May Day rally at Hillsborough Park. He was a frequent street speaker and also joined a local group on the London hunger march.

He was also involved in the Abbey Brook Trespass a few months later. This was organised by the Ramblers' Rights movement he helped to set up, which included about twenty local clubs. He and about twelve others broke away from the main group to trespass over to Foulstone Delf and were threatened by keepers with pit props who urged the police to arrest them. There are stories that Arthur disguised himself at the protest because he was a marked man.

In 1934 he went to Moscow to attend the International Lenin School on a nine-month course. Newsum was unemployed when he joined twenty-five Sheffield men to fight with the International Brigade in Spain in 1936. He was killed within days of arrival, during aerial bombing at Cordova in January 1937. A memorial service for him at the City Hall highlighted the group's activities with a gymnastic display, jazz band and a one-act drama. His death at the age of twenty four was a blow to Sheffield YCL but they rallied round with a demonstration and organised regular Sunday collections of food for Spain from local estates.

Joseph Norman (1908-)

Joe and his twin brother George were born in Hulme and his father was a carter in the cotton industry. The family moved to Salford in 1914 and his first full-time job at the age of fourteen was at a mill, where he led a deputation which resulted in 40% wage increases for himself and two hundred others. He next found employment in engineering at Metrovics, Trafford Park, where he and his brother took up boxing in the lunch hours.

While unemployed in 1930, they joined the Royal Naval Reserve and enjoyed success in boxing tournaments. Joseph turned professional and had sixteen fights at featherweight and lightweight between 1930 and 1936. From an early age he was active in trade unions and politics. Joe was a member of the Workers' Art Club and local chairman of the Unemployed Workers' Movement organising sport. He went with the BWSF boxing team to Russia and was so popular, after winning all his fights, he was invited to make a tour of Red Army camps where he sparred with soldiers, and was known as 'The Professor'.

Following the death of his friend George Brown he enlisted with the International Brigade in 1933 to replace him in the fight against fascism. During the battle to take Teruel fortress, a young reporter beside him was shot through the head. Joe was taken prisoner in 1937 along with 140 others and spent a harrowing time in concentration camps. They had to endure terrible conditions such as being kept in a large dungeon below street level. Many of his fellow prisoners were executed and he twice faced a firing squad, but for some reason his life was spared.

He was freed in 1938 after an exchange of Italian nationalist prisoners, and returned to a great welcome in Manchester. Norman said the Republican Army was well-clothed and led, and every soldier got ten pesetas a day - forty times as much as the rebel troops were paid.

Joe married Vera Chadwick on his return to England, and found work at Irlam Steel Works and then Crossley Motors. He volunteered to train as a nurse at Crumpsall Hospital. Later he moved with his family to Northumberland because of his son's poor health. His wife became the head of a village school and Joe worked as a keeper and assistant shepherd for the County Council, and also for the local river board, building roads and flood banks. He organised boxing classes for young shepherds aged between twenty and thirty.

They later moved to Corby, Northamptonshire, where Joe worked at the steelworks. He was involved with the local Labour Party and continued to help form union branches. He was also elected to the National Executive Committee of the International Brigade.

Eric Oliver (1912-1998)

By EILEEN CLEMENT

Eric Furness Oliver was the youngest of three brothers, and they lived at Millhouses, Sheffield. Eric joined the Ramblers' Association when it was formed in 1935 and was a staunch supporter of 'The Right to Roam' and the National Trust and was proud to take part in the Trespass.

Eric met my mother, Kath, when they worked in the same office. They married in 1937 and moved to Birmingham where Eric was an insurance underwriter. During the war he was a fireman. They had three daughters

Joe Norman

Joe Norman

Eric Oliver

Working Class Movement Library

Oliver family

Oliver family

Eric Oliver

and, after Eric's retirement, they moved back to Totley near Sheffield. He loved the outdoors and we had many family walks in the Worcestershire countryside when he taught us the names of wild flowers, trees, birds and insects. On one occasion on entering a glade on the hills Eric surprised us by doing a handstand. Many of our walks were not straightforward paths as we often went off on a tangent to discover more. *Trespassers will be prosecuted* and *Private - No Entry* notices seemed like an invitation to Dad.

My father was a keen gardener, enjoyed reading *The Countryman* and the *Geographical Magazine* and always had the *Daily Telegraph*. He was fond of poetry and odd rhymes and often recited *The Ancient Mariner* and *The Owl and the Pussycat*. My children used to stay with their grandparents and went on walks with Dad. In the early 90s when Eric was over 80, he and Oliver would be dropped off 8-10 miles from home and walk back across the moors, stopping at a pub for a beer and fruit cake and cheese. On another occasion, Eric crashed down on his back in the springy bed of heather, causing my son to think he had collapsed, much to Eric's amusement. 'We always used to crash in the heather for a rest' he said.

Harry and Jane Orr

Harry (1901-1988) was born in Woolwich because his father was in the army, and spent his childhood in Malta. His parents were from Sheffield and by the 1920s they returned there and Harry trained locally as a civil engineer. He met Jane, his future wife, when they were both members of the Clarion Rambling Club in the mid-1920s, when Harry was on the committee for transport. Jane (1906-2002) was from South Collingham near Newark and came to Sheffield at the age of sixteen and worked in the lace department of Coles department store.

Harry and Jane

Orr family

They spent their weekends rambling in the Peak, particularly enjoying the beautiful countryside in the Upper Derwent Valley. They took part in the Trespass just prior to their wedding in May at Collingham.

They continued to enjoy the outdoor life, walking and camping in Europe before and after WWII, then later staying in hotels around the Mediterranean. When they were married they lived at Oldham, then Harry's civil engineering work took them to Mill Hill in London, where they lived for the rest of their lives. However, the Peak remained a special place for them, and their ashes were scattered at their request on Win Hill where they had courted.

Jean Pettinger (1918-1986)

Jean (Heath) had been encouraged to go on the Trespass by her socialist-leaning father who owned a women's clothes shop in Lincoln. Her mother founded Chatterton's Pork Pie shop nearby. Jean was born in Lincoln in 1918 and met her future husband, Sidney, at the West Lincoln Cycling Club after 1932. They married in 1939 and migrated to New Zealand where they had four children.

In 1965 she returned for a nostalgic walk up Kinder with her son Richard who remembered her weeping for her father who had died not long before in England, and who had inspired her to go on the Trespass. She also marvelled at the number of people on Kinder while on her walk, and greeted her fellow ramblers like long-lost friends. Jean died while seeking cancer treatment in Mexico in 1986, and her family came to England to be part of the Trespass 50th anniversary celebrations.

Jean Pettinger

Aileen Plant (1913-2009)

By GLYNIS GREENMAN

As soon as Aileen, from Stockport, was able to walk, she developed a strong sense of exploration, and she didn't take kindly to being told where she could and couldn't go. Her chief hobby became escaping from the confines of her garden, and the supervision of her mother, and by the time she started school she was well known to the local police who would find the little girl wandering about quite happily on her own and return her to her long-suffering family.

As she grew up one of her special pleasures was rambling at weekends with friends or family. It was a welcome escape from the drudge of daily life and routines. At that time large tracts of the moors were not open to public access because landowners wanted their land dedicated to grouse shoots and they did not want 'trespassers'. It was not the politics which inspired Aileen but the fact that ordinary people were not allowed to roam the open moors and she joined the group of around four hundred walkers, revelling in the freedom offered by the march. There were scuffles and protests and arrests, but Aileen was not involved. She was a trainee teacher and had her budding career as a nursery teacher to consider.

Aileen Plant

Aileen spent her life as a nursery schoolteacher, becoming head teacher at Reddish Vale nursery. She was keenly interested in nursery school education and its potential and worked hard for the Nursery Association until well into her eighties. She never married but she felt the nursery school children were her family, many of whom returned to visit her long after they had left. Sometimes childlike herself, she enjoyed being with children, often more than with adults, and she adored her nephews and nieces. When they had children of their own Aileen eagerly took them under her wing as well. She had a strong sense of family and always insisted her surname was a shortened form of the ancient royal Plantagenet family.

During World War Two Aileen undertook fire-watching duties. She also learned to drive, but never took an official driving test. As she got older she drove her ancient Lada into Derbyshire for afternoon tea with friends. Unfortunately, she was easily distracted, and her driving skills often left much to be desired. She would drive in the middle of the road, commenting, when other drivers yelled at her, that people were not as polite as they used to be. She never had an accident, but she had little road sense and gained the distinction of causing one local driving instructor to jump from her car in consternation at her lack of awareness of other traffic.

Aileen had a life-long love affair with the camera, and recorded every occasion, work, family, holiday or personal. Her collection of photographs and slides was legendary; and there were obligatory slide shows at every family gathering. As children we got used to the much-anticipated Christmas lunch being put on the table, and as we were about to eat would come a cry of 'Hold it!' By the time she had finished photographing it all, the poor turkey had gone cold.

Plant family

Aileen Plant celebrating her 100th birthday

Her passion for photography could cause trouble. She finally got her longed-for chance to travel when she retired in the 1970s. She flew all over the world, visiting China, Russia, Australia, New Zealand and the United States. It was in Russia that she got herself into a potentially dangerous situation. Russian history fascinated her, and she had always dreamed of visiting Moscow and the Kremlin. She was warned to be extremely discreet with her camera, but Aileen was not about to give up her cherished principles of freedom.

On arriving in Moscow, she headed straight for the Kremlin, and, walking through the gates, began taking photographs. Kremlin guards, guns drawn, surrounded her in a flash. Aileen was not fazed. She told them it had been her life-long dream to visit Russia and she wanted some mementoes of her trip. She gave them a short lecture on their own history and told them that she had a bust of Lenin on top of her gramophone at home. The Russians let her off with a warning, but Aileen wasn't finished. She insisted on a photograph with one of the guards and persuaded his colleagues to take it.

However, at heart Aileen was really a home bird and she lived in the same Stockport house from 1922 to 2009. She never lost her wanderlust but, by the time she was in her nineties, she satisfied it with endless recordings of the travel and nature programmes shown on television. She became a 'night owl', often going to bed at four in the morning and not getting up until midday. Aileen lived her whole life guided by her principles of freedom and the right to wander at will, and, although it was sometimes difficult, one had to admire her grit and determination.

George & Gwendoline Revill

They were part of the Spartacus Rambling Club which joined the Trespass. Married the previous year, George and his wife Gwendoline (1911-1982) walked from Sheffield to one of the BWSF camps at Rowarth, spending a night under canvas on the journey. They were met by Benny when they reached Rowarth and during their first night there several tents were blown down. The following day they were joined by other members of the Spartacus Rambling Club. George, born in 1908, was one of the original members of the Spartacus club formed in Spring 1932 during a ramble in the Cordwell Valley. He was chair of the organising committee for the Abbey Brook Trespass. By 1939 he was listed as a telephone operator and lived at Ecclesall Road, Sheffield.

Charles Richardson

He was part of the Sheffield contingent who came over Kinder to meet the Manchester group. He was also a member of the Clarion Ramblers who did not officially support the Trespass. After the meeting following the Trespass they returned to Edale to catch the train home. Once while camping, he was arrested by the police after keepers accused him of tearing down branches to make a fire. Even though Charles and his friends protested they only used deadwood, they were fined ten shillings.

Monty Rosenfield (1917-1944)

He worked in the clothing trade and was a leading member of the Cheetham YCL. In 1936 he, his brother Abraham and two others were each fined 20s at Manchester Police Court for fighting after a fascist meeting at Cheetham, claiming they had been provoked. At the age of nineteen he went to fight in Spain with the International Brigade, hiking over the Pyrenees to join the regiment. Major Sam Wild, the commander of the Manchester men, praised him for his efforts in the conflict.

During WWII he was awarded a Military Medal for bravery in Italy at the Anzio beach-head where he was seriously injured. He was sent home to convalesce but spent his time in hospital giving lectures to the other troops. As soon as he was passed fit, he returned to the front line where he was killed in August 1944. A memorial to him was unveiled three years later at Failsworth cemetery. He had been a good sportsman, rambler and camper and popular because of his great enthusiasm.

Inset: Monty Rosenfield
Below: Rowarth peace camp.
L-R Rosenfield, Sydney Boler, Solly Simmons, Hymie Kyte, front Benny Goodman

Working Class Movement Library

Manchester Archives

Benny Rothman (1911-2002)

Memories of my militant father

By HARRY ROTHMAN

Harry Rothman

My father, like all individuals, was a product of the social milieu in which he grew up. The most significant aspects which moulded him were his Jewish origins, working-class life, experiences of anti-Semitism, struggles against fascism, and membership of the trade union movement and the British Communist Party. Finally one must add his marriage to my mother Lilian Crabtree, not of the Jewish faith but a Rochdale mill-girl, the youngest of a large and close knit family. Karl Marx said 'social being determines social consciousness' and I will here try to show how my father became the man he was. Of course, as his son I cannot escape the charge of a certain degree of subjectivity, though I would argue that this also serves to provide me with insights not easily available to outside observers. I say all this as a preamble for there are those who, with all the force of hindsight and historical judgment behind them, are shocked that this icon of 'freedom to roam' was a communist and militant trade unionist, and remained so all his life.

My father often spoke of his parents' origins in Romania and the many and widespread Jewish relatives. They were not alone in Manchester which had at that time a large thriving Jewish community, in which lands of origin initially remained of significance, each group having their own synagogues. One of my aunts told me with a laugh how Romanian Jews thought themselves superior to the Lithuanian Jews. In other words they stuck together, especially in marriage. Bernard's family were orthodox Jews and associated with other members of the Romanian Jewish community in Manchester. Although they kept basic religious customs and festivals he told me his father had little time for religion, indeed was an atheist. Nevertheless, Bernard said as a boy he did attend Shul Hebrew classes like his peers preparing for bar mitzvah; also the language of his home was Yiddish, the language of Romanian Jews along with other Ashkenazi Jews. Clearly my father was steeped in North Manchester Jewish culture and traditions, and I recall when I was a child occasionally returning from visits there with rye bread and bagels which were then unobtainable in Timperley.

Below: Benny (right) and his sisters Phyllis, Leah, Rose, and brother Gershon

Harry Rothman

My father seems to have gone to a good primary school, and to have benefited from growing up in a bilingual environment. He says his maths primary school teacher was especially good, and he learned a fair bit of algebra there. He won a scholarship to Manchester High School for boys, and did very well in his studies but sadly left at 14 because his mother needed him to go to work. His father, who ran a hardware market stall at Glossop and Shaw markets, had died aged 54 on Bernard's 12th birthday, June 1923; his estate was valued at £180. Not much for a widow with five children, so Bernard was expected to go to work as soon as he was eligible to leave school.

Harry Rothman

Becoming a member of the working class

My father's first job was with Tom Garner's Garage. Why he went to work in the motor trade rather than the clothing business isn't clear, and he did say the family disapproved of his choice. Was this the first sign of rebellion? He managed to persuade his grandmother to buy him a bike, which allowed him to get to work more conveniently than the tram service. The bike also allowed him to travel and take trips out of the city. Previously he rarely got beyond the Elizabeth Street or Heaton Parks, but he now began to ride into Cheshire, and took his first holiday in Snowdonia. His love of cycling and the open -air never left him. He rode bikes into his eighties.

It was at that time he began cycling, rambling and camping with friends. Although he left school, like many others of his generation, he attended night school. In 1928 my father took classes in advertising, salesmanship, and economic geography. There are class notes he made at the time which clearly show he took this education seriously, developing a self-disciplined approach to study which he retained all his life. The subjects studied included: basic English grammar and rules for composition; how to deal with problems and problem-solving; techniques for memorising; reasoning and rules for logic.

One of his workmates, a communist Scots mechanic Bob Donne, sharing father's interest in economics invited him to a debating group he frequented at the Clarion Cafe on Market Street. There he met people who changed his life. My father told the climber and writer Jim Perrin, 'These were very exciting meetings with a good mix of people - and I soon drifted into the Young Communist League.' Other personal influences may have included his Uncle Arthur Solomon, who claimed to have known the Irish revolutionary James Connolly, and his Aunt Ettie who introduced him to Robert Tressell's 'The Ragged-Trousered Philanthropist', the iconic novel which converted many to socialism.

British Workers' Sports Federation

Once in the YCL, my father began his ascent as a political activist and soon had his first brush with the police, being fined for obstruction whilst chalking slogans on pavements and walls; the fine was a week's wages. Part of the YCL activity was to try to attract youth to their movement, if not directly then by association, in what today would be called a 'front' organisation, the British Workers' Sports Federation. The BWSF ran a wide range of sporting activities such as football, cycling, rambling and camping, and had international connections through the Soviet-based Red Sport International.

My father's 'black book' of local contacts from this period included over 370 names and addresses, referencing their sporting interests, politics and affiliations - such as YCL, Clarion or BWSF. Also in this notebook are sections on 'Suggestions for a Camping Site' and 'List of Items Needed for Camping Trips'. The BWSF was especially strong in the Manchester area and seems to have been a focal point of my father's activities prior to the Kinder Trespass.

My father's account of the Kinder Mass Trespass is provided in his memoir *The Battle For Kinder Scout* (2012), and in the ninety years that have elapsed since, there has grown around that event a nebulous cloud that allows a variety of interpretations of its significance, which will be ever-changing as different generations perceive it through the prism of their own experience. That it is of importance is without doubt. Certainly there had been other earlier mass trespasses, and there would be more to come, sometimes taking the action into new and deeper political directions.

Young Communist and antifascist

My father made a good attempt to defend himself at his trial but along with his fellow accused he was sentenced to prison, in his case for four months. He always felt that these convictions were unjustified and reflected the class biases of the courts in his day. His immediate family felt shame that he was in prison, a family disgrace. As for his period in prison, it wasn't too bad, he told me. He said many of his fellow inmates sympathised with the actions of him and his comrades; he said, in particular, one very tough professional criminal who had been relocated to Leicester prison from Dartmoor after the notorious Dartmoor prison riot of January 1932, was helpful. His vegetarian diet regime was respected, and he was able to go to Sunday service in the chapel - one way of getting out of the cell - despite an objection that he was Jewish. He also took the opportunity to study, learning Gregg shorthand - which he felt was a very useful skill for future negotiations. My father also mentioned that while he was in jail, he was visited on a few occasions by people who sympathised with his case and felt that it had been an injustice.

Harry Rothman

Top: Page from Rothman's black book containing contact details of members of CP, YCL, BWSF, or just interested in camping, rambling or sport. Although it cannot be verified, many of those listed could have been on the Trespass. The book, thought to have been compiled between 1932-3 also had notes from courses he had attended.

Above: Mis-match - Benny sparring with an unnamed person at a 1935 peace camp.

When he got out of prison his former employer Tom Garners had no room for him anymore and he was on the dole. He began to enter political activity with the YCL at that point and moved to Burnley, where there was a big strike of textile workers, the 'more loom' strike. He had been sent there by the Communist Party to build a branch of the YCL, using the approach that had been successful in Cheetham through sport and other social activities. However, after some months it became clear this was not a success and he returned to Manchester and a motor mechanic's job at Syd Abrams' garage.

Top: With friends at Matlock Bath
Below: Benny had always been an avid note-taker

During this period he was engaged in working with the YCL in various ways, including helping to edit their new weekly newspaper *The Challenge*, with John Gollan, then the national leader of the YCL. Part of this work was to develop supporters and sympathisers through the BWSF; there is as I have already mentioned an address book of my father's from this period. In Cheetham the YCL built up a club with around four hundred members called the Challenge Club, in which my father played a very active role. In one sense it was a social club with a wide range of activities such as gymnastics, canoeing, boxing, cycling, rambling and camping. On the other hand it gave them a strong body of fit young people willing and able to take on the task of combating the fascists as they began to meet and demonstrate in Manchester. Their aim was to make it impossible for the followers of Sir Oswald Mosley's British Union of Fascists, with their poisonous anti-Semitic ideology, to establish themselves as a force in Manchester.

An important aspect of the anti-fascist opposition was to prevent and disrupt BUF meetings and rallies to split the working class on ethnic and religious lines. The struggle became physical at times, and on one occasion fascist stewards threw Bernard over a balcony. Fortunately his fall was broken by the bodies of their own supporters below. I cannot stress how important the anti-fascist struggle was to my father and his Manchester comrades, a number of whom went to fight in the Spanish Civil War. He said he'd volunteered as an ambulance driver to Spain but the offer was refused, and he had to be content to work campaigning for money and support.

Harry Rothman

In this period my father and mother became closer, and I expand later on their relationship. I must mention one story of my mother's which shows another facet to the social and political activities of the Left in Manchester and Lancashire: this was theatre. She was involved with a workshop, (I think it was the Clarion Players), of Joan Littlewood, the famous playwright and producer, and Jimmy Miller (Ewan MacColl) her husband. It is alleged that MI5 kept Littlewood and MacColl under surveillance at their home, one spook reporting 'A number of young men who have the appearance of communist Jews are known to visit. It is thought they came from Manchester.' My parents remained in contact with MacColl and he attended several Mass Trespass anniversaries.

Above: Benny, Metrovicks works committee

Trade union man

My father became an active member of the Amalgamated Engineering Union (AEU) and wished to move from a garage to a factory environment with more scope for union activities. He was already in 1935 a delegate to the Manchester and Salford Trades Council, and he managed to get work at the aircraft company A V Roe (Avro). When they discovered he was a communist, however, they sacked him. Fortunately Metropolitan Vickers (Metro-Vicks) in Trafford Park was expanding to meet the looming war with Germany and were recruiting skilled workers. He was able to get a job working there until he was victimised in 1952. Five Metro-Vicks workers became Members of Parliament. In those days the Labour Party actually selected workers to stand in Parliamentary elections; and a further three, including Hugh Scanlon (later Lord Scanlon of Davyhulme), became leaders of the AEU.

My father played an active role and was elected to an important union position in the factory, representing several thousand workers from the West Works on the Works Committee for over ten years. In 1952 the management sacked him and three others on a trumped-up charge. The struggle, initially involving a strike over his victimisation, dragged on for several years but he was never able to get his job back.

As my father discovered, once you have been sacked for union activity you are placed on the 'black list', - people who shouldn't be employed - which was circulated to employers. As a result he was out of work for some time. He did get work, initially at Meldrum Brothers of Timperley, and after they closed at the British Rayon Research Association in Heald Green. This was an industrial research centre which studied ways of improving and using rayon for the textile industry. He found working with scientists very interesting and congenial, and was excited by the work he did on fluidised beds - this is a means of getting solid particles to flow like a fluid, a phenomenon with many applications.

In 1956 my father got work with Kearns-Richards in Broadheath until he retired in 1976. He continued trade union activities as a shop steward, chairing the works' shop stewards committee, and being involved in national and local struggles, long after retirement, to save jobs as British manufacturing began its great decline. He actively supported the miners' strike, and spoke up against the National Front. Eventually his union, by then renamed as the AUEW, awarded his sterling work as a trade unionist with, in 1980 The Gold Badge, and its highest award the Special Award of Merit in 1990.

The family man

My parents married at Christmas 1937. Tragically, my mother's mother aged 64, had a fatal heart attack a few days before, hardly the most auspicious beginning. My mother Lilian (Lily) Crabtree from Rochdale, was the youngest of a family of thirteen, eight of whom were alive in my childhood. The family had a tradition of socialism, father Paul claiming to have met Keir Hardy, and Lilian and at least two of her brothers, George and Bob, were in the YCL, attending the rambles and camps.

My mother worked in the card room of a cotton mill, and was for long periods the only member of the family in work, a situation that placed great emotional strain on her, leading to occasional periods of depression; she was, nevertheless, usually a jolly woman and a beauty when young. Mother bore three children: I was born in 1938, Marian in 1940, and Paul who died at birth in 1952, that annus horribilis when father was sacked from Metro-Vics. They eventually had five grandchildren, and ten great-grandchildren.

My father was welcomed into the Crabtree family, who had no anti-Semitic prejudices. Unfortunately, my father's family were bitterly opposed to the match, and felt that he had shamed them by marrying outside his religion. The Rothman family cut him off and for over twenty years he only saw his brother Gersh and Uncle Arthur Solomon, finally seeing his mother just before she died.

Harry Rothman

Lily and Benny

The war dominated my parents' early marital years. They moved to a nice semi-detached house on the newly-built Riddings Estate in Timperley, where they stayed for more than fifty years. Bernard left home at a very early hour to cycle the seven miles to Metro-Vics and returned late after a long hard shift. Sometimes my mother was in work, and her father Paul lived with us for a while and acted as a babysitter. Bernard, ever conscious of the need to protect his family, built his own bomb shelter in the garden. It seemed solid enough to stop all but a direct hit, and, until he demolished it to build a garage, it also made a great den for the local kids. Bernard was in the Home Guard and he kept his rifle and bayonet in a corner of the hall. Once Marian and I stole them and paraded round the block - after that he locked them up.

Whenever they could, my parents went rambling in the Cheshire country-side and Peak District. For holidays we went camping, and, for a period after the War my father continued organising camps for supporters of the Daily Worker in the Lake District. Generally we took camping holidays

Harry Rothman

there, and in Snowdonia, and North Wales, and we climbed all the main summits as children. For a few years he owned a small wooden chalet on a farm in Whitegate, a Cheshire village. My father had an abiding interest in English rural life, and its many strange and beautiful seasonal customs such maypoles and rush-bearing. He was passionate about natural history, and father and mother were enthusiastic members of the Altrincham Natural History Society, which had regular nature walks by the River Bollin for bird and wild flower spotting. Sometimes we would visit Cotterill Clough nature reserve near Ringway - before the modern airport existed.

In our home there was constant political discussion, and most of our visitors were comrades. Generally these were communist fellow workers and union members, but some, to Marian and me, seemed rather exotic; there was Emily who rode a giant motorbike carrying her husband on the pillion, a pipe-smoking lady psychiatrist, a former West End chorus girl, a cosmic-ray physicist, and a friendly linguist who coached me through my O level French. Once an Indian doctor, on 'party business' stayed overnight, possibly the first Asian I'd ever seen. After 1956 - the Hungarian Revolution and Krushchev's revelations about Stalin - many of the non-working-class members left the local communist branch. My parents and a hard-core of trade unionists remained steadfast in their faith to 'the movement' and carried on their day-to-day struggles, in the unions, CND and the 'peace movement'.

A central part of my father's endeavours involved keeping up with the news and fulfilling his propagandist role. He sold the *Daily Worker*, later renamed *The Morning Star*, at his work place, and had a paper round of regular weekend readers, some of whom also took the *Soviet Weekly*. He also assiduously read *Labour Monthly*, especially *Notes of the Month* which provided the latest party policy changes. He even took *The Manchester Guardian*.

Receiving AEU award from Lord Scanlon

My father had a sizable library of more than five hundred books, which included all the Marxist classics and volumes from the Left Book Club. His collections also included much on technical engineering, science books, and natural history - including the early volumes of the New Naturalist series, many OS maps, atlases, and other reference books. His literature included Shakespeare, Dickens, Burns, Jack London, O. Henry and Howard Fast, and several Soviet novelists. He loved comedies such as J. K. Jerome's 'Three Men in a Boat', laughing out loud as he read them. Mother also enjoyed reading, often perusing dictionaries for hours. He enjoyed my comics, such *The Dandy* and *Beano*, from which his favourite characters were Lord Snooty, Pansy Potter, and Desperate Dan. He also invested in a set of *Arthur Mee's Children's Encyclopedia*, quite expensive for a working man, buying a volume every month, and Marian and I read and enjoyed them, gaining an educative general knowledge, despite its underlying ideology that the British Empire was progressive, just and liberal.

Physically Bernard and Lily were both small, he five feet three inches, and mother an inch shorter; both possessed strong characters and formed a good partnership. Lily was kind, and generous to a fault, and all too willing to express her feelings, whilst Bernard was stoical and less willing to show his feeling on the surface, and a natural leader. Lily could handle responsible roles but didn't seek them. They were abstemious, neither smoked or drank, and Bernard had been, prior to marriage, a strict vegetarian. Later he recanted. Lily was the cook and he had to eat what she provided. They didn't own their home until late in their marriage, and finances were tight. There was no way in which Lily could have had the luxury of being a 'housewife'.

For most of their marriage my mother went to work. She said she had had nineteen different jobs, including working in a cotton mill, a turner in an engineering works, a dinner lady. One job involved working with asbestos, and another led to industrial-induced dermatitis. She was also a qualified St John's Ambulance nurse, which helped when she became a carer, first to an old family friend and finally to Bernard. This gave her a certain degree of economic independence, reinforced by the custom my father followed of handing her his weekly wage packet unopened. That said, she always seemed to accede to any of my father's needs for 'expenses'. My mother, though sometimes exasperated by my father, was also unbelievably kind and tolerant of his lifestyle. She shared his politics obviously but that was but one facet of his mercurial character.

He was a man of unbounded interests and hobbies within which we all had to live. Some of these are worth describing since they say much about the man. He would have loved to have been a professional photographer, and he sometimes freelanced as a sports photographer for the *Daily Worker*. In this digital age we forget the paraphernalia of photography, cameras, accessories like flash, light meters, tripods and of course, the dark room, with enlargers, dishes, photographic paper, bottles full of hypo and developer. Also magazines and books on the latest equipment, techniques and styles. All this had to be accommodated in their small home. The bathroom was commandeered for hours at a time, no-one was allowed in, and even when not in use it stored photographic equipment. Many photographs took the form of slides and transparencies which he enjoyed projecting, necessitating more gear, projectors and screens. After he retired he gave public slide shows on natural history and politics.

My father was a music lover, and as soon as he could afford it, added a radiogram to the radio, which he listened to constantly. He was a fan of Paul Robeson, both for his singing and political courage. He got a piano, which just fitted in the small front room, and would occasionally play. He had a pleasant singing voice, and a repertoire of radical songs from camp-fire days, and couldn't resist yodelling. Distant ramblers were often surprised to be hailed with a mighty yodel from across the valley, which could be a bit embarrassing. He could play the trumpet, whistles, mouth-organs, although he had had no formal musical education. His preference was for light classical music, and traditional Yiddish music.

Harry Rothman

Benny's photos of Emil Zatopek at White City Manchester during the Britain v Czechoslovakia athletics meeting, for the Daily Worker 1955

Benny and Lily at Healey Dell

He was also a technophile, an early adopter of new technologies and gadgets if he could afford them. These included the first ballpoint pen, a pressure cooker - which terrified my mother, Teepol - a laboratory grade detergent, for washing dishes, and DDT, which probably poisoned pets as well as fleas. From army surplus stores there came a veritable torrent of equipment, and also antiques and clock mechanisms from junk shops. My father enjoyed making things, in wood and metal. This involved building sheds to work in and store his ever-growing collection of tools. Eventually the rear garden contained three sheds, a green house, and a garage, and my mother used to complain he had turned it into a 'shanty town'. Fortunately their home in Crofton Avenue was a corner house with a relatively large garden.

He owned over time a succession of bicycles - including a tandem for Lily, who never learned to ride a bike safely, a motorbike and side car, a caravan, and cars. Generally in later years his motors were Russian or Czech, which we thought was taking political loyalty to extremes. However, he was perfectly able to repair any of their mechanical defects. All this provided him with the mobility and transport he needed for multitudinous activities. In later years having toured all over Britain, he and my mother travelled in their caravan through France, Central and Eastern Europe. They visited Australia, where Gersh, his brother, and numerous relatives of mother lived.

Before it was covered in sheds the garden was a source of home vegetables, and during the war he kept hens that provided us and neighbours with supplies of fresh eggs. He had an incubator in a bedroom for hatching chicks, a source of wonder for my sister and me. He also grew an amazingly large productive grapevine which extended along the walls of their utility room. He leased a series of allotments, especially in his years of retirement, working in them until poor health forced him to give up. My father was fond of animals and over the years we had a dog, many cats, rabbits, tropical fish, and a budgie, which was actually mother's pet.

The Green turn

The working class, its institutions and industrial base began a long decline after the 1970s and '80s, and then came the dramatic collapse of the Soviet bloc. Coincidentally Environmentalism became an increasingly important political current. Consequently the form of his politics changed and he began to stress more green values which, of course, had always been there, in the Mass Trespass and the struggle for the Right to Roam. Although my father was politically a red, it was always tinged with green. Furthermore, when he retired from work, his union and party work was greatly reduced.

In 1970 I was completing my book on pollution in industrial societies, *Murderous Providence*, and had a perpetual conversation with him about ecological and environmental issues. We agreed on the profound importance of the environment and that the Left and the Unions had paid

Harry Rothman

Harry Rothman

it insufficient attention. He began to raise green issues in his union meetings, with what effect I can't say. Environmental topics frequently featured in the column he wrote for a local newspaper. In the initial column arguing the need for a post-Cold War peace dividend he wrote '*Among threats to Britain, and in fact to the planet, are threats of global warming and irreversible damage from pollution. Can't the spare mental and industrial resources be directed towards dealing with the very real dangers to our present and future existence?*'

In 1982 the National Trust bought Kinder Scout, and my father became the first secretary of the Kinder Scout and High Peak Advisory Committee, I have been told this was not popular with some interested parties, but he took the position seriously and devoted attention to helping to create new paths. There was a new access struggle in 1989 when the Water Bill threatened to close access to open country owned by water authorities. An important, ultimately successful campaign was waged to safeguard the right to walk on these lands.

A highpoint of the campaign was the Rivington Pledge Committee, of which Bernard was secretary. Their pledge, to trespass if access was denied, was recited by over 3000 ramblers at a protest rally on 7th May 1989 at Rivington near Bolton.

My father also became increasingly appalled by the environmental damage created by new highways cutting through fine countryside and sites of scientific interest. One such was Twyford Down, and he was a principal speaker at the Protest Rally on July 4th 1994. He later wrote:

Top left: Benny holding a copy of the 1989 Rivington Pledge declaration, designed by his daughter-in-law.

Above: Opening of the Midshires Way 1994

Below: It seemed impossible to imagine for many years that Benny could be given such an honour by the rambling establishment.

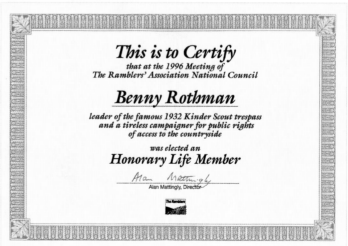

Harry Rothman

This is to Certify
that at the 1996 Meeting of
The Ramblers' Association National Council

Benny Rothman

*leader of the famous 1932 Kinder Scout trespass
and a tireless campaigner for public rights
of access to the countryside*

was elected an

Honorary Life Member

Alan Mattingly
Alan Mattingly, Director

The Ramblers

'I arrived at the Twyford Cutting a day before the scheduled Mass Trespass in opposition to the Criminal Justice Bill and this gave me an opportunity to look at the site where such destruction of the environment had taken place and where the history of the fight to oppose this devastation had been made. It also gave me the opportunity to meet up with the people who had led this now famous campaign of opposition...[accusing the contractor's security] of warlike hostility to any opposition... like an army of occupation in hostile territory.'

This was to prove to be his final protest before he was incapacitated by a series of strokes.

The memory of the Mass Trespass had begun to enter a wider social consciousness by the time the 50th anniversary arrived and the media began to take an interest. Chris Brasher made a TV film, and several others followed, and my father gained new friends and acquaintances in the media, and associated climbing circles. I'm not sure how many anniversary rallies he attended before he became ill in his eighties - quite a few. He became an icon and celebrity to the outdoor movement. Students came to interview him, he did mini-lecture tours, a play was written and performed by his friend Mike Harding. A blue plaque was placed on his old home in Timperley, a train was named after him, as was a mountain in Greenland, and a mural was placed in New Mills Station. In 1996 The Ramblers' Association made him an honorary life member.

Benny leading the way at the Trespass anniversaries

Harry Rothman

Harry Rothman

Harry Rothman

Victor Wall family

Harry Rothman

Benny and Lily

Finale

Benny suffered a severe stroke when he was 83, in 1994. He never fully recovered though for a time he was able to travel around in a wheelchair. Indeed his last court appearance was from his wheelchair to present, and win, the case for keeping open a local footpath in Timperley. Lily looked after him as his carer until eventually it was clearly too much. They sold their house in 1996 and moved to a house in Billericay where Marian had her home. There they were lovingly cared for by Marian and her husband Frank. As is often the case the carer died first. Lily passed away on 29th March 2001, aged 86, and within ten months Benny had died aged 90 on 23rd January 2002.

Lily and Benny share a common grave at Great Burstead Cemetery near Billericay Essex. That summer I made a pilgrimage to Kinder with my friend Alan Bond, who had served with Benny on the Kinder Scout and High Peak Advisory Committee, along the route of a path they had designated. When we reached the Downfall I sprinkled half his ashes watching the wind blow them over the gritty rocks and peat bogs he loved. Now he was not only on Kinder he was part of Kinder.

Keith Warrender

Marion and Harry Rothman at the unveiling of the plaque on Benny's former home in Timperley in 2012

Harry Rowley

Harry Rowley (1919-1991)

Born in Manchester, by 1939 he was employed as a cotton piecer, living at Churchill Street, Chorlton-on-Medlock. During the last war he was a conscientious objector. Afterwards he was a rubber worker and lived in Wythenshawe. Harry and his dog were present at the 1982 Kinder Trespass anniversary celebrations.

Arthur Schofield (1910-)

Born in New Mills, he was a keen sportsman and was invited for a trial at Blackpool FC. His father refused to let him go saying he already had a good job with a future at the local calico printworks. He'd also advised Arthur to steer clear of strong drink and fast women.

He enjoyed walking and a favourite ramble was to the Hope Valley via Jacob's Ladder. He made many unsucceful attempts to get to Kinder Downfall, then he and friends finally made it onto the plateau one snowy day in January 1931, only to be met by three keepers who escorted them off, miles out of their way. He took part in the 50th Trespass anniversary celebration leading the way out of Hayfield. Interviewed later on TV he claimed he was lucky not to have been locked up with the other Trespassers.

After marrying Mabel Pope in 1937 they lived for some time in Carlisle where he was clerk at a textile printing mill. On their return he went to work at Courtaulds, Hyde until he was 65 then finally employed at a smaller textile firm in the town.

Arthur Schofield

*Trespass vets L-R:
Standing, Jimmy Jones.
Sitting, Arthur
Schofield and Bella
Costello at the 60th
Anniversary event*

Albert Shirtcliffe (1908-1992)

Albert was born in Sheffield and by 1939 was living with his parents at Woodthorpe School, Sheffield where his father was the caretaker. Albert was employed as a baths attendant. By the time of his death he was living in Balby, Doncaster and listed as a retired chief swimming instructor.

John Simmonds (1906-1997)

Born in Manchester, the eldest of six children. During WWI he had to look after his younger siblings. He worked at Clayton Aniline and used to walk with a few friends on Fridays from Manchester to Derbyshire to spend the weekends in the Peak. Around 1916 he was also chairman of Hayfield Choral Society.

He married Edith in 1929, daughter of the owner of the cafe at Stones Head, Hayfield, and by 1939 was listed as a riveter, living at Stones Head. He used to serve at the cafe, and it was there he got to know Benny Rothman and his friends. He was a local councillor for about two years, and enjoyed ballroom dancing well into his seventies. When he was in his eighties, he was said to have been the oldest walker to complete the ninety-five mile West Highland Way from Glasgow to Fort William with overnight stays in hostels. At the age of eighty-six he was still a keen rambler, walking twenty miles a day. He enjoyed taking his grandchildren on Derbyshire walks, always singing songs with them.

John Simmonds

Edith Stringer

At the time of the Trespass she lived in Miles Platting and was a member of YCL. She and friends used to camp every week in an ex-army bell-tent at Hayfield. She went at the age of eleven to the protest with her elder brother Walter and sister Nellie. On the day of the Trespass, Edith was scared by big notices which read *Trespassers will be prosecuted* and thought she would go to prison. Edith later lived in Chorlton.

George Sumner (1911-2000)

From Salford, he was a friend of Jimmy Miller. In 1939, George was listed as a calico printers' designer and living in Duke Street, Salford. As one of the surviving Trespassers, he was invited to the unveiling of the plaque at the former New Mills Police Station in 1994. He was a member of the British Workers' Sports Federation and said 'We had been fighting to get across Kinder for many years, but every time there was grouse shooting we could not go up there. We never expected it to turn violent but the gamekeepers had sticks and they started the trouble'. He and his wife moved to Cleveleys where he was active in the local Labour Party, as well as Blackpool Trades Council and the British Pensioners' Trade Union Action Association. George was also a member of the Blackpool and Fylde arts associations.

Edith Stringer

Evelyn Taylor (1913-1998)

Evelyn, born in Northwich, grew up in Knutsford and had always been a keen walker. She worked in the engineering industry in the 1930s and was dismissed from Ferguson and Palin for her union activities, before a strike brought about her re-instatement.

Evelyn Taylor

Evelyn acted as the election agent for George Brown, the Communist candidate for Openshaw in 1934. (See George Brown). Her heckling against fascist leader Oswald Mosley resulted in her being frog-marched by stewardesses up the aisle of the Free Trade Hall at a meeting. Benny Rothman who was also present described her as 'a big lass' who lashed out and knocked over some of her escorts. She was fined £25 but refused to pay and spent time in Strangeways. She was also arrested during a peaceful meeting at which she laid a wreath at the Cenotaph in St Peter's Square, Manchester.

She worked for underground movements which were in opposition to the various fascist dictatorships and undertook the dangerous work of taking aid and messages to clandestine groups. She married George Brown but he was killed during the Spanish Civil War. Then she married Jack Jones who was to become a notable union leader. He was a friend of her former husband and had been seriously injured himself while fighting in Spain.

By 1939 she and Jack were living in Coventry where he was a trade union official and she worked in aero engine production. She was also a shop steward and secretary of her union branch. The following year the family home was demolished by enemy bombs. She remained active as the Labour Party ward secretary, as well Secretary of the local CND and took part in the Aldermaston marches. She attended the 1984 peace conference in Paris after it had been abandoned by Britain and America, and was in frequent contact with the singer and peace campaigner Paul Robeson.

In 1963 when Jack was transferred to his union's London headquarters Evelyn joined Dulwich Labour Party. She became a JP and juvenile court magistrate before being removed by Lord Hailsham, the Lord Chancellor. She campaigned for left-wing causes in the local constituency, but was criticised for holding a £700-a-year role with a development company, after her husband had highlighted some other MP's interests. Evelyn was a vociferous critic of the litter problem in Camberwell but could not blame the street cleaners as they belonged to her husband's union.

Joe Thomas (1912-1990)

Joe was born in North London, the son of a cobbler and leather worker, in a Primitive Methodist household. He joined the YCL in the 1930s and was involved in the Workers' Olympic Movement of 1936. In 1943 he joined the socialist Commonwealth Party and became one of its organisers, then from 1946 to 1952 the Socialist Workers' League.

He got involved with the trade unions in the early fifties and took a leading part in the dockers' strike when the dockers were refused their demand of twenty-five shillings a day basic pay and a forty-hour, five-day working week. He was editor of the *Workers' Review* from 1967, and by 1972 involved with *Workers' Voice*.

Thomas joined the *Guardian* as copytaker, where he was father of the SOGAT Union. He always had a cigarette in the corner of his mouth, and intrigued his younger colleagues with his associations with some of the great figures of the Left, such as novelist George Orwell. He was a founder member of the London Workers' Group which helped to educate refugees, and the Movement for Workers' Council in 1987. Joe was said to have been a hard worker who helped many to get their wages and work conditions upgraded, and established procedures for employer negotiations.

Joe Thomas

Michael Tippett (1905-1998)

Tippett, the famous composer who was knighted for his services to music, was the life-long friend of David Ayerst, the *Guardian* correspondent at the Trespass. They met in Oxford through their common interest in the writings of Thomas Butler, the writer and satirist. Tippett had been active in left-wing politics in the 1930s when Ayerst became a journalist. During his first visit to Manchester, Ayerst invited him to come along with him to the protest at Hayfield.

Tippett wrote about the day of the Trespass: '*At a pre-arranged signal everyone left the path. Suddenly the black figures of the gamekeepers appeared over the hill. David sent me striding on ahead to see what was happening and in consequence I was struck by one of the stones being thrown (by a keeper?) which David duly noted.*'

Tippett then went back to receive treatment for his badly cut hand. After the Trespass was over, he and Ayerst passed through the police cordon in the village by means of his press card. The divisions in society which he experienced at the Trespass prompted him, shortly afterwards, to join an organisation which supported unemployed miners.

Michael Tippett

Victor Wall (1909-1998)

Victor was born in Halifax, the son of a tramway employee. In a letter to Benny Rothman in 1991, he wrote 'I was twenty-three in 1932 and my strong reflection of the Trespass is that I took the whole affair nothing like as seriously as you and others appeared to do. For me it was something of a lark. My weekend rambles almost invariably involved trespassing, often on Kinder itself, and this added tension to all other hazards. On one occasion my girl friend and I strayed on to the wrong side of a Territorial Army shooting range, and I was never again so near to receiving a bullet (albeit a 'friendly' one) even during my army service in the East during the Second World War'.

Wall family

Victor had contract work with Ferranti at Oldham as an engineering designer between 1928 and 1933. From 1933-1934 he taught at Oldham Technical College, and then Hollins Central School. He went on to Wigan Mining and Technical College where he lectured in maths and engineering. As he was in an essential profession, he was not allowed to enlist for the British services during the war and so he served with the Indian Army where he was commissioned as a major between 1941-1946.

After the war he was assistant master at Oldbury Technical School, and then at Hackney Technical Institute. Wall had links over many years with the Workers' Educational Authority giving talks on Astronomy and Industrial Archaeology.

He was a lecturer and guide at London's Science Museum between 1956 and 1976 where he delighted and enthused young and old audiences with his presentations on a wide range of subjects including: atomic power, space-travel, iron and steel, meteorology, relativity and number magic. Sometimes he was advertised as 'Major VC Wall'. He was also a Fellow of the Royal Astronomical Society. His most popular lectures were on Astronomy and he lobbied for the Star Dome at the museum.

SCIENCE MUSEUM
South Kensington, London SW7 2DD

**EASTER HOLIDAY
LECTURE DEMONSTRATIONS**

THE WORLD OF CURVES

LECTURER: VICTOR WALL, TD, C Eng, MIMechE, FRAS

BRACHISTOCHRONES
SPIDERS' WEBS
NAUTILUS SHELLS
SUNFLOWERS
CURVE STITCHING
MOTOR CAR WHEELS
HANGING CHAINS
COMETARY ORBITS
AND MANY OTHER CURVES IN
NATURE AND TECHNOLOGY
WILL BE DISCUSSED

Victor Wall was often seen on television appearing with science topics on Tuesday Rendezvous, the tea-time children's programme in the early 1960s presented by Muriel Young and Bert Weedon. While on that programme he met the Silver Beatles soon to become the Beatles. He also took part in other programmes such as Questions in the House, a science-based programme, Late Night Line-up and The Sky at Night. In addition, he acted as an advisor for other TV science productions.

Victor was married three times, and his interests were astronomy, fellwalking and foreign travel. In a letter to Benny Rothman in 1982, he said he had walked all over the country including the Pennine Way and Cotswolds. He added he always kept wire cutters in his rucksack for the barbed wire on rights of way footpaths.

He was a man of many talents, an accomplished pianist, and attended the Trespass anniversaries in 1982 and 1988 when he was 'proud and happy' to meet up with Benny again.

Wall family

Victor Wall at the Science Museum

George Westfield (1916-1937)

Born in Liverpool, he moved to Manchester where he was a member of Cheetham YCL. He worked in the clothing trade, and was a keen rambler and camper. He took an interest in military history and was killed fighting with the International Brigade at Embro Fountains.

George Westfield

Working Class Movement Library

Frank Wilson (1908-1933)

He was born in Sheffield to George and Isabella. George was listed in 1911 as a butcher's blade minder, and they lived in Burgoyne Road, Sheffield. They were said to own a coal-delivery business and a shop. George and his sister Doris loved walking in the countryside and both went on the Trespass, against the wishes of their mother.

Frank was a founder member of the Spartacus Rambling Club in 1932. He was a member of the Young Communist League, the Esperanto Club and Friends of the Soviet Union, and employed as a foundry labourer.

He died aged twenty-five of septicaemia from a carbuncle on his back. Two years previously he had been treated in hospital for a skin condition. A crowd of about four hundred witnessed his burial at Burngreave Cemetery, Sheffield. He was described as a prominent member of the YCL and the British Workers Sports Federation's rambling section. George Fletcher, local bakery owner and communist, gave the speech at the graveside, which was followed by the singing of the *Internationale*.

Wilson family

Frank Wilson

Wilfred (Wolfie) Winnick (1907-1972)

Wolfie was born in Stockport, one of ten children. By 1911 the family were living in Broughton, and his father, Abraham, was a mantle maker. The Winnick family lived for many years on Shirley Road, Cheetham Hill.

Wolfie developed boxing skills at the YMCA in Manchester, and boxed as a welterweight in the army. He worked in the Merchant Navy on his way home from Australia on one of his two trips. He was discharged from the Merchant Navy in 1927.

He was Benny Rothman's 'minder' and a leader of the Trespass, and could be clearly seen in press photographs of the Trespass scuffling with keepers. Instead of returning to Hayfield with the main group, he made his own way off the moors. The following day a photograph clearly identifying him appeared in a newspaper and so he met up with his friend Sol Gadian, who gave him money to go to London to stay with his band-leader brother, Maurice, on Park Lane for a few months, until events died down. On his return, he was employed at a raincoat factory.

Wolfie was beaten up while heckling at one of Mosley's Blackshirt meetings at the Free Trade Hall. He married Annie E Barnes in 1934 in Manchester. They met at a Communist summer camp where she was

Winnick family

Wolfie in Spain 1938

a chef. When they were courting, they used to cycle at weekends to meet up half-way between Manchester and Leicester, where Annie lived.

In 1937 he went to Spain to fight with the International Brigade. He had been moved by a newsreel of the bombing at Guernica, and within a few days had been sent to Arles. He and the other volunteers were trained in the use of firearms, and the techniques of warfare. They learned how to dismantle and assemble guns under blankets or blindfolded, because in war they would have to do it in the darkness. As an instructor forcefully put it 'No-one's going to hold a candle for you, if your gun jams in a night attack!' Being left-handed, he had difficulty in firing a rifle and was demoted to the 'Awkward Squad' with others who weren't good with firearms. He suffered concussion in March 1938 and a shrapnel wound to his left arm and elbow in the August.

Winnick family

Wolfie in Kenya 1944

In 1939 he was listed as a heavy clothing machinist, living in Fallowfield, although he wanted to find an engineering job away from the rag trade. During war-time service in the Army he fought behind enemy lines in Burma, and while stationed in Kenya, he climbed Kilimanjaro. After the war he was employed at a tailor's making suits and dresses. He also worked from home with material obtained from his brother Joseph who had a market stall selling cloth from the mills.

Later he was given money by his elder brother Maurice to set up a scrap metal business which was very successful. W Winnick Metals Ltd was at Elizabeth Street, Broughton, and he worked closely with two brothers-in-law who were also in the same business. He was said to be a considerate employer. Most weekdays, he used to cycle to the YMCA at lunch-time to play tennis, and drove there at weekends.

His son Peter said that his father used to take his family on walking and camping holidays. He didn't seem to pursue his political ideas later on and left the Communist Party in 1956, due to its attitude to the Hungarian uprising and its support for the Soviet Union. Wolfie played 'fives' and tennis at the YMCA all his life. He was a very outgoing and popular character, and his party piece was to recite *The Rubaiyat of Omah Khayyam*. Benny Rothman didn't reveal Wolfie's name and his role in the Trespass out of respect for him until after Wolfie's death.

Mendel family

Wolfie and Annie

William Womersley (1903-1969)

His mother Ida ran a draper's shop, composed of two terraced houses, on Bond Street, Sheffield. Her sister, Annie, was the mother of journalist and media personality Malcolm Muggeridge. William's father, George, was a cabinet maker who joined the RAF in 1918 as an aircraftman. William was a member of the Clarion ramblers and edited the club newsletter, contributed poetry and placed ads in it for hiking equipment. By 1939 he and his wife were living at the shop and he was listed as a speciality salesman. William was a religious man and gave his four children a church upbringing.

During the last war he worked in Iran as a civilian worker on unspecified projects. After the family home on Bond Street was destroyed by enemy bombs, the family went to stay with relatives in Lincolnshire.

He was a Labour activist, and involved post-war in organising housing in Sheffield and Dronfield, and in the formation of Sheffield's Green Belt. He lived for the rest of his life after the war in a council house in Dronfield.

William Womersley

Len Wood (1908-2000)

Len was born in Ashton-under-Lyne. He loved walking and cycling on long weekends in the Peak, leaving on a Friday and returning on Monday. He worked as a Rexine spreader at ICI, Newton, Hyde, then during the last war as a driver in Germany before returning to his old job at ICI. His main interest was in gardening, growing tomatoes and chrysanthemums.

Len Wood

COUNTRYSIDE CAMPAIGNERS

Edwin Royce

While GHB Ward and the Sheffield Clarion club are well-known to ramblers, perhaps less familiar is the work of Edwin Royce in Manchester. Royce was a tireless advocate of access to mountains, and Tom Stephenson labelled him as 'one of the grand old men of the open-air'. Alongside Ward, Stephenson, Barnes, and Morton he was one of the great pioneers in the fight for countryside access.

Royce was born at Slaithwaite near Huddersfield in 1881, the son of a grocer. He remained single all his life and lived with his sister Amy in Levenshulme. Later he moved to Rusholme. His many interests included being president of the Manchester Geographical Society and a member of the Manchester Literary Club. He loved walking and there were few places in Britain he had not visited, as well as taking many trips abroad. He gave lantern slide lectures on his walking experiences from around the world.

Great passion

His great passion was to see unrestricted walking on the hills and he devoted his life to the cause. It led him to take the roles of president of the Manchester Ramblers' Federation, vice-chairman of the Peak District and Northern Counties Preservation Society and vice-chairman of the Ramblers' Association.

He was not in favour of the Mass Trespass, and memorably described the events of 1932 as 'more than the usual froth and bubble'; however he dramatically changed his stance on direct action in later life. He edited the Manchester Ramblers' Federation handbook, published between 1923 and 1938, which though less well known than the Clarion Club publication was a similar mix of walks, updates on Federation work, progress of Parliamentary bills and Peakland history. He contributed to a number of other publications and went on to edit *Northern Rambler* for six years.

Neglected Peak District

Royce was a well-known speaker at ramblers' meetings, and at the 1933 Council for the Preservation of Rural England conference at Buxton, he said: 'Why should we be satisfied with what our forefathers were satisfied with? We ought to be making progress, but we are losing ground - losing footpaths in the district. This is a society for the prevention of cruelty to scenery, and there are two kinds of cruelty - active cruelty and cruelty by neglect. The Peak District is a thoroughly derelict region; never in its existence has it been so neglected as it is today. Its bare valleys were once full of timber. Between Baslow and Longdendale there were 50,000 sheep: today there are 5,000.'

In 1937 he quoted Professor Stapleton's comment in his book *The Hill Lands of Britain* - 'In so far as the masses of people in this country are concerned, the glorious general scenery provided by our uplands might as well be on the Moon or Mars, for the amount of pleasure and health it actually dispenses'. Royce was a frequent writer to the newspapers, arguing the ramblers' case regarding the problems and dangers with the various Access to Mountains Bills. He fearlessly campaigned not only against private landowners but also Manchester and Preston Corporations' restrictions of access to ramblers.

In his *Daily Herald* column in 1938, Tom Stephenson described how Edwin Royce continued the battle, 'crossing swords with dukes and landlords and editors of sporting journals'. Royce had told him about an experience in the Highlands after setting out on a walk. First, he was stopped by the agent of the estate and informed he was in the wrong glen, there was no right of way and the track on the map did not exist. Ignoring this advice Royce went on his way, only to be confronted by the landowner himself, who was more polite than his agent but insisted there was no

Keith Warrender

Royce memorial on Lantern Pike looking towards Kinder

track and he would lose his way in the bog. The man offered to take Royce to his destination by car. Royce was not to be deterred and found a track, as he had hoped, and completed his walk.

Royce was a speaker at the Winnats rallies and founder member of the Standing Committee on National Parks in 1936. He was co-author of a report opposing the water authorities' restrictions for walkers over water-gathering grounds, and also a signatory to the letter protesting about the 'Trespass Clause' proposed for the 1939 Bill.

Pennine Way

Royce was heavily involved in the early planning of the Pennine Way. In 1938 he co-presented the concept of the long-distance trail to a conference of outdoor organisations at Hope. He and Tom Stephenson in 1939 prepared a brief for rambling clubs to make a preliminary survey of the trail. By 1943 Royce and Ward, as their influence waned, were being outvoted by some of their younger colleagues who wanted to replace the 1939 Act with new legislation rather than work with the present regulations. Ward referred to an unspecified injury of Royce in the 1944/5 Clarion handbook, which had curtailed his walking activities.

During 1945, Royce started to doubt whether access to mountains legislation would ever be passed

by Parliament. He wrote to Tom Stephenson about taking drastic action. As he was shortly to retire and had no family or dependants, he was prepared to trespass so regularly that he would be imprisoned, which would attract publicity and possibly renew the demand for new legislation. He didn't carry out his threat and died in hospital in December 1946.

Lantern Pike

His many friends and associates raised funds to purchase the thirty-two acre Lantern Pike site, overlooking Hayfield and Kinder which was given to the National Trust in his memory. One hundred and fifty people climbed to the 1,100ft summit to witness the unveiling in the fading light of an October evening in 1950. The memorial was a direction indicator hewn out of stone from a local quarry.

Various dignitaries paid tribute to Royce's life and work. Harvey Rhodes, MP and president of Manchester Ramblers, remembered how Royce whose interests ranged from geology and geography, to literature, the arts and music would go out of his way to do acts of kindness. Royce's old friend GHB Ward, also present, perhaps summed up Royce's life when he said 'I loved Edwin Royce and his years full of continuous work, writing and lecturing for freedom of mountain, moor, path, an unravished scene, without desire for monetary reward, job, political fame or publicity'.

COUNTRYSIDE CAMPAIGNERS
Phil Barnes

Barnes family

Phil Barnes was a life-long dedicated campaigner for improved access to the countryside, as well as conservation of the rural environment. He was born in Peckham, London in 1900 before the family moved to Sheffield when he was eleven. After completing his education he was conscripted into the Duke of Wellington's, West Riding Regiment in 1918. A year later he was medically discharged and began training as a draughtsman in Sheffield at Cammel Laird, then became a professional photographer in advertising. His rock climbing photographs were later used in guide books of Stanage.

Frequent trespasser

Barnes described himself as a socialist, climber, dedicated rambler and frequent trespasser. Photographs show him out walking in his distinctive velvet jacket. He was a member of the Sheffield Clarion ramblers and on the committee which purchased the Longshaw estate in 1927. He founded and led the voluntary wardens at Longshaw which was the forerunner of the system operated in national parks and other areas.

In 1934 he produced the impressive *Trespassers Will be Prosecuted* publication in support of the Access to Mountains Bill. The book, beautifully illustrated with Barnes's own photographs, highlighted the lack of footpaths over the moorland of Kinder and Bleaklow and the problem of privately and publicly owned land being restricted to walkers. The book also dealt with the landowners' claim that ramblers disrupted their grouse moor interests. There is a section on the previous lack of progress of the Access to Mountains Bill, an outline of the lost public rights due to the Enclosure Awards and photographs of the trespasses on Kinder and at Abbey Brook. Most importantly, Barnes's photographs show how much fine countryside and historic sites were being denied to walkers. On the final page, he urged readers to do everything they could to help the passing of the Act. Manchester Ramblers' Federation ordered two hundred copies of the book for its members.

Barnes was in something of two minds over accessing moors such as Kinder. He spent his entire career trying to protect wilderness areas and found it difficult to reconcile the opening-up of these peaceful places with the inevitable invasion of visitors. Writing to Bert Ward, he said: 'I'm afraid I care for Kinder so much that I am perhaps taking a selfish view but, frankly, I would rather stay away from the hills myself and leave them to the tender mercies of the shooter and keeper than see the delicate beauty of the cloughs vulgarised by picnic parties...'

In 1927 Barnes became the first technical assistant at the Sheffield and Peak District branch of the Council for the Preservation of Rural England, before moving to the Lancashire branch of the CPRE in Preston in 1935 to become its Secretary. He played a leading role in public inquiries in Lancashire, and established a good reputation for proposing acceptable compromises between the demands of preservation and the public need. Most local authorities supported the CPRE financially and the county council provided him with office accommodation and consulted him on planning matters.

Green buildings

Throughout his career he was committed to minimising the impact of new planning schemes on the countryside, including the development of the National Grid and the building of Skelmersdale power station. He was involved in the proposal for access to a moorland ridge walk at Boulsworth Hill in Lancashire in 1955. Barnes also took part in discussions between Manchester and the Lake District authority to take more water, and at the time of his death, he was urging that pylons, in a scheme taking electricity over the Pennines, should be positioned below the skyline where they were less visible. One of his legacies was to persuade a holiday home developer on the banks of Lake Windermere to paint the buildings in green to blend in with the surroundings - a practice which has become more widespread.

At public enquiries he challenged the threats from opencast mining, water pump-ing stations and ugly power lines. He fought to preserve greenbelts and historic properties, and establish walking trails objected to by grouse shooting interests. His lifetime's work for the preservation of the countryside was recognised with an MBE in 1961.

As well as working for CPRE, Barnes was heavily involved with the Access to Mountains Act, working with the Ramblers' Association and giving presentations to Parliamentary committees both before and after the War.

In a 1939 initiative described by Tom Stephenson as 'a supreme effort', Barnes organised within three days a letter signed by twelve leading access campaigners to be sent to the press and six hundred MPs, outlining the objections to the forthcoming Parliamentary Bill. As his frustrations grew over the Act, he wrote an article for the 'Progressive Rambler' in which he listed the Act's deficiencies, criticised the weak leadership of the Ramblers' Association and commented that progress could only be made under a sympathetic government.

Pennine Way proposals

In 1943, he gave evidence to the Central Advisory Water Committee of the Ministry of Health on access to water-gathering grounds in uncultivated mountain and moorland country. It was his 1946 document on access to uncultivated ground presented to the

Barnes family

Countryside Committee which was recommended for approval as a White Paper. Probably his last big project for the Ramblers before his death was the opening of the Pennine Way in 1965. Earlier he had opposed proposals to re-route the trail between Laddow Rocks and Black Hill. While dealing with all these national and regional issues, he was also well-known for his talks to local groups.

At the age of forty-seven, Philip married Margaret Schofield in 1947. He died aged sixty-six in 1966.

COUNTRYSIDE CAMPAIGNERS

Stephen Morton

Stephen Morton born in 1905 in Sheffield, was the son of Ernest, a commercial traveller selling eggs. His interest in walking began when he joined the Rotherham Rambling Club. In 1926 he became the first secretary of the Sheffield Ramblers' Federation formed from eighteen groups. He resigned in 1931 but five years later became its Hon Secretary. Morton was involved with GHB Ward in forming the National Federation of Ramblers and convened the first meeting in 1931 at Longshaw.

Stephen married Rachael Stewart in 1931, and worked for his father who was then the manager of the Continental Egg Supply Company. He worked five and a half days a week, not finishing his invoicing until 10pm. Later he worked for Thomas Robinson who tried to curb his long working days, and finally for his son-in-law where he ran the accounts department.

Breakthrough?

On the day of the Kinder Trespass, Morton was unaware of it, until he met local journalist Pip Bolsover at Hope Station, who queried if he was joining the protest. Morton was about to lead a walk some miles away in the opposite direction, and as there was some optimism that they were about to have a meeting with landowners he declined to join the Trespass. He contended the Kinder and Abbey Brook trespasses were political in origin but later accepted it might have been better if the mainstream rambling groups had supported the Kinder Trespass. Although Morton and others feared the Trespass would set back the negotiations, in reality, agreement was many years away.

In his *Wayfarings* column in the *Sheffield Daily Independent*, October 1937 it is clear Morton thought landowners were unwilling to compromise, even if ramblers agreed to keep away from the moors during the grouse breeding and shooting months. Morton and his fellow ramblers were encouraged by the opening up of land by the Chatsworth Estates in 1937. This had been the result of meetings between interested parties in 1932 in London, followed by a regional meeting at the Grand Hotel, Sheffield in 1934. The agreement was subject to some restrictions but they had hoped other landowners might agree to walkers' access.

Morton was a leading figure in the Access to Mountains campaign, and in 1939 addressed an RA London meeting criticizing amendments to the forthcoming Parliamentary Bill. He was a signatory of Phil Barnes's letter to MPs rejecting the new proposals in the 1939 Bill, and involved in the formation of new legislation to replace it.

His regular column for walkers in a Sheffield newspaper provoked many skirmishes in print with 'old friend' Henry Walker of Bradwell over walkers' rights. He spoke several times at the Winnats rallies, and wrote the obituary of his close friend GHB Ward in the Clarion handbook, although they had a serious disagreement in the late 1940s over implementing the pre-war Access Act which Morton thought was unworkable. To avoid any ructions in the Federation, Morton resigned but returned eleven years later, after Ward's death as RA President for South Yorkshire and North Derbyshire.

Key roles

Morton held a number of key positions including on the executive of the CPRE which he helped to launch. He was on the National Trust estate management committee, and became a member of the Peak Park Planning Board in 1956. Thirty years later at the National Park Cavedale rally, he and fellow access

Morton family

Peak District National Park Authority

Benny Rothman, Tom Stephenson and Stephen Morton at the Cavedale rally 1986 organised by Roly Smith

campaigners Benny Rothman and Tom Stephenson were brought together. Morton spoke of his frustration that the National Park Authority did not have enough finances to make all the access agreements they wanted, and that the battle for access had not yet been won.

Trespasser

Throughout his life, he had never been afraid to trespass on disputed routes, and had reputedly thrown a gamekeeper into a stream during an altercation. Another moorland confrontation resulted in his having a three-week stay in hospital. By the time of the 1982 Trespass Celebration he had changed his views on direct action. After years of frustration Morton had come to the conclusion, like Edwin Royce, that there was a case for direct action because landowners were deliberately prolonging negotiations to avoid making any change.

Morton contacted Benny Rothman in late 1981 volunteering his support and services for the 50th Celebrations the following April. He wrote: 'Whatever may be said, and much has been said, this is the

event that is foremost in the public mind when access to the hills and moorlands is mentioned and it is therefore one of the most historic days in the ramblers' calendar ... I understand fully how you felt, in fact at a recent meeting between the Peak Park Officers and outdoor representatives I found myself threatening further mass trespasses to the moors ... if they continue with their bureaucratic nonsense to inhibit access to 75% of the high moorland within the Peak. Though the Peak National Park Authority have secured some 56% of all access agreements over the whole country, this is only 25% of the moors within their own borders.'

Morton added:'... although I was inclined to be critical (of the Trespass) at the time, yet I never doubted that we were all fighting for the same cause. ... From my point of view the fight is unfinished and I hope someone will just say that at your celebration. I am willing to give what help an old man can'.

In a letter to Benny the following year, with the Trespass Anniversary approaching, he wrote that the event had given him the opportunity to express what he had been wanting to say for many years. He was going to warn people that their 'child-like faith in governments, councils and boards had lulled them to sleep over the years and they didn't want to listen to old 'has beens' like himself trying to persuade them that the battle had hardly begun'. At the question and answer session at New Mills Town Hall, on the day of the anniversary, Morton was concerned that he was the only real access campaigner on the panel.

Sheffield Ramblers organised a walk to join the rally, and from this SCAM - Sheffield Campaign for Access to the Moors - was founded, which Morton supported.

Recognition

Morton received various recognitions for his years of work for the access cause. A plantation at Lenny Hill on Blacka Moor, Sheffield was named after him and a plaque built into a triangular rock commemorating the long service of the popular ramblers' leader was installed in 1971. He was awarded honorary life membership of the RA in 1986, and a seat in Chesterfield bears his name. At the age of eighty, he attributed his longevity to walking, even then averaging ten miles' walking daily and outings with a Wednesday walking group. He was said to be good company on walks with interesting things to say. There were a number of passions in his life: despite working long hours, he was a dedicated family man, Sheffield Wednesday season-ticket holder, walker and activist, regular

contributor to the local newspaper, active member of the Fulwood Society, and a man of great Christian faith. Despite a number of setbacks with his health and the death of his wife he overcame them with courage and never complained. He was a man of immense drive but also integrity.

After Stephen Morton's death in 1988, his access friend, Benny Rothman, was invited to be the speaker at the Memorial Lecture organised in Morton's honour by SCAM at Sheffield Town Hall, with his family present.

Morton (centre) with Victor Wall and Benny Rothman at the 50th anniversary celebration

Above top: Morton planting a tree in his honour at Blacka Moor 1971
Above: Morton given honorary life membership of the Ramblers' Association 1986

The walker's grouse

Benny Rothman wrote 'Our grouse is grouse' because game birds were at the heart of the controversy over greater moorland access. Press reports used to read: 'the moors were reserved for the pleasure of the grouse shooters'. Walkers weren't entitled to the pleasure of walking in wild places and exploring the terrain because they would disturb the grouse. It was only on the 'Glorious Twelfth' that the grouse could be roused and the shooters would have their 'pleasure and sport' dispatching the birds in their thousands.

But did the presence of walkers adversely affect grouse numbers? It was not until the 1930s that the established wisdom began to be challenged. In a 1932 report to a meeting of the Longshaw Wardens, countryside campaigner, Phil Barnes, said that public access to these moorlands had not brought about an exodus of moorland birds, as many had prophesied. He pointed to the example of a curlew which had nested for three years within a hundred yards of a busy wayside pub. In his 1934 book Trespassers Will Be Prosecuted he pointed out that despite increased number of ramblers on the moors since the First World War, newspaper reports over the previous twenty years had not indicated a decrease in game bags, in fact 1931 had been a record year.

Barnes observed that wildlife had not been adversely affected on the Longshaw Estate after being open to the public for six years. The same could be said of Blacka Moor, also 'none the worse' after two years. It was reasonable to conclude that numbers of grouse depended more on the condition of heather, disease, the weather during the breeding season, and sufficient numbers of birds left at the end of the season to breed.

Dr Joad in his 1945 Untutored Townsman's Guide to the Countryside also cites the example of Ilkley Moor where, after many years of public access, grouse continued to thrive. This was confirmed

in a 1935 article about grouse-shooting in the Ramblers' Federation Handbook, at Ilkley, which noted there was a footpath within two hundred yards of the nesting grouse, but neither this nor the noise of nearby guns and the yelling beaters disturbed the birds. Dr Joad posed the question of why ramblers had to be kept off grouse moors:

'Why can you not have both ramblers and grouse? It is not altogether clear. It seems, however, that sportsmen are very fond of grouse. I don't mean merely that they are fond of their dead bodies when they appear cooked on the table; they are fond also of their live bodies when they fly over the moors. They have an affection for their targets and don't like them to be disturbed. Now the grouse, it is said, would be disturbed by the trampling feet of many walkers. I have heard speakers lash themselves into a fine frenzy of noble indignation on the score of these outraged feelings of the grouse.

'We are asked, for example, to picture the plight of the young grouse, parted by the wicked walker from his parents. With what unction have I been invited to consider his condition as, startled by the heedless walker, he flies lonely and disconsolate over the moor, until, after hours of wandering, he drops with fatigue and dies from hunger and exposure. The mildest of these oratorical flights pictures the grouse growing up nervous, wasted creatures, because of the walkers' invasion of their haunts. Grouse, subject to interruption by walkers, do not, it is said, grow plump; on the contrary, they grow wary, restless and neurotic. And therefore? Therefore they are not such good targets for the guns of 'sportsmen'; they are not so easy to shoot. (A fact of some importance, when the 'sportsman' is only a stock-broker on holiday.)

'It is, indeed, difficult, as one listens to these arguments based upon a tender compassion for the feelings of the grouse, to realise that they are being put forward by those whose sole concern

is to ensure that the birds shall be easy to kill.
Stripped of hypocrisy, the argument runs as follows:
'We desire that there shall be as many grouse
as possible, that they shall be as plump as possible
and that they shall be as unsuspecting as possible,
in order that our bag may be as large as possible.

'The wary vigilance so lavishly employed
in excluding walkers owes much of its inspiration
to the desire for a large bag. The craze for record
bags is of comparatively recent origin.
A 'sportsman' does not now go forth upon the
moors and shoot a stray grouse when he sees it.
He lurks, in company with other 'sportsmen'
complete with loaders,
behind a wall of butts,
while hired men drive
frightened birds in serried
masses upon their guns.
As a result enormous
numbers of birds are killed.

'In one of these holocausts
on the Abbeystead Moors
near Lancaster, as many
as 2,929 grouse were shot
by eight guns in a single
day. . . .

Willow Publishing

1870 red grouse print

'And in order to facilitate this slaughter of birds
during a few weeks each year, the public are not
only excluded throughout the whole of the year
from hundreds of square miles of moorland adjacent
to thickly populated areas, but are regaled with
arguments designed to show that the exclusion
is dictated out of consideration for the welfare
of the distressed victims, arguments which testify
to the intelligence of those who propound no less
than they insult the intelligence of those who are
expected to be taken in by them.'

Marion Shoard's *This Land is our Land* includes the
experience of a former Yorkshire huntservant:
'How can two or three people walking across
several thousand acres of moorland disturb the
grouse? I can't see how they can, and I've been
in the country all my life. You're not likely
to stumble over a grouse nest - if you do it's
a chance in a million. Most game birds - pheasant,

partridge, grouse, if you come to them when
they're nesting, they lie ever so low and only
when you're on top of them will they move. Mostly
they won't, they'll remain stationary. Unless you
actually stand on the nest you haven't disturbed
them and if you do disturb them they'll perhaps
fly away twenty yards, they'll settle down and
then they'll run back through the under-growth
to their nest. So why close a whole moor down
for fear of disturbing a bird for a few seconds?'

Nicholas Picozzi's 1971 key study confirmed this.
Broods of grouse were counted on six moors with
varying degrees of access, over three years. It was
found that grouse bred just as well on moors where
people had unrestricted
access. The survey also
found that most people,
in spite of access agree-
ments, kept to main foot-
paths. In 1976, RS Gibbs
at Newcastle University
interviewed farmers,
land-owners, sportsmen
and other interested
parties and concluded
that the impact of access
by the public on upland
areas was extremely
small. The following year
the Duke of Devonshire told a meeting in Sheffield
how grouse numbers had risen despite allowing
walkers on his moors. At a Peak National Park
conference in 1979, the head keeper of a 23,000
acre estate in Lanarkshire reported that neither
grouse nor sheep had suffered from the presence
of large numbers of visitors at weekends and bank
holidays.

The Red Grouse Action Plan published in 2013 by the
National Red Grouse Steering Committee concluded
that if a brood was disturbed by anything, they would
scatter and then re-group within an hour. The bigger
nuisance was the use of off-road vehicles which
caused great problems during the nesting season.
Through the findings of various reports and studies
over the years, it seems the fears of landowners which
kept the great mass of people off Kinder for so long
were simply unfounded and completely unnecessary.

When Joe sacked a bungling beater

TOM WAGHORN

Gamekeeper Joe Townsend was furious. 'You're fired' he raged. Not a single grouse had been shot on the drive. He paid me the full daily beater's allowance wage of ten shillings (50p) and organised a lift for me back to Glossop.

As a hillwalker and naturalist I adore the red grouse. I love to see them leap into the air on spreading wings and descend steeply, extending their necks and feet and fanning their tails. Above all I cherish their barking call 'Go-back-back-back-back'.

In the late 1940s I was less enlightened. As a fifth-former at Glossop Grammar School I was hired in the summer holidays as a beater on aptly-named Bleaklow and part of the northern section of Kinder. A small group of us would be picked up in Glossop by open-topped lorry ... and so to the work we relished. A sandwich lunch was sometimes served by Joe and two or three adult beaters in a shooting cabin. Here we learned that the shooting fraternity never talk about 'the Glorious Twelfth'. Just 'the Twelfth' if you please!

Joe Townsend

Few walkers were around on the moors in mid-week in those days. Joe was a fine organiser. A line of beaters waving white flags on six-foot sticks and with an adult at each end, drove the grouse to the shooting butts ... and to eternity. Many of the poor creatures were only winged by the hail of leadshot. And I'll never forget the horror of seeing them lying in the heather, bloodied but still alive, and watching the male beaters and gunmen picking them up by their feet and banging the birds' heads on leather boots to dispatch them.

So why was I sacked? It was a typical day of hill fog, about 1800ft up on Bleaklow. We were to do two drives in the morning and three in the afternoon. The butts, semi-circular and built of gritstone and peat by Joe and his colleagues, were arranged back to back. After one sweep, the beaters would swing round and drive the grouse to the second set of butts. I became lost in the fog with a fellow school beater and separated from the main party of flag-wavers. When the grouse saw us, they did a clumsy U-turn and flew back over the flags.

Beating career over! But, shame on me, I must have been unique in being both a beater and trespasser. Pre-Pennine Way, groups of us were enjoying those magical Peakland acres of heather, bilberry, cloudberry, cotton grass and that cloying peat with the consistency of thick black porridge.

And brushes with gamekeepers. Joe Townsend was firm but not aggressive like most of the other tweed-clad keepers. 'Harry the Terror' on the Woodhead moors comes to mind. (Joe's main hate was the visitors who started fires.)

The annals of Manchester's Karabiner Club tell of members being chased off the Scout well into the Fifties. Years later Karabiner stalwart Len Stubbs often dropped a Sunday paper at Joe's Snake Cottage at the foot of the Pass. 'We had many a brew there' say the records. I've no doubt that Joe was repaid with his favourite cigarettes.

Forgive us our tips and trespasses

MIKE DENT Rucksack Club Archivist

'Everyone knows that the Rucksack Club bribed keepers.' Thus was the President, John Beatty, accosted on attending, by invitation, the 75th anniversary celebrations of the Mass Trespass. So what are the facts?

Since its early days, the club, formed in Manchester one hundred and twenty years ago and now a national body with three huts and more than five hundred members, has always supported access to mountains. At the same time it has sought to cooperate with Peak District landowners to gain permission to walk and climb on 'forbidden' grouse moors.

From 1911 to at least 1925 tips were given to keepers privately or out of Club funds. In that latter year, for instance, the club authorised 'payments' to Kinder keepers Marriott, 15s (75p) and Barnes, 10s (50p).

This would seem to be perfectly in line with the customs and conventions of the day. If one visited a country house as a guest it would be normal and expected practice to tip the butler and the chambermaid. And the keepers on a shoot! Presumably similar ethics would apply if a party was out rambling or climbing with the landowner's permission.

The club's prized privilege was the occasional one granted by James Watts Jnr to climb on the gritstone of Kinder Downfall. (Was it just a coincidence that a prominent Rucksacker, Harry Gilliat of Cheadle, was employed by the landowners, S & J Watts, in central Manchester? He is reputed to have walked to work every day,

rain or shine, and back in the evening. Five miles each way, wearing shorts, of course!)

Things didn't always go to plan for club or landlord. One year in the Twenties 'was disastrous for the moor owing to fires, the caterpillar plague etc,' the club was told by Watts. 'I have decided to give it a complete rest next year, not even using it myself.'

There is no specific mention of the Kinder Trespass in club records. However, oral evidence passed down suggests that a number of members took part in their private capacity, but others were completely opposed to the action.

The club had usually enjoyed good relations with Sir Philip Brocklehurst, the Antarctic explorer, a guest at the 1925 annual dinner, whose family owned the Roaches. Somehow an access rift developed between both sides. On the weekend following the Kinder Trespass the club, led by the eminent surgeon Wilson Hey, staged a deliberate protest at the Staffordshire crags. Sixty-four members and friends of the Rucksack Club and a Midland club took part. But, unlike on Kinder, there was no violence in that mass trespass. Eventually Sir Philip relented and the once strictly-preserved Roaches were climbable again.

So what happened on the Scout after the 1932 Mass Trespass? Rucksackers and Bogtrotters seemed to enjoy unusual access freedom. Both were highly praised by the estate gamekeeper, John Watson. His opinion of the 1932 trespassers is unrepeatable ...

KINDER LANDOWNERS

Watts family

The Kinder plateau was owned by several families, and any walker who intended to cross it legally, needed to apply for permission in writing to each of them. The Watts owned the western flank, including Kinder Downfall and Kinder Low. The Duke of Devonshire had the northern and eastern sides, along with most of the plateau, while the Champion family held a section of the plateau and land around Grindsbrook. The owner who had the greatest notoriety among ramblers was James Watts because he aggressively asserted his land ownership rights.

He ceased issuing permits to ramblers for a number of years and used legal means to prevent GHB Ward and others from setting foot on his estate. His solicitors were responsible for the issuing of an unpopular 'wanted notice' seeking the identity of people photographed on Kinder for a reward of five pounds.

Farlands purchased

James Watts senior came from a family of Manchester merchants. His father had been Mayor of Manchester and High Sheriff of Lancashire, but he took little part in public life, concentrating on the family firm S and J Watts and Co. The business premises, an impressive warehouse on Portland Street, Manchester, is now a hotel. Watts lived at Abney Hall, Cheadle, and in 1879 purchased Farlands at Kinder set in five acres of land as a country retreat. It was previously the home of William Walker who wrote and published the 1878 guide to footpaths around Hayfield.

Watts had acquired a substantial portion of the Kinder plateau by about 1894 when it was reported to be in 'new hands'. In 1901 he arranged for a special clause to be inserted into Stockport Reservoir Works Bill to protect his 2,500 acre estate and grouse moor.

Kinder damage

It was during his time as Vice-President of the Peak District and Northern Counties Footpaths Society that his ownership of a section of the Kinder plateau was publicaly acknowledged. As a member of the Society, he made sure the Hayfield to the Snake footpath didn't cross his land, and during a meeting in 1897 he complained about damage done to his stone walls and people being caught illegally walking on his moor. Watts repeatedly stated that there were no footpaths on Kinder and that people had no right to be there. While it is true there was an absence of paths as such, a route around the perimeter of the plateau would have satisfied most ramblers, and not interfered with the grouse moor. Watts supported

Ian Watson

Three generations of the Watts L-R Jack, James junior and James senior

155

Ian Watson

Upper House - Watts' luxurious country home at the foot of Kinder

the re-opening of the Snake footpath but resigned from the Society after it voted to back access to mountains legislation.

Upper House

With the construction of the Kinder Reservoir, Watts felt unsafe living below the level of the dam, and relinquished Farlands and properties at Bowden Bridge in 1905 to live further up the valley at Upper House. He upgraded the farmhouse into a splendid country residence and planted many trees and shrubs to give privacy and enhance the landscape. Watts enjoyed showing guests around one of the rooms which contained relics found on Kinder. He also travelled about the country with his friend Fletcher Moss taking photographs for Moss's *Pilgrimages to Old Homes* series of books published between 1901 and 1920.

Watts was a man of contradictions as he supported the concept of land nationalisation yet greatly restricted public access to his land. While it remained in his ownership, he made sure it yielded as much profit as possible through grouse shooting. He complained in 1900 that the entire income of the

Kinder Estate was paid out in income tax, super tax and rates. For one who professed a dislike of land in private hands he nevertheless actively acquired more acreage, purchasing the Highfield Estate, Edale, in 1896, and over fifteen acres around South Head, Chinley, in 1921. This was in addition to the four hundred acres he owned in Lancashire. In 1910 he stated he had been a Liberal and Radical all his life, and agreed with the land reform ideas of influential writer Henry George. Watts said he believed in the principle of land nationalisation and would be happy to see a change in the law if everyone had to give up their land.

Kinder a shooting range?

On several occasions Watts tried to offload Kinder, first to the War Department in 1900 as a shooting range but his offer was not taken up. Then the following year he offered Kinder to Manchester Corporation as a country park for the city, but the councillors turned it down as the cost of £30,000 to build approach roads and erect railings around it was considered too expensive. At his death aged eighty in 1926, a newspaper stated 'Many ramblers were indebted to him for permission to enjoy access to Kinder' although as one seasoned rambler wrote in 1901, the permits were usually granted after the shooting season had ended in December for a four-month period when the moors were at their wettest and dreariest. It was also pointed out that Kinder was the only mountain in the UK that was not fully accessible to the public.

Agatha Christie

James Watts junior took the same approach as his father, and so at the time of the Trespass it remained a 'no-go' area for ramblers. He maintained his father's grouse-shooting interests, and earlier in 1930 a newspaper reported that James Watts and party were anticipating 'good sport' on the Kinder Scout moors. His wife Margery (Madge) was the elder sister of Agatha Christie, and the great author was a frequent visitor at the Watts's and used the Abney and Kinder estates in her writing. Madge herself was a talented writer of plays and magazine articles. Watts was said to have had a good relation-ship with his sister-in-law and suggested various changes to her novels, which she heeded.

James Watts junior's son 'Jack' was less formal than the earlier generations and more likely to eat with the grouse-keepers than with the guests at lunch on a grouse-shoot. He didn't enjoy shooting and used to trail his gun like a walking stick, muttering comments about other members of the party. He became a Conservative councillor in Manchester, frequently campaigning against what he considered to be wasteful public expenditure. However he seemed to back the wrong issues, such as voting against the building of the Town Hall Extension and Ringway Airport but supporting an aerodrome at Platt Fields or on the roof of Central Station!

Access agreement

Jack sold Abney Hall to Stockport Council in 1955, and also that year he and his father gave agreement of access to their 3,354 acres of Kinder to the Peak Park Planning Board. This finally gave ramblers legal access to go over most of the Kinder plateau. In 1959 Jack was returned as MP for Moss Side and described as one of the most colourful characters in northern politics,

as well as gaining a reputation as a raconteur. He died suddenly in 1961 in London aged fifty-seven following complications from a fall.

National Trust sale

The legacy of the Kinder estate fell to Christie's grandson Mathew Prichard, film producer and philanthropist, whose company MCT Prichard Estates sold the Kinder Estate to Martin Salmon, a local farmer from Whitwell, in 1978 for about £250,000 when he outbid the Peak Park Planning Board. There were some concerns that ramblers' rights of access could be eroded with the sale. Finally in 1984 it was given to the nation when the National Trust bought it off Salmon for £600,000.

The National Trust stated their aim was to restore the over-used moorland to its former beauty. They had received £315,000 from the National Heritage Memorial Fund, £75,000 from the Countryside Commission and £50,000 from the bequest of Maurice Fry. The remaining £200,000 was to be raised with a special Kinder Scout Appeal. The estate included farms at South Head and the Ashes and a resident flock of sheep. The Watts's old residence, Upper House at Kinder, has since been converted into a hotel.

James Watts senior

The Glorious Twelfth

PAM GEE

The 'Glorious Twelfth' (see page 153) was celebrated in some style during the 1930s on Mr James Watts' Kinder estate. One of the gamekeepers described a typical shoot of around 1935:

'Preparations went on for days before as we cleaned and renovated the shooting cabins, repairing the ravages of Winter. Butts were rebuilt with fresh turf and disguised with clumps of heather and bilberry. Few people knew of the cabin at Cluther Rocks as it was camouflaged with green and brown paint so it would merge into the background. Made of wood with heavy iron shutters, this cabin was not as luxurious as the main stone-built cabin, called 'Sidebotham's', where lunch was eaten.

Two or three days beforehand, the Watts family with their cook, butler, housemaids and kitchen-maids, would be installed at Upper House. Villagers watched out for the huge, black, chauffeur-driven Daimler which made many journeys through Hayfield from Abney Hall Cheadle. Hampers of the best quality foods were brought from the Hall for the guests. Hams, fowls, sides of beef, cheese and cake were packed in grease-proof paper and wrapped in linen cloths. Select wines and spirits with their appropriate glasses in fine crystal had to be packed very carefully for these must be carried right up onto the moor without being broken.

Transporting all the food and drink for the guests and beaters was a big headache for the gamekeepers who had to organise the day. Horses and carts could only get a short way up the tracks, then the hampers had to be unloaded and carried the rest of the way. A local farmer was paid seven shillings for collecting a barrel of beer from 'The Sportsman' on Kinder Road. When he had driven his horse and cart as far as he could, the heavy wooden barrel was loaded onto a stretcher between poles and two stalwart men were given the job of manhandling it up the hill. Meanwhile a side of beef, bread, butter, cheese and fruit cake were stored at Sidebotham's cabin for lunch.

The table looked beautiful when set. Mr Watts was the ideal host and everything had to be perfect for his friends. The linen was spotless, the glasses polished and the cutlery, though not the best solid silver of everyday use, had to shine. The day before, the knives, made from best quality steel, were ground 'to a fine edge' sharp enough to shave by in a large, wheel-shaped grinder. This was hard work as the machine needed to be turned steadily so that the blades rubbed against the emery paper inside. Even the water for the guests to wash in had to be carried up. Probably very few of them thought for a moment of the immense work that went on behind the scenes to make a successful day.

Three or four guests would stay overnight but many close friends and a few neighbours arrived on the day of the shoot from their country houses. The Fitzherberts from Tideswell, the Bromley-Davenports from Capesthorne Hall, Colonel Heath from Macclesfield and Mr Bagshaw from Chapel-en-le-Frith came year after year.

On the morning of the shoot everyone assembled in the courtyard of Upper House. It looked a bustling, noisy muddle with gamekeepers, guns, guests, beaters and dogs all sorting themselves out into groups ready for the onslaught on Kinder and the grouse. Jack Watts disapproved of 'massacre shooting' and used a single-barrelled gun, whereas the others used double-barrelled weapons. The drives were very difficult over the extremely rough ground and though most of the beaters were local lads, some of them had never

Capstick family

Kinder shooting party

been on these moorlands before. Many found the day too exhausting and were reluctant to volunteer again. After the first drive a welcome bottle of beer and a slab of cake gave them a fresh burst of energy before lunch.

This meal was the highlight of the day. The game-keepers and beaters sat outside around the mill-stone tables on specially made circular seats designed to fit neatly round the tables. An enormous side of beef, 20-30 lbs in weight, was brought out by butcher Charlie Torkington who had cooked it and always carved it. Generously thick slices were handed round to be made into sandwiches that were more beef than bread. Then the hungry men put away chunks of cheese and slices of cake washed down with mug after mug of beer. More than enough was provided for the most ravenous of appetites. After this the beaters were reluctant to move and some of them would be a little unsteady. Then occasional loud comments such as 'He couldn't hit a town if he was in it' might be heard, before the speaker was hushed.

On a poor day, when visibility was bad and rain and mist with low cloud blotted out the surrounding hills, the formidable Moss drive was a very daunting prospect. Even with teens of men it was difficult to keep in line and they were instructed to call constantly to the man on the right to make sure no-one went astray. Time after time someone would get lost, only discovered after a head count back at the house. Then the tired keepers, who knew every stick and stone of the estate, returned to blow whistles and call until an answering shout led them to the unfortunate man. Though always told to stay still if lost in the mist, they would wander, sure they knew the way, but the lie of the land steered even the most expert away from the home direction over towards Edale, Fairbrook or the Snake. The old routine of following a stream seldom did them any good either for water runs in all directions from the top of Kinder Scout. One man, found after a long search, had utterly exhausted himself trying to climb the steep-sided groughs. He was wet through and almost unconscious.

For the beaters it was a well-paid job with the bonus of as much food as they could eat and plenty of free drink. The ten shillings a day was a good wage when for 60 hours in a mill he took home £3

Keith Warrender

Goulburn Family

Top: Upper House, almost hidden by trees beyond the reservoir
Above: Kinder grouse on sale at Goulburn's, Manchester

or a shilling per hour. Back in the courtyard the grouse were laid out to be counted while everyone had a final drink and held a post mortem on the day's shoot. A brace of birds was put into the boot of every guest's car' with an extra pair for a special friend. The rest were sold to Goulburn's, Manchester's most exclusive provisioners, where they would be well hung before sale.

Mr Watts knew every inch of his land which he loved dearly. He was an early conservationist hating any changes that might spoil its wild beauty. While at Upper House he planted thousands of trees and when persuaded to have a telephone installed, went to great expense to have the poles and lines completely hidden. A carefully-designed generator avoided unsightly overhead cables across the moor. However there were times when he would economise as when his well-worn Harris tweed suit was sent back to his tailors to be turned ready for the next season. Also his Armstrong-Siddeley with his monogram on its black sides was run for years after the old Daimler broke down. It was sent to the original Gorton garage for a complete overhaul until, as good as new, it was sold in 1958.

For the grouse no expense was spared. One never-to-be-repeated season a ton of quartz grit was brought to the moor as he thought that the mill-stone grit was not hard enough for the grouse gizzards. The gamekeepers toiled up and down with rucksacks full, leaving heaps of the new grit in the feeding areas. The grouse ignored most of it, which may still be there to confuse the geologists of the future.

At Christmas the keepers were instructed to take a pheasant, hare or a bottle of whisky to the tenant farmers on the estate. Never a grouse, for Mr Watts felt they would not appreciate a well-hung bird. Unfortunately, the outbreak of the Second World War altered everything and changed a great many lives, so that the 'Glorious Twelfth' was never celebrated in quite the same style again.

Extract from *KINDER PEOPLE* 1985
Reproduced by kind permission of the author

KINDER LANDOWNERS

Champion family

THOMAS NOEL

The Champion family arrived in Edale in the 17th Century, hailing from Wirksworth. John Champion was installed as rector of Edale Church - at that time a small chapel on the east side of the Grindsbrook road, opposite the modern church which was built in the 1880s. His grandson, also John Champion, was also installed as rector. They lived originally at what is now the Old Parsonage at the northern end of Grindsbrook, but had to move to larger quarters in Nether Booth when John and Margaret Champion had fourteen children in the space of seventeen years. They were not great landowners for this period.

One of these children, William Champion, became a snuff manufacturer in Manchester. In 1860 he married Constance Bentley, daughter of Robert Bentley, the owner of Bentley's Brewery in Rotherham. As his only heir, Constance derived great wealth from the tied pubs in Rotherham and Sheffield as well as brewery sales to free houses, but also from the patent that her father and his two brothers had taken on their 'cold stone press' method of brewing.

This patent was eventually sold to the Bass company in Burton. With the proceeds of the sale, William and Constance bought a 'sporting estate' in Norfolk (Riddlesworth Hall) and also some 2000 acres of moorland on Kinder Scout in the 1880s. They remodelled Grindslow House in Grindsbrook into a summer shooting lodge and William's sister Anne Champion lived there and kept the house while they lived mainly in Norfolk.

From this point William Champion invested large amounts in his own moorland but also in the Hope Valley in general. He planted the land-

Thomas Noel

Grindslow House, belonging to the Champion family. The owners of Grindslow were the first landowners to grant a way for walkers from Edale

Thomas Noel

*William Champion,
Manchester manufacturer,
and his wife Constance,
the daughter of a
Rotherham brewery owner*

scaped coppices in Grindsbrook Valley which give so much pleasure these days, even with their non-indigenous conifers and larch stands. Whenever he spotted an opportunity he would move into action. When it seemed likely that the upper end of Edale Valley would be flooded to make a reservoir, he bought the land in Upper Booth. For a while he owned the Blue John mine in Castleton, and his house in Norfolk, as well as his daughter's house by marriage in Devon (Rockbeare Manor) still contain beautiful Blue John architectural pieces.

When the railway was built he bought and remodelled the Church Inn (now the Rambler). At the same time he invested in various community projects: he donated land for the current Church and vicarage, a building for the village Reading Room (now a private residence), and new housing for staff on the estate. Vestiges of the Norfolk craftsmen's work can still be seen in the East Anglian porch on Grindslow Lodge.

It appears he did not sit easily with neighbouring landowners, either in Derbyshire or in Norfolk. In 1901 he and his cousin Arthur organised a mass petition to the Duke of Rutland to protect the rights of graziers on his grouse moors to the North and East of Edale. His wife Constance

probably did not enjoy her life in Norfolk much either. She 'invalided herself' according to those who remembered her, and was wheeled about in a chair by a companion from Rotherham.

When the original Elizabethan manor at Riddlesworth caught fire in 1899 she forbade anyone to clear its contents, saying, 'let it burn'. However, with her wealth, her husband William built an even bigger mansion, with a special wing of twenty-two bedrooms for visiting cricket teams and their valets. Riddlesworth Hall has been a boarding school since the second War, when a girls' school from Folkestone was evacuated there, and the Champions and their daughter Dorothy moved to her husband's house in Devon.

William Champion was a keen sportsman. He was the Billiard Champion of England. His game book shows enormous shoots in Norfolk and smaller ones in Edale. In those days a shoot was a leisurely affair. There were three shooting cabins on the Edale Moor, traces of two are to be found at 'bungalow corner' on the old Pennine Way up Grindsbrook, and the 'Four Jacks' cabin above Upper Tor. Meals would be served in each and the grouse would be driven off the moorland into the valley, as well as along the Kinder Plateau above Nether Tor where faint traces of the butts can still be seen. Help was drafted in from the whole of Hope Valley. Cheeses came from Hope, preserves from Edale, and a full kitchen garden was kept by Jack Belfitt (one of the four Jacks) to provide fresh produce well into the 1950s.

The railway brought visitors and William's grand-daughter Delia Follett permitted access in the 1930s so that the Pennine Way route could be accessed through the Grindsbrook Valley. Thus the Nags Head pub, owned by the Heardman family, became the official start of the Pennine Way. Unfortunately the pressure of walking boots led to severe erosion on the soft gritstone trail so the route had to be transferred to the West up Jacob's Ladder - probably much to the relief of sodden ramblers for whom the boggy plateau trails were notorious.

William and Constance Champion had one daughter, Dorothy, who married Colonel Spencer Follett from Rockbeare Manor in Devon, They had one daughter, Delia, who married Brigadier Eric Griffith-Williams, whose appetite for shooting was curtailed after his traumatic experiences in both World Wars. They had a daughter Caroline who married Gerard Noel, also a Devon lad, who became the National Trust Director for the Mercian region. He took great interest in the nascent National Park and enjoyed collaborating with the authority to enable sensitive access for members of the public while protecting the landscape. He too was not particularly a shooting man but he would organise one day a year for family and friends. The days of driven grouse were long gone, so the smaller gang would set out on foot and drive the birds before them. If they shot twenty birds they would be quite satisfied and that persists to this day, shooting for the pot more than anything else.

Gamekeepers have tended to stay long. Arthur Lowe is remembered as the keeper who presided over the moor at the time of the mass trespass. It did not affect Edale in any great measure as access had already been granted by Mrs Follett, but he was protective of the nesting sites off the footpaths. In fact in 1945 he sent Gerard Noel packing when he found him wandering there during a trip out from Manchester University.

Years later Gerard married Caroline Griffith -Williams and became Arthur's employer. He never mentioned their first meeting to Arthur!

Robert Townsend became farm manager in the 1960s and very little gamekeeping was done until 2009 when his son Geoffrey took over. The current landowner, Tom Noel, joined up with the National Trust and PDNPA in the 'Moors for the Future' project, so conservation efforts trump all other activities on the moorland, trying to regenerate the blanket bog which has been severely depleted by acid rain and grazing. Sheep are now grazed for landscape management rather than farming profit, allowing wild-seeded trees to take hold in the cloughs and grasses to regenerate on the plateau. Thanks to the footpath efforts of PDNPA and the landscaping investment from the EU, this is starting to show promising results, with once bare patches of peat greened over and starting to flourish as peat-generating moss banks again.

Edale Moor has its own micro-ecology determined by its altitude and its exposure to prevailing winds. It is inaccessible to vehicles, so all conservation work takes time and effort. The hope is that, in future generations, it will be a haven of biodiversity, a carbon sink and an enduring destination of peace and wonder for visitors.

Jack Belfitt at Four Jacks' cabin

163

KINDER LANDOWNERS

The Duke of Devonshire

Edward Cavendish 1895-1950,
the tenth Duke of Devonshire

The northern section of Kinder belonging to the Duke of Devonshire was opened to ramblers in November 1953 following agreement between the Peak Park Planning Board and the trustees of the Chatsworth Settlement which had been created in 1946 by the tenth Duke to help his family.

The tenth Duke of Devonshire died in November 1950, just a few weeks prior to the date when death duties would not have to be paid on the whole estate. As a result over £3 million was handed over to the Inland Revenue from the sale of properties and works of art. Ownership of the Kinder estate was given to the nation and administered by the National Trust.

A man who loved his work

EVA LAWSON

My father, Joe Townsend, (see photograph page 153) was gamekeeper for the Duke of Devonshire at the Snake Pass for forty years, and spent the last five years of his working life for the National Trust. He was proud to be employed by the Duke, and I still have his medals, and cap from Chatsworth. He lived on his own for thirteen years, before marrying my mother, and later moved to the Snake Cottage.

During the 1946-47 blizzards, he walked to Glossop fourteen times and carried the old wet battery for the radio, flour, and yeast. He would go one day and walk home the following day. I remember that when he got back, his moustache and eyebrows were covered in ice.

My father helped the neighbours with the shearing. What great get-togethers they were. His lunch was a cheese sandwich (my mother made them so thick that one sandwich did for two) and a bottle of cold tea. He was proud that he never missed a shooting day. My father did not like a tie, but on the shoot it was the done thing to wear one, but it always ended up in a mess. So one of the shooters bought him a plastic one on elastic. It looked so real at the front he thought it was great, and said the other ties throttled him.

When my father said something he meant it... as many a walker has found out to their cost. He was a character and everyone enjoyed a chat with him. He had a wealth of knowledge of the Snake Valley and his job. His love for his dogs was very strong.

● Dad was young at the time of the Trespass, but Benny Rothman visited him several times. It was interesting to listen to them. On his last visit, when Dad was bedfast, they laughed and talked about the old times and shared memories.

Shaking hands with the duke

JIM PERRIN

The Duke speaking with Mrs Gillett in 2002

Seventy years on from the great Kinder Scout Mass Trespass of 1932, one of the heartwarming and inspiring annual gatherings that Roly Smith has been organising for years now took place in the quarry at Bowden Bridge, from which the original Mass Trespass set out. Its leader then - stepping in at the last moment when the appointed man lost his nerve in the face of a heavy and forewarned police presence, notebooks and truncheons in hand - was a twenty-year-old Manchester man who worked in the motor trade - Jewish by descent, tiny in stature and fiery in rhetoric. He was my dear old friend and comrade Benny Rothman, who served four months in Leicester jail for his part in the crucial event in the history of the struggle for access to England's open country.

At the time of the 70th Trespass anniversary, Benny was two months dead (the last words he spoke, while sitting on a sofa at his daughter's home in Billericay watching a slick barrister Tory shadow minister mouth his habitual mendacities on tv, were reputedly 'Lawyers! Liars!')

The 2002 event was held in a marquee in the Bowden Bridge quarry. Outside it, a protest was under way from the Countryside Alliance, whom the police had to restrain from intimidation of the mostly elderly attendees. The usual suspects were there to address the faithful - our redoubtable Kate Ashbrook from the Open Spaces Society; the Stockport MP Andrew Bennett; folk-singer and comedian Mike Harding was at hand to lead the singing of 'The Manchester Rambler'. And I'd been drafted in to deliver a eulogy for Benny.

But before I spoke, a frail, elderly gentleman, immaculately dressed (he was the only one wearing a tie), rose to speak, and his contribution stole the show. He was Eton and Cambridge educated; had won an MC in the Italian Campaign; was a Tory MP, one of the richest men in the country; bookshop proprietor, owner of racehorses and of Chatsworth House and Estate (for free public access to thousands of acres of the latter he'd signed an agreement with the Peak District National Park Authority in 1991). His name was Andrew Cavendish (1920-2004), the 11th Duke of Devonshire.

What he did that day would be unthinkable to a contemporary member of his caste and political persuasion. He came to the microphone and, in a clear and emotional voice and tones of sincere humility and contrition, he apologised for the actions of his father, the 10th Duke, in excluding ramblers from the Peak District moorland, which had resulted in the imprisonment of four of those who took part in the Trespass.

He had, if you like, walked into the lions' den of militant access campaigners, and made the apology for his father's role to an unforgiving community grieving for the recent loss of their figurehead. The audience was hushed, astonished by what they'd heard.

Listening to him, I was both moved and persuaded of his absolute integrity. On impulse, before I began to speak, I walked over to him, shook his hand, thanked him, and then returned to the microphone and gave my eulogy for Benny, knowing that he, passionate and selfless fighter that he was, was also a man of magnanimity, who would have smiled his grave smile, and nodded his wise old head, and approved of what he saw.

No Longer Trespassers on Kinder

Keith Warrender

Right of access to 6,000 acres

In splendid spring weather here at Edale yesterday about a hundred ramblers gathered outside an inn to hear the first access land in the Peak District National Park formally 'declared open.' No tapes were cut, no gates were opened with golden keys - it is hard to know how to deal ceremonially enough with a large part of the slab-sided and excellent mass of Kinder Scout - yet it was a golden day in the history of the open-air movement.

Roughly six thousand acres of the Kinder massif have now been made officially 'accessible' after negotiations with the landowners, which means that for the first time ramblers and rock climbers can divert themselves on this extensive stretch of moss and moor without fear of being regarded as trespassers. Though the byelaws which go with the agreement - a copy more or less of the 'Country Code' normally followed by the country-lover - do not allow them to 'drive a vehicle, light a fire, hunt, fish, or shoot' there without the leave of the owner of the land. If they do, or if their actions are a nuisance to others, they will have to answer to the wardens' service, and this was the second feature of today's inauguration.

Each week-end and Bank Holiday from today on, a group of wardens, all but one volunteers from local rambling clubs, men and women who know the Park well, led by a full-time warden employed by the Peak Park Planning Board, will be patrolling on and around Kinder Scout ready to act as friendly guides to the rambler and also ready with a warning in cases of hooliganism.

No 'organised' Look

This does not mean that Kinder is going to get an 'organised' look. As one warden said, stowing a minute apple core carefully back in his ruck-sack (we were sitting in the middle of a monstrous moor where one could have thrown almost a truck-load away without feeling a litter-fiend): 'You couldn't organise Kinder with an army of policemen and we don't aim to be that.' In fact they are very obviously ramblers themselves, wearing merely a green arm band and a paper 'warrant of authority' in their pockets. They are supplied with a compass, a map, and first-aid kit. They are also insured by the Peak Park Planning Board. Their experience and capacity to help are their own. 'You are friends of the rambler, not park keepers,' officials of the board emphasised in their brief speeches before we moved off.

One of to-day's wardens, a man of seventy-seven who has known Kinder in all weathers, spoke of it feelingly as 'a great day' and he gave vent to the same idea in various phrases as, we puffed up the slopes of Grindsbrook Clough for the day's patrol. For him, he said, doffing his first sweater 'as usual' at the thousand-foot contour line as he rested on a familiar boulder, to-day marked the end of '60 years of trespassing' - and not of the timid kind either, one gathered.

Gamekeepers, mostly friendly but sometimes not, protecting the grouse shoots, have often in the past barred the way to this open space, even to the most gentle-minded of rambling clubs. Most of to-day's wardens had such memories of disturbed walking. The job now is to show the landowners that with the new freedom they are less liable to vandalism than before.

Tactful wardenship

At a rendezvous on top, at the 2,000ft mark, the wardens paired off, with a patrol of about ten miles each to carry out. This enabled the top of the plateau to be fairly well covered and the access routes - the easiest and well-known means of getting on to the access land - to be kept under supervision from the edges of the heights. Since anyone diverging from these is likely to walk over arable land or stock pasture, they would have to be warned about it if necessary. But no one, apparently, strayed.

When they returned to the Edale base at twilight there was only one incident the wardens had to report. Someone had left a small section of picnic on the moor and apologetically cleared it away when the warden pointed out his sin. The offender was back five minutes later to mention that his girl friend had blisters on the heel. And so the first warden's first-aid kit was broached. Numerous ramblers asked wardens for a good route when they were doubtful, and the armband seemed to have shown its worth.

By an un-named reporter
MANCHESTER GUARDIAN Saturday 17 April 1954

John Beatty

Streams leading down to the packhorse bridge at the foot of Jacob's ladder

'No man has the right to own mountains'*

ROLY SMITH

Before the coming of the iniquitous Enclosure Acts of the 18th and 19th centuries, most open country, mountains and moorland was common land, where anyone could graze their sheep, cut heather or peat - or simply walk and enjoy the view.

There had been many previous abortive Parliamentary attempts to win back the cherished freedom to roam, from the first bill promoted by Liberal MP James Bryce in 1884, to the falsely named Creech Jones Access to the Mountains Act of 1939. Inadequate provisions for site-by-site access agreements (most in the battlegrounds of the 1930s in the Peak District) were also made in the 1949 National Parks and Access to the Countryside Act.

In 1985, the Ramblers launched its *Forbidden Britain Day*, highlighting non-access moorland with well-publicised rallies. By 1991, this annual event was seeing organised trespasses on a scale not seen since the 1930s, and active pressure groups like the Sheffield Campaign for Access to Moorland continued the campaign.

Paddy Tipping, MP for Sherwood, Nottinghamshire, a champion for freedom to roam and a former president of the Ramblers, promoted several private members' and ten-minute rule bills to urge the government into action. So when eventually a sympathetic Labour government was elected in 1997, the Ramblers were primed and ready. Pledges for action had come from candidates of all parties before the election, confirming that they would back the right to roam, and the promise had been included in the Labour Party manifesto.

In 1999, Environment Minister Michael Meacher confirmed the intention for legislation in a speech to the House of Commons, saying it would be a lasting tribute to the memory of former Labour leader John Smith. After some procrastination in the House of Lords, the resulting CRoW Act finally became law on November 30, 2000.

Before the implementation of CRoW, many landowners, including moorland owners and the Country Land and Business Association (CLA), had expressed fears of a rise in rural crime, disturbance of wildlife and moorland fires, all of which have proved groundless. Perhaps the most positive thing to come from CRoW is the fact that owners and users are now talking to one another through Local Access Forums, on which all interests are represented.

The Ramblers' *One Coast for All* campaign contributed to the passage of the Marine and Coastal Access Act of 2009, which called on Government to create a 2,800-mile path around the entire coast of England by 2020. The first section of the England Coastal path opened at Weymouth in June 2012, and work on extending the path continues, but it is still a long way short of that ambitious target.

In 2011, the Ramblers launched the *Branch Out* campaign in opposition to the Forestry Commission's plans to sell off publicly accessible woodlands in England. The campaign persuaded government to rethink their plans and it continues to advocate increased access to woodlands.

The situation in Scotland, where de facto access to open country had always been allowed, was slightly different. Following intense lobbying by Ramblers Scotland, led by former director Dave Morris, a Land Reform Act was introduced in 2003, which established a statutory right to be on land for recreational, educational and certain other purposes and also the right to cross land. These rights have to be exercised responsibly as specified in the Scottish Outdoor Access Code, and there is currently an on-going review of open access in Scotland.

Many people believe England and Wales should adopt the proven Scottish model, or even the Swedish one of *allemansrätten* ('all man's right'), which gives walkers the right to roam anywhere, subject to a common-sense set of restrictions.

But have no doubt that the threats remain. A recent Government consultation paper appears to be yet another attempt to make trespass a criminal offence, something which was first suggested over eighty years ago in the hated Access to Mountains Act of 1939.

'The Manchester Rambler' song by Ewan MacColl

Above: Looking towards Kinder Reservoir from the plateau

Below: The 50th Trespass anniversary at Hayfield

Milestones
on the road to access

ROLY SMITH

1217: Charter of the Forest re-establishes rights of access
to royal forests for freemen and commoners

1235: First enclosures sanctioned by Parliament

Between 1604 and 1914: More than 5,000 individual Enclosure Acts
passed, enclosing 6.8 million acres of once common land

1824: Association for the Protection of Ancient Footpaths in York founded

1826: Manchester Association for the Preservation of Ancient Footpaths
founded

1845: Another General Enclosure Act allows appointment of Enclosure
Commissioners who could enclose land without Parliamentary permission

Rights-of-Way Society formed

1865: Open Spaces Society formed (as the Commons Preservation Society)

1876: Formation of the Hayfield and Kinder Scout Footpaths Association

1884: James Bryce introduces first Access to Mountains
(Scotland) Bill to Parliament

Forest Ramblers' Club formed to retain Epping Forest as an open space

1888: Bryce presents second Access to Mountain Bill

1894: Peak District and Northern Counties Footpath Preservation Society
formed in Manchester

1896: Mass trespass on Winter Hill, Lancashire

John Beatty

Cairn on Kinder Low

1898: Bryce unsuccessful again with an Access to Mountains Bill

1900: Sheffield Clarion Ramblers founded by GHB Ward

1926: First Winnats rally

1931: National Council of Ramblers' Federations established

1932: Mass Trespass on Kinder Scout, resulting in imprisonment of five ramblers

1935: National Ramblers' Association founded

1938: Access to Mountains Bill proposed by Arthur Creech Jones

1939: Access to Mountains Act, including controversial clause which made trespass a criminal offence, passed

1945: Dower Report published, proposing National Parks, National Trails and access agreements

1949: National Parks and Access to the Countryside Act passed

1951: First National Park, in the Peak District, designated
First access agreements negotiated

1953: Peak Park Planning Board complete access agreement
with the owners of the Chatsworth Settlement for 5,624 acres
of the northern section of Kinder, including Seal Edge
and Blackden Edge

1954: Free access to part of Kinder begins

1955: Access to 3,354 acres of Kinder Scout belonging
to the Watts family agreed with the Peak Park Planning Board

6000 acres belonging to the Chatsworth Settlement
and the Youth Hostels Trust become accessible
after agreement with the national park authority

● **Walkers gain free access to the whole of the Kinder plateau
after access agreed for a further 1000 acres around Grindsbrook
and Golden Clough**

1965: Tom Stephenson's Pennine Way, Britain's first
long distance path, opens

1982: National Trust buys Kinder giving open access in perpetuity

2000: Countryside and Rights of Way (CRoW) Act passed,
giving access to open country

2003: Land Reform (Scotland) Act gives the public the right of access
to any land for recreational, educational and certain other purposes

2005: Right of access came into effect across the whole of England

2009: Marine and Coastal Access Act approves an England Coast
Path, to be completed by 2020

2012: Wales Coast Path opens

2020: Twentieth anniversary of CRoW Act

Covid 19 pandemic national lockdown

2022: 90th anniversary of the Kinder Scout Mass Trespass

Kinder Downfall in the 1920s

Kinder Tor

Kinder

Final thoughts

Ninety years on from the Trespass, the story of Kinder is ongoing. On the following pages, we've invited people with different experiences and perspectives of Kinder to share their memories and opinions on future opportunities and threats towards conservation and access to the countryside.

Forbidden Kinder - the black perspective
MAXWELL A AYAMBA

The Mass Trespass in 1932 will forever be remembered as one of the most important landmarks in British history even among those who were originally against it, for playing an important role to publicise the class struggle against land ownership and access in the UK. The fact that in 2021 we have the freedom to roam only 8% of the English countryside since the mass trespass eighty-nine years ago is an indictment of the contestation and politicisation of the English rural countryside space. Benny Rothman and his compatriots must be credited for their heroism to battle for the right to roam over lands labelled as forbidden. From my perspective, the significance of the mass trespass is tantamount to social justice and a human rights issue to access a shared space for the benefit of everyone irrespective of race, class, social status or gender.

However, with 92% ownership of these spaces which constitute public assets still in the control of the aristocracy, farmers and landowners, it suggests the Kinder narrative remains an insurmountable battle. Although the Julian Glover Review launched in 2019 is advocating access for everyone, there are question marks as to what extent this will change the status quo.

As an immigrant from Ghana and visibly a black man in a predominantly white space my first experience of Kinder was in 2006, that is despite living in Sheffield since 1996. I can still vividly recollect that very freezing bitter cold morning of 11th November 2006. As the first black Board member of the Ramblers' Association (2005) and co-founder of the *100 Black Men Walk for Health Group* (2004), I and our walking group was invited to join Griff Rhys Jones to re-enact the mass trespass at Kinder 75 years ago. This was my first experience of and exposure to Kinder and the story behind this famous space.

Coming from a country where land is the embodiment of our source of livelihood made me question the rationale behind why in England some people should be denied access to the land for walking as an escape from pollution in the cities. Sadly, millions of people from Black and Ethnic Minority communities just like myself prior to experiencing Kinder, have no knowledge about the mass trespass and the struggle for access and freedom to roam. Even though the Trespass, and subsequent work by the Ramblers' Association, resulted in legal access for all, some sections of British society remain marginalised, if not excluded from these spaces. To many of Britain's eight million minorities the countryside appears something of a middle-class white space.

This perception is the more reason why the national play, *Black Men Walking*, inspired by our 100 Black Men Walk for Health Group and produced by Eclipse and Royal Theatre production in 2018/19, became a very popular hit across theatres in England - *We walk. Though we are written into the landscape you don't see us. We walked England before the English.*

The play was a political statement and subtle reminder that Black people, though they may appear invisible in the British rural space, have always been part of the landscape. And though the Mass Trespass was a class issue, access now is a race and privileged issue. Overturning attitudes heavily entrenched in traditions of land ownership though is still ongoing; it is the racialisation of rural spaces such as Kinder that has also become the new narrative.

Maxwell A Ayamba is a PhD Research Student in Black Studies, at the Department of American & Canadian Studies University of Nottingham, M4C/AHRC. He is an environmental journalist, who worked previously as an Associate Lecturer/ Research Associate at Sheffield Hallam University (SHU). He is the Founder and Projects Co-ordinator of the Sheffield Environmental Movement (2016) and Co-Founder of the 100 Black Men Walk for Health Group (2004) which inspired production of the national play *Black Men Walking*.

Celebrating and cherishing hard-won rights

DAVID BLUNKETT

As former Home Secretary, you would not expect me to be in favour of trespassing. After all, trespassing is breaking the law! But I have to be clear. If I'd been alive 90 years ago, I would have been with the walkers on Kinder Scout, taking part in the Kinder Trespass peacefully, and I emphasise peacefully, protesting.

These were not middle-class anarchists. They were not disrupting other people's lives, costing other people dear, nor, for that matter, did they have nothing to lose. Some of them had a lot to lose. Jobs were on the line and, in fact, as we know, some people were dissuaded from taking part precisely because they had been threatened by their employers, including the local authorities, if they continued with the protests that had already taken place.

This threat was to remain real until 1949 when at last the original protest and those throughout the 1930s, yielded fruit in the form of the Countryside Act. It is, of course, worth bearing in mind that by 1949 there were only twelve major rights-of-way that those from Manchester, Sheffield, Derby and Nottingham, could use.

The lung - for that's what it was - that allowed people to breathe, to be 'free' to explore and enjoy the glories of nature, was confined to those with wealth and privilege, with land and the law on their side.

So, there are times when legitimate protest has been crucial in changing minds, opening-up freedoms and establishing what, years later, we take for granted. All of us stand on the shoulders of those who came before us. Men and women who were prepared to take a risk and stand up and be counted for something they believed to be their birth-right. All these years later, and those rights are so often taken for granted. All the more reason for a reminder of the sacrifice that was made and how important it was that people were prepared to put their own heads on the block that we might enjoy the beauty of the Peak District.

During the months of the pandemic, and in particular at times of 'lockdown', we've been reminded, once again, of what we are missing, and what was missing from the lives of those who, until just over seventy years ago before the 1949 Countryside Act was passed, found themselves subject to a law that restricted their movement, forbade them from walking in the countryside and, of course, reminded them of the exclusivity of land ownership.

Today, our task is both to remind ourselves of that struggle, to educate the need for respect and care of the countryside and celebrate and cherish those hard-won rights. As in the public mind the Kinder Trespass of 1932 stands out, so should we celebrate the first publication of Clarion Club, and the work of GHB Ward in 1921 when he reflected on the previous years of campaigning, which ultimately led to the Countryside and Rights of Way Act 2000. I'm proud to have been a member of the Cabinet which, finally, and after so much resistance, genuinely opened up the right of access, and the freedom to roam.

As a small child, from five years old I had no idea, on those wonderful occasions when my dad was not working, and we were able to picnic in Derbyshire, that we were the early beneficiaries of the creation of the first ever National Park. This year we will be able to celebrate that very special occasion and to recall the first, but not the last, Mass Trespass.

Born and bred in Sheffield, **David Blunkett** was Home Secretary, Education and Employment Secretary and Work and Pensions Secretary in Tony Blair's 1997 Government. He was granted a life peerage in 2015 and is now president of the South Yorkshire & North East Derbyshire Ramblers. RS

Kinder reminiscences
HENRY FOLKARD

'What's it called?' I asked, looking at an unknown lump of higher ground in the distance. 'It's called Kinder Scout'. 'I've never heard of it' I said. There was little reason why I would have heard of it, being born in Essex. I was not impressed. It looked monotonously flat. Yet there Kinder Scout was. You could not ignore it. Its very presence lodged itself in my mind.

One day I just thought I would go up Kinder. 'You will have to go to Edale' I was told. There was a nice-enough looking valley up from Edale, which kind of led you on to see where it went. But then the anticlimax: you got to what passed for the top. I had never seen anything like it - but then why should I have? A monotonous plateau in every direction of dissected bog with no view once you left the valley rim: only more of the same. When you tried to walk over it, things got worse. Steep banks of peat, much of it devoid of vegetation, were desperate to walk across, making you lose all sense of direction. When you thought you were on a path it disappeared, and if it snowed you very quickly had no idea where you had come from, let alone where you were going.

But considering this to be a mountain, the objective was to get to the top - I will never know where I did get - apart from being thoroughly disorientated, disappointed and lost.

The saving miracle was that at some point I came by chance upon a place where I could see a view other than unending bare bog, and, better still, recognise where I had come from in the valley below. 'Did you enjoy your walk'? I was asked. Answer came there none. So why did I ever go back there? I really don't know. But then, I don't need to know. Why should you need to know an answer for everything in life? Kinder can be strangely captivating. It is just enough to know that I did go back, and have been going back for over 50 years.

Some things don't seem to change. Being lost on Kinder is one. The first time I was lost was not to be the last. But then being lost is more about a state of mind than failing to be at some preconceived point of orientation. Kinder has a compelling sense of place that grows on you. It's being there that matters, not any precise whereabouts.

So I went up Kinder another way, and then over it, and across it and around it in both directions and up it from the north, the south, the east and the west - still getting lost most of the time, but that was part of the enjoyment - knowing that you were contented, but not needing to know just where you were. I climbed its Downfall in winter and many of its buttresses in summer. Then the magically-sculpted rocks at Seal Stones, the Wool Packs, at Fairbrook and round Sandy Heys, in changing lights and at different times of day were waiting to be discovered, with their different shapes and profiles suggesting different things for different people.

As Kinder unfolded itself over the years the familiar changed, little by little but relentlessly. The contrast between the cloughs and the plateau dwindled. It became a sad place, bare bald flanks merging into a characterless top, with trashed eroded paths and huge expanses denuded of vegetation. Playing in peaty bits had been fun, navigating boggy stretches difficult, walking trackless wastes special. It seemed the red grouse were not there like they had been, and where were the meadow pipits? Bare stalks of dead heather passed for vegetation and popular paths spread across wide swathes of decimated land. Trees in the cloughs dwindled, along with whatever else had grown there. Kinder's essence, its character, deserted it, eaten by sheep - the Sahara of the Peak.

So came the National Trust, and *Moors for the Future*, and the restoration and resurgence of the land we had loved. Grasses, and acid-loving plants and even the mother of the peat, sphagnum moss, began to be re-established, a triumph of vision, dedication, effort and European funding. It is too easy to take so much for granted, yet now there is so much to be grateful for. It is for those of us who enjoy it to respect it, and to nurture its delicate and precarious survival. That responsibility goes further - for we who value it and have learnt to understand it are its eyes and ears. Each one of us is the guardian of its future.

With the sense of place unfolding, a sense of history asserts itself. Kinder has a presence that exerts a fascination across generations. From the beginning of time archaeologists can point us to places where there is evidence of habitation or burial or hunting or whatever, and less easy to document but no less real is the way it will have imprinted itself on the psyche of the communities who live around it. Indeed it was the community's, and they had rights of grazing and pannage, whilst everyone else was free to wander at will. All that changed, really very quickly, with the Enclosures. Where what had been everybody's became somebody's, and worse, somebody's to the absolute exclusion of everybody else. It was the wealthy and the influential who enclosed it for their own pursuits, and because they were also the architects of the law of the land they made sure their own interests were encapsulated in that law. It was a law which suppressed everyone else's rights. It is, thanks to the great campaigners for open access from Sheffield and Manchester - Bert Ward and Benny Rothman - that the legacy has not persisted on Kinder at least, though it tries to be rife elsewhere.

It is perhaps no accident that the access movement, which reached a climax with the great Trespass in 1932, led by Benny, should focus on Kinder. It hovers on the horizon where you can see it from parts of those two cities, tantalising you. Their proud gift to the common good was enhanced and enshrined by the Peak District National Park Authority soon after its establishment, with their pioneering negotiation of access land, and carried forward by the National Trust and those private landowners who 'own' Kinder now, with the strength of the protection of the Countryside and Rights of Way Act. We have a proud inheritance to remember, to respect, to safeguard and to hand on to the next generation. It's something we all can and must do.

Kinder's compelling essence exerts its own fascination, and draws you to it, imprinting itself on you. As Bill Emmingham, founder of the Woodcraft Folk, once said as he looked up at Kinder from the train returning him to Sheffield. 'I'll be back'. And Kinder said to him, 'I'll be waiting for you'. It's time to go up there again. I wonder if I ever have really got to the top of it?

Henry Folkard is Access Officer and representative of the British Mountaineering Council on the Kinder and High Peak Advisory Group. He was a member of the Peak District Local Access Forum for fifteen years and also active on the Stanage Forum. RS

Willow Publishing

Ice grotto, Kinder Downfall

The Trespass history is still relevant

JAN GILLETT

'My father went to prison' was always an attention-getter when I was a child in the 50s and 60s. However, I didn't use it often as the explanation left other kids bored. Who cared about going to prison for the right of access to some distant hills when we just went where we dared in our neighbourhood? Later on, we went on field trips and there seemed to be access all over the place, so what was the fuss about?

My father, Tona Gillett, did go to prison in 1932 when he was nineteen. He didn't refer to it very often, when he did it was to downplay it, and claim it helped him revise for his engineering exams. To be fair, he didn't talk about his past very much at all; those were traumatic times for youngsters growing up in an economic slump watching fascists taking over in Europe. The Trespass wasn't too big a deal for him, not in the same league as his later marches in London in resistance to Oswald Mosley's gangs. It wasn't until the 1970s after the *Look Stranger* programme, and then 1982 that the event, and Tona's part in it, gained a life in the media.

Our reticent dad was still not very forthcoming about it, and it was really only clear to me what had happened when I inherited his letters on his death in 1992. In fact it appears that the very extra-ordinariness of the whole episode meant that it was not the trauma it might have been. He received complete support from his parents. They were Quakers, used to clashing with the establishment. After all it was a non-violent event, and they and many other people supported the idea of open access; it was just the manner of the protest that was an issue. A prison sentence was such an over-reaction that the Trespassers felt justified in what they had done. Dad received very supportive references for his application to Cambridge University and life moved on.

Where does this leave us, now that memories of the Trespass are at best second-hand? On the plus side there is more recognition than ever before of the 1932 event. The Ramblers' Association and the National Trust long ago came round to supporting it and taking the speakers' platform at anniversaries. But the land-owning establishment of England fiercely maintains its right to exclude the rest of us when it can.

The Trespass history is still live and relevant. Around the world are populist governments thriving by attacking hard-won freedoms of all kinds. Our work is never done. It seems only a matter of time before the English press attacks the right to roam legislation.

What can we do to pre-empt this? Part of the problem is evidence that roaming across the countryside is harmful to the very environment itself. Litter, fires, erosion of pathways, dogs worrying farm animals, motorbikes, four-wheel drive vehicles and so on can cause catastrophic damage and cost to the landowners.

So, as one of the few surviving links to the imprisoned trespassers, I don't try to speak for my father, but I do know he was upset about the behaviour of such vandals who followed in his footsteps. I have two things to say:

1. We must maintain our vigilance and efforts to preserve the rights to roam which go without saying in so many other countries.

2. We need to take a lead in demanding a coherent set of behavioural requirements that conserve the very things we so treasure. We must be associated with policies that lineup with the two crises of extinction and climate. Our parents and grandparents campaigned for walking as a life-affirming activity. We need to concentrate on getting support for that and taking responsibility to ensure it causes no damage.

Jan Gillett is the son of Tona Gillett, one of the arrested and imprisoned 1932 Trespassers, and has been a loyal supporter of the Spirit of Kinder events for many years. RS

The spirit of Kinder
TERRY HOWARD

My 'first footing' on Kinder as a child was sheer elation after a gruelling climb up one of the stream beds which led to the plateau. I could see for miles around and felt as though I was on top of the world. It inspired me for all of my life. It was a challenge met not offered to so many young people. The story of the Kinder Trespass of 1932 was an inspiration which guided me along the 'Access Trail'.

I have been on Kinder in the worst of weather where icicles hung from my beard, I have seen myself projected onto clouds by the sun which covered the valleys in a temperature inversion, glided along with the breeze over the peat as though my feet were not touching the ground. Many young people have followed me up onto Kinder to enjoy 'bog trotting', route finding and the pure physical challenges offered, and enjoyed.

I have taken Kinder 'virgins' from various groups and communities onto the plateau they have heard so much about to help fulfil a dream. Their elation could only be measured in knowing how much they enjoyed the experience and how it helped them in their lives. Of later years I recognised how most ancient burial sites in the High Peak looked towards Kinder and yet none has been found on the plateau. Many ramblers have had their last remains spread on Kinder. Is it because ancient people and ramblers wished or believed their spirit would wander over Kinder for eternity?

It would seem the 'bog trotting' and 'grough jumping' days are sadly going and being replaced, as some may say, by a garden-like, surface through revegetation. We have known for a very long time the effects of over-grazing by sheep, industrial pollution, draining and even boots have impacted on Kinder; other popular areas have also suffered the same. The problems and issues are being met, not through banning people as in the past, but enlisting their co-operation on the new and varied management and revegetation schemes. Unfortunately, some methods have attracted criticism by introducing alien materials, such as plastic.

Kinder as I knew it has changed and so have many other places I loved and enjoyed. But to protect these special places for future generations choices have to be made which do not keep people out. The spirit of Kinder still lives in me and we must encourage more people to share in that same spirit.

Terry Howard, is an access campaigner, walk leader with Sheffield Ramblers, founder of SCAM and organiser of many trespass walks leading to the CRoW Act. KW

Keith Warrender

Kinder - a special place in the National Park

ANDREW McCLOY

Kinder Scout has a significance for the Peak District National Park that goes beyond any simple height classification or definition based on geology or landscape. Arguably there are more shapely hills and certainly quieter and more wildlife-rich locations, but for me Kinder Scout's essence and its key relationship is - like the National Park's - all to do with people.

The Peak District's huge urban hinterland, with an estimated twenty million people within one hour's journey, makes this comparatively small area of moorland and dales incredibly precious. The 1949 legislation that established the Peak District as Britain's first National Park recognised the mounting post-war pressure on its 555 square miles from damaging economic development, as well as the need to safeguard and ideally to extend public access to this vital natural resource. From the beginning, Kinder Scout was talismanic. Although the 1932 Trespass did not in itself lead directly to the creation of the National Park (there were other events that contributed and some notable campaigners like CPRE's Ethel Haythornthwaite who played a more instrumental role) the Trespass nonetheless lodged the 2,000ft gritstone plateau in the public's consciousness.

It was no coincidence that in 1953, two years after the National Park was formally established, the first new access agreement to be struck by the Authority covered 5,624 acres of land owned by the Duke of Devonshire on southern Kinder, as well as some additional areas belonging to the Youth Hostels Association and local farmers. The first visitor information point in the National Park was established, albeit informally, by Fred Heardman in the dining room of his Edale pub,

and there is a great photo of him standing with some young ramblers by a table full of books and pamphlets, pointing animatedly to a large map of Kinder Scout on the wall behind.

My own relationship with Kinder Scout is, like so many others, very personal. I have yomped across the middle on the Four Inns challenge walk, skirted carefully round the edge on the first day of my Pennine Way adventure, then at other times simply wandered the paths around its high outer edge to get different perspectives on the National Park: bustling Edale, remote Ashop, distant Manchester. It tells me so much about the make-up of this complex National Park. For instance, the trains pulling into Edale station remind me that generations of ramblers have come here for weekend adventure; but so, too, do the flagstone paths that are now a feature of Kinder's southern and western edges. Which brings me back to people.

The 70th anniversary of the Peak District National Park in 2021, played out against a sobering backdrop of the Pandemic, was a time not so much to dwell on past achievements but for us to consider how and where we go from here. And if we needed evidence that the National Park still mattered then it was right in front of us. As the lockdowns unfolded, crowds of people surged into the Peak District, evidently desperate to get away or be outdoors or perhaps simply reconnect with nature. They camped illegally on the Dark Peak moors; cars were parked all over the place; a lot of litter needed clearing up; and one or two required helping off the hills.

But regardless, National Parks like the Peak District were there when the nation needed them most. And hills like Kinder Scout once again acted as a magnet - a source of physical, emotional and spiritual comfort. The Peak District National Park has always been a pioneer, and I'm clear that for us to enjoy another seventy successful years we have to adapt and respond to the changing world around us. It means showing leadership on nature recovery and climate change, such as the work of the *Moors for the Future Partnership* which is making such a difference restoring the damaged peat of the Dark Peak. Kinder Scout, which was

John Beatty

Final approach to the steep ascent of Kinderlow End

one of the first projects, slowly reversing the long-term effects of pollution, overgrazing, fires and erosion. But we must also be more imaginative and inclusive when it comes to helping everyone enjoy the National Park. Iconic locations like Kinder Scout should be accessible to all and not limited by someone's income, cultural background or other real or perceived barriers. How many residents from Moss Side or Darnall head for Kinder Scout these days, I wonder? But inevitably more people mean more pressure for Kinder Scout. Balancing the fragile habitat and delicate ecosystem of this National Nature Reserve with the public's hard-won freedom to roam all over it is an ongoing challenge; and as we found in 2021 the task of educating a new wave of urban visitors in responsible countryside recreation can be daunting. But it's a challenge that we'll rise to and it's a price we must pay if the Trespassers' legacy of access for all is to be honoured, and if we want a new generation to connect with this special landscape. Once this happens there's a good chance that many will go on to actively care for it; and some are likely

to develop a special bond of their own with Kinder Scout and even trace the timeline back to 1932.

A couple of years ago I remember chatting briefly with a group of teenagers I bumped into on Kinder Scout. They were on their Gold Duke of Edinburgh's Award expedition and were friendly, confident and entirely at ease on the open paths and moors. After all, they knew no different. Kinder Scout had always been open to them; and anyway they were all born after the Countryside and Rights of Way Act 2000 brought in the so-called right to roam in open country. It's why the Kinder Scout story needs telling and re-telling; and it's why it remains a special place in the National Park.

Andrew McCloy is chairman and a Parish Council-appointed member of the Peak District National Park Authority. He is a published author and previously worked as a Press Officer for the Ramblers' Association in London. RS

Enjoying our land freely
STUART MACONIE

At the top of my stairs at home, I have a picture given to me by Ramblers GB when I became their president. It's an illustration of the moment in 1932 when the groups of walkers who'd climbed Kinder Scout from Manchester and Sheffield came face to face with the gamekeepers who were there to 'protect' the grouse moors. It's a great picture. Of course, they could have given me a Heaton Cooper painting of a Lakeland tarn or a sketch of a Cornish seascape.

I'd have loved any of those. But the Kinder poster is particularly apt. Ramblers GB arose from the actions of the Trespass and I have always been enormously keen that we remember our roots, which are not just in the joy and companionship of country walking, but in protest, dissent and campaigning.

The details of the Trespass will no doubt be covered in greater detail and with greater expertise in this fine book than I can do justice to here. Suffice it to say that several hundred walkers (a couple of thousand if you believe PR man Ewan McColl), angry at being turned off Bleaklow a few weeks before by lackeys of the Duke, decided to take a stand.

'Kinder was thick with keepers' according to Trespass leader Benny Rothman 'The professional ones just shouted and waved their sticks. It was the silly buggers that waded in.' The more practically minded among us may realise of course that having spent all week in difficult and dangerous conditions in factories and down coal mines they would not necessarily be frightened of a man in a stupid deerstalker. In the ensuing melee that followed, one keeper was mildly injured but a 'riotous assembly' was deemed to have occurred and the jury at Derby assizes found five defendants guilty.

Rothman got four months in Leicester jail. The others got lesser sentences. One of the five, Tony Gillett, was a university student from a wealthy banking family. Incredibly, he was offered the

2019 Castleton Spirit of Kinder event. L-R: Maxwell Ayamba, Jon Stewart (NT), Margaret Manning (Chair M/c and High Peak Ramblers' Association), Mags Metcalfe (M/c Ramblers), Ruth George MP, Jarvis Cocker, Roly Smith (front), Stuart Maconie, Lynn Robinson (BMC president), Salle Dare (M/c Ramblers) and Henry Folkard (BMC).

John Beatty

chance to apologise but he refused and so was sent to prison too.

The public outcry to these draconian sentences, applied with subtly political and racial bias, was such though that the blue touchpaper of the right to roam and access movements was lit. Now whenever I take out one of my beloved OS maps in mountain mists or lashed by rain on a soaking moor or later by crackling fireside with a warming dram I think of Benny Rothman and his mates. Because for over a decade now, all over these battered maps I see great expanses of sandy yellow where previously there was antiseptic white space and 'keep out signs'. That yellow shading stands for Open Accesslands; great swathes of our country lowland and upland once forbidden to me and you that is now open to us all.

The freedom to walk here unmolested and without asking permission was won by the bravery and fortitude of many, but begun by the Kinder Scout trespassers. When I was there a couple of years ago at the *Be Kinder* event with Jarvis Cocker, Jeremy Deller, David Blunkett and several of the contributors to this volume, we toasted them with custard creams and tea in the Methodist Church in Edale and later with something stronger in the pub. I remember them every time I pass the poster on my stairs on the way to the loo. I think Benny would like that.

Amazingly there are still those who don't accept the achievement of the Kinder Trespassers. When I wrote celebrating them in the Daily Mirror a few years back, the son of one of the gamekeepers complained that I was venerating troublemakers and lawbreakers. (Presumably, he took a similar view of the Suffragettes).

The Wikipedia entry on the Trespass cites a Yorkshire historian whose dismissal of the protest dwells rather tellingly that many of the trespassers were Jewish and left-wing. He adds that middle-class people had long enjoyed the delights of Kinder without resorting to trespass by the simple expedient of 'tipping the gamekeepers'. If ever a point was missed, it is surely here. We should all be able to enjoy our land freely without tipping gamekeepers or tugging forelocks.

Author and broadcaster **Stuart Maconie** is president of the Ramblers and has been a regular speaker at the annual Spirit of Kinder events. At the 2012 event, he claimed that the 1932 Mass Trespass should be on every school curriculum. RS

The key role of Kinder
HILARY McGRADY

It's hard not to be captured by the spirit of Kinder. There's plenty to draw you in - the history, the landscape, the scenery and the sheer joy that it brings to so many people. But looking to the future, it is the enduring relevance of the site that makes it so special - and makes the job of protecting it for future generations so important.

Whilst specifics may have changed, the reasons underpinning the fight for access at Kinder have clear parallels with those challenges we face today.

The first was the need for space, the freedom to roam. The events of 1932 sit against a wider history that encompasses the likes of the Enclosure Acts, as well as a period of increasing urbanisation. With a disconnect between city dwellers and nature, and little obvious solution without reform, the ramblers looked to the grand landscape which lay within easy reach of the city.

Ninety years on and there has clearly been much progress. The fights of the 1930s preceded landmark gains: the creation of National Parks and Areas of Natural Beauty, national footpaths and trails, and more recently the Countryside Rights of Way Act. Kinder is today enjoyed freely by thousands each year, earning its place as one of the nation's most loved outdoor attractions.

But for many the benefits of spending time in nature are still impossible to reach. The barriers are many and diverse - from how to make the first step into a space that you don't know or feel welcome in, to the physical issues of transport, and quality of space within reach.

Lockdown brought this into sharp light: reminding us of the importance of green space, whilst also showing the inequality of access. One in eight households have no garden, and thousands live in grey deserts with no accessible green space nearby. In the poorest 20 per cent of households, nearly half don't have a car, making transport difficult to wilder nature beyond town or city.

Against this context places like Kinder therefore remain vital - still providing a place to escape to from Greater Manchester, Sheffield and beyond, accessible by train and bus. The large numbers

Keith Warrender

who rushed to visit once lockdown had eased are testament to this service. Looking to the future we must ensure that this access is not only protected but available to everyone.

As well as the need for space, 1932 was also a response to environmental pollution. Many of those who joined the Trespass came from towns and cities blighted by smog. Manchester was particularly notorious: John Ruskin had spoken of 'Manchester's devil darkness', labelling the city the spiritual home of pollution. Just a year before the Trespass, winter smog took the lives of over four hundred and fifty of its residents.

To escape to Kinder therefore represented not just freedom to roam, but a literal respite from the city's polluted air. This was cited explicitly by Benny Rothman at the Trespass trial: 'After a hard week's work in smoky towns and cities, [we ramblers] go out rambling on weekends for relaxation, for a breath of fresh air, and for a little sunshine'.

Today, coal smog may no longer be visible over our cities and factories, but climate change is one of the greatest challenges of our generation, and as we work to tackle climate harm Kinder again has a key role to play.

The secret lies today not in Kinder's air, but in its soils, and the blanket bog that covers most of the plateau. In good condition, bog not only sustains wildlife, but it also traps carbon dioxide. If bogs are degraded however, as has historically been the case, due to the legacies of industrial pollution, overgrazing, and moorland fires, the peat dries out, becomes vulnerable to erosion and as a result releases carbon, turning from a store to a source of emissions.

The iconic landscape is therefore still playing a vital role on the frontline against environmental threat. To allow nature to play its part, we need to help it recover, in turn protecting Kinder for future generations. We need nature now more than ever - and it needs us to help it survive. Work is already under way. Tens of thousands of tiny sphagnum moss plants have been planted across Kinder and the High Peak, and reseeding

of vegetation has recarpeted bare peat. Thousands of small gully blocks have been installed across the landscape to raise the water table and slow water flow, stopping erosion by keeping the bog wet and reducing flood risk as the moor absorbs more water during heavy rains. Thousands of native broadleaf trees have also been planted, with woodland areas created to benefit biodiversity and encourage natural regeneration.

There is plenty more to do - efforts at Kinder are part of the wider High Peak Vision, a fifty-year strategy for the area's moorlands. But we can already see that changes are making a real difference. Those visiting Kinder over the last thirty years will have seen the transformation of the once-exposed 'moonscape' of bare peat into a green landscape now covered in healthy vegetation. They may have also noticed the increase in wildlife as nature returns, from the song of the curlew to the sight of iconic raptors - an achievement celebrated by the site's designation as a National Nature Reserve in 2009.

In 1932, the Kinder trespass sat in a wider context, in many ways the culmination or expression of two fundamental pressures - a lack of space to breathe, and the blight of pollution. The hills above Hayfield and Edale promised fresh air, clear skies and the sight of nature, attracting the ramblers.

Today the site is so special not just because that history took place, but because the questions posed ninety years ago remain so relevant today. Protecting this incredible place for future generations will require careful management, but I've no doubt that it can continue to provide just the space we need - the spirit of Kinder continuing.

Hilary McGrady was appointed Director General of the National Trust in 2018. She has worked for the Trust since 2006, joining as regional director for Northern Ireland, later becoming regional director for Wales and the London and South East region. In 2014 she was appointed the Trust's chief operating officer, leading its operations and consultancy teams. Hilary spoke at the 2019 Spirit of Kinder event, dubbing Kinder 'The People's Mountain.' RS

Memories of Kinder

FIONA REYNOLDS

It was in 1982 that I first joined the Kinder Trespass reunion. In fact I think this was the first big reunion, to mark fifty years since the original event. Crowds were to gather at Hayfield, for a ceremonial march up the hill, led by Benny Rothman and others who'd been present in 1932.

My friend Hazel and I were excited to be joining them. Together we constituted the entire staff of the Council for National Parks, the charity founded in 1936 as the Standing Committee on National Parks, to press for legislation. It was, truly, a Council, formed of the many countryside and access charities who had believed that joining together to press for National Parks legislation was more likely to succeed than each working independently.

In that they were right, and the passing of the 1949 National Parks and Access to the Countryside Act was a landmark moment. It was, also, something of a disappointment to those directly involved as there were so many compromises from the vision declared with such articulate skill by John Dower in his 1945 White Paper. Among many disappointments was that access to open country was much less widely secured than had been hoped by champions of the Act.

By the 1980s, though, CNP's preoccupations were with defending the Parks from live threats such as moorland ploughing (Exmoor), conifer afforestation (Brecon Beacons), road improvements (Lake District and Dartmoor) and other intrusive developments, and there was much to do. To strengthen our voice, we set up the Friends of National Parks, to enable people to support the charity as individual members, and we decided the Mass Trespass celebration was the perfect moment to launch the campaign. So Hazel - the artistic one - designed and printed hundreds of leaflets urging people to become a Friend of National Parks, and our job for the day was to hand out as many as we could. We did, in fact, succeed, but the experience was memorable for many other reasons. Above all we were both captivated by the impact of hundreds of people, walking together in solidarity for a common cause.

Benny Rothman, tiny and strong, headed the snake of walkers. He'd been arrested on that memorable day in 1932, when the gamekeepers with their sticks halted the walkers; and with his big smile and enormous walking boots he was only too ready to lead the procession fifty years later. Hazel and I worked the line, handing out leaflets and enjoying the repartee. Every now and again someone would strike up with Ewan MacColl's *Manchester Rambler*, or *This Land is our Land*. It was a heady, lively atmosphere created by like-minded people walking peacefully to remember a remarkable band of pioneers and to argue for a cause still not won.

It was my first exposure to the mass passion that access to the hills inspires, and my own first foray up Kinder, but far from my first experience of the hills. My parents were keen hillwalkers and every holiday for us five girls would be to Snowdonia, or the Lake District, or sometimes Skye. We all loved mountains. My parents had lived in Sheffield before they married, and in the mid-1980s happily moved back there, so expeditions to Kinder (up the ice-laden Downfall; wading through deep peat in pouring rain and - just occasionally - a stride in glorious sunshine) became a regular treat.

I returned to join several of the Kinder Trespass reunions over the years, Kinder in effect becoming a thread running through my working life. I left CNP in 1987 to join CPRE, which has its own strong Peak District heritage; and in 2000 I became Director-General of the National Trust, which owns large parts of Kinder and the Dark Peak.

By then, though, we had realised that the peat uplands were in a catastrophically declining state, as the peat dried out and was eroded away, emitting rather than absorbing carbon, and destroying a fragile and valuable ecosystem. Kinder, and the Trespass, meant a huge amount to all of these organisations, and I was proud to return, wearing a different hat but the same heart: powered by the love of high places and the joy derived from being free to walk them.

One of the most moving reunions was in 2002 when the 11th Duke of Devonshire, himself then 82, made an historic public apology to the massed walkers in Hayfield, expressing his regret for the actions taken by the gamekeepers in 1932, instructed by his grandfather. He spoke too of his support for the Countryside and Rights of Way Act 2000, which, he said, 'had done something to redeem that evil', finally providing free access to land defined as open country. His speech was a tremendous moment, and his last remarks were drowned by cheers from the crowd: he certainly knew how to pick his moment.

I was there then, and again in 2012, the 80th anniversary. Then, in my last year as DG of the Trust, I spoke alongside my friend Kate Ashbrook, President of the Ramblers' Association, and rambling stars Stuart Maconie and Mike Harding. Benny wasn't there - he had died in 2002 at 90 -

and by then few of the original trespassers were still alive. By now the agenda was as much about the urgent need to restore the peatland as access, and a consortium of organisations including the National Trust and the Peak District National Park had launched an ambitious *Moors for the Future* project. But the freedom to walk there, with the joy it brings, remains one of the powerful reasons why Kinder Scout has such meaning and value to people today.

The conservation challenge of the upland peat is not yet solved, though its urgency is well understood. And the annual Trespass reunion continues, drawing in an ever-wider audience, the mood vibrant, the atmosphere electric, as we remind ourselves, with each passing year, of the enduring value of the freedom to roam in beautiful countryside.

Dame Fiona Reynolds was Secretary CNP, 1980-87, Director, CPRE, 1992-8 (Assistant Director 1987-92) and Director-General, National Trust, 2000-2012. RS

Keith Warrender

Fish-like rock formation on Kinder

The Peak and Northern Footpaths Society
DAVID SISSONS

The Peak and Northern Footpaths Society, under its former name of the Peak District and Northern Counties Footpaths Preservation Society (PD&NCFPS), was formed in 1894 for footpath preservation, not for trespass off footpaths, and it was therefore not within its remit to attend or support the Kinder Mass Trespass. However, its footpath preservation work played an unwitting part in the Trespass, in that the society's first success was the 1897 re-opening of the Snake Path from Hayfield to the Snake Inn. When the Trespassers walked up the Kinder Road from Hayfield past the Kinder Reservoir, most would have joined this Snake Path at the foot of William Clough, and their subsequent meeting at Ashop Head would have followed the Snake Path uphill.

The Manchester Association for the Preservation of Ancient Footpaths had been set up as long ago as 1826. The more locally-focused Hayfield and Kinder Scout Ancient Footpaths Association (H&KSAFA) had from 1876 waged a twenty-year campaign to re-open the William Clough path from Hayfield to the 'Snake Inn' by way of William Clough and Ashop Head, bordering on Kinder Scout.

It was not only thirsty ramblers from Hayfield who found themselves unable to use this footpath to patronise the Snake Inn. Methodists from Hayfield were prevented from using it to attend their annual 'Love Feast' in the Alport Valley, and Sunday worshippers from the village were unable to attend the chapel. Ten years after this chapel's construction, the Duke of Devonshire closed the footpath on grounds that it crossed his grouse moors and, supposedly, members of the public using the path would interfere with the grouse-shooting of one of his tenants, a mill owner. The campaign initiated by the H&KSAFA was continued by the PD&NCFPS and in 1897 brought to a successful conclusion.

Most of the rambling organisations, including the Manchester Ramblers' Federation, opposed the Trespass, even though Sheffield Clarion Ramblers had been trespassing on Kinder for years. A generation gap, class divide and political difference were perhaps felt by the organisers of the Mass Trespass, and this comes across in Benny Rothman's 1982 account: 'It is easy now, after fifty years, to look back and see the mistakes made by the Trespass organisers. We should never have antagonised the the Ramblers' Federation and rambling leaders who had worked hard over a long period. We should have used our youthful zeal and energy inside the rambling movement, but of course, the faults were not all on one side'. There may be a lesson there from the past as we deal with the present and look to the future.

Today the PNFS continues the struggle to protect walkers' rights and to keep rights of way open. Rights of way are threatened with erasure in 2026 if they have not been registered on the definitive map, and the Deregulation Act 2015 will give more powers to landowners to divert or close paths. Rights of way are also put at risk through neglect, as a result of highway authorities' much-reduced resources, and building developments.

Contemporary 'radicals' - the climate change protesters and modern day trespassers - also pursue goals outside the constituted aims of PNFS, and, like their predecessors, the Society tries to achieve change within the framework of the law, (though that doesn't rule out trying to effect changes to the law). PNFS today continues to 'work hard' to protect and improve rights of way, aptly described as a 'labyrinth of liberty' (Robert Macfarlane, *The Old Ways*, Viking, 2012).

David Sissons was a long-standing member of the Sheffield Campaign for Access to Moorlands (SCAM) and the Peak & Northern Footpaths Society. He is an expert on GHB Ward, and his book *The Best of the Sheffield Clarion Ramblers' Handbooks* was published in 2002. RS

The courageous stand of Rothman and friends

COLIN SPEAKMAN

Benny was a remarkable individual, modest, mild-mannered with a sense of humour, but this disguised an inner steel. His was a binary world - the privileged wealthy few who owned the land and went grouse shooting, and the rest of us, the ordinary folk, including those who choose to tramp the hills. He always had a passion for supporting the underprivileged. In 1990 I joined Benny on what we called 'Benny's Bus', an open-top bus trundling around the Wythenshawe council estate, Manchester, to promote the weekend Wayfarer bus service to the Peak District National Park to local urban communities.

Yet the rambling establishment didn't always fully appreciate Benny. Even that other great hero of working-class radicalism, Tom Stephenson, once told me he believed Benny had put back the cause of access to open country by antagonising landowners and the political establishment. In reality, with parallels to George Floyd and the Black Lives Matter movement, the harsh and unjust treatment meted out to Benny and his colleagues for the simple act of walking on the open moorlands of England gave the outdoor movement its martyrs and galvanised opinion. The act of defiance and the official reaction to those events of 1932 burned in the public imagination. This allowed the wily and pragmatic Tom Stephenson to include those key clauses in the great 1949 National Park and Access to the Countryside Act that brought in the first legal Access Agreements. But it also paved the way to the far more radical 2000 CRoW Act Access we enjoy today.

Benny's and his young colleagues' passionate act of protest on Kinder had repercussions not just in the Peak District but all over England. This was especially true in the Yorkshire Dales where the

Duke of Devonshire's vast shooting estate of Barden Moor and Fell were strictly off-limits to walkers, with access only allowed by permit, which had to be obtained in advance and then under strictly-controlled conditions. Even the passing of the 1949 Act didn't force local authorities to act. It took a series of rallies organised by the Ramblers on Ilkley Moor before, finally, grudgingly, the Barden Moor and Fell Access Agreement was signed; even then it was implemented in stages from 1967 onwards, eighteen years after the 1949 Act had been passed.

Harry Rothman

Benny Rothman

Without the courageous stand by Benny and his colleagues not only would we not have had the Barden Access Agreement, but also the great CRoW Act, which in 2005 opened over 60% of the land in the Yorkshire Dales National Park to public access, would not have happened.

With a Government who once again challenge our civil liberties, with talk of criminal trespass legislation, there is little doubt that we need just the kind of young hotheads, like Benny was in 1932, to defend our freedoms, and not just that of walking in freedom and dignity to the summit of Kinder Scout.

Colin Speakman is perhaps best known as the creator of the Dales Way long distance path in the Yorkshire Dales. He is also an acknowledged expert on public transport and established the Dales Rail project when he worked for the Yorkshire Dales National Park in the 1970s. RS

Information sources

The origins of documents are often acknowledged in the text.
Other sources of information as follows:

Kinder becomes the forbidden mountain

Various newspapers and *Kinder Printing company; Its Strange History* - Sam Garside

Origins of the Kinder Trespass

Rothman Archives, the Working Class Movement Library, Salford -
Benny Rothman's 1982 account and his other interviews on the Trespass
Various newspapers

The Kinder Mass Trespass re-examined

Benny Rothman's accounts
Hayfield recreation ground - Hayfield guide leaflet, Hayfield Civic Trust
The Kinder Reservoir and Railway - by Jean and Ken Rangeley, Derek Brumhead,
New Mills Heritage Centre 2008
Various newspapers
Sol Gadian's account of the Trespass
Gordon Simmonds re Stones Head tea room
The Battle For Kinder Scout, Willow Publishing 2012

The Trial re-examined

Worker Sportsman journal and various newspapers

Jacob's Ladder meetings and Winnats Rally

Various newspapers

John Anderson - the walk that led to jail

Documents provided by Anderson's descendants and various newspapers

Forgotten for forty years?

Various newspapers and magazines

The Trespass - a turning point?

Various newspapers, Stephen Morton letters to Benny Rothman, Rothman collection,
Working Class Movement Library, Salford
A History of the Peak District Moors - David Hey, Pen & Sword Local 2014
Forbidden Land - Tom Stephenson, Manchester University Press 1989

The Trespassers

Trespassers' descendants- see full list in the acknowledgments, various newspapers,
the 1939 National Survey and archives from the Working Class Movement Library, Salford
Life and Times of Joe Thomas - Alan Woodward, Libertarian Socialists 2010
Forging the Faithful - The British at the International Lenin School - Labour History Review
Class Act, the cultural and political life of Ewan MacColl - Ben Harker, Pluto Press 2007
George Brown, portrait of a Communist leader - Mick Jenkins, North West Communist
Party History Group 2007
Journeyman - Ewan MacColl, Sidgwick & Jackson 1990
The Fox Golfing Society - Harry Morris 1983
Non Conformity in the Manchester Jewish Community - Rosalyn Livshin 2015

Acknowledgments

The author offers his grateful thanks for all the generous help given:

Maxwell Ayamba
Julian Batsleer
Margaret Barlow
Nial Barnes
Michael Barnes
Ann Beedham
Jo Bird
Rica Bird
Roy Blackman
David Blunkett
David Bobker
Victoria Browne
Janet Capstick
Eileen Clement
Dorothy Collins
June Cooper
Hilda Curnow
John Davies
Mike Dent
Paul Druck
Adam Dyster
Henry Folkard
Harold Frayman
David Gadian
Pam Gee
Harriet Gillett
Jan Gillett

Neil Gore
Tina Gould
Glynis Greenman
Donald Helman
Terry Howard
Hazel Humphries
Julie Humphreys
Veronica Jackson
Hilary Jones
David Kaiserman
Sheila Kelly
Mrs Kemp
Vivienne Kind
Eva Lawson
Rosalyn Livshin
Tony Lloyd MP
Ian Logan
Mike Luft
Hazel Maxwell
Andrew McCloy
Hilary McGrady
Phil Mendel
David Merrington
Jackie Nesbitt
Stuart Nesbitt
Thomas Noel
Jane O'Neill

David Orr
Jim Perrin
Richard Pettinger
John Poole
Philip Poole
Josephine Costello-Procter
Pat Reid
Fiona Reynolds
June Rose
Roz Rose
Harry Rothman
Andrew Screen
Peggy Seeger
Judy Skelton
Marion Shoard
Gordon Simmonds
David Sissons
Colin Speakman
Mrs Summer
David Toft
Ann Walker
Ian Watson
Barbara Whitley
Andrew Philip Widdall
Peter Winnick

Thanks also to the staff at Manchester Archives & Local Studies, Derbyshire Record Office, New Mills History Society and the Working Class Movement Library, Salford

The author acknowledges the kind permission given by:
Sidgwick and Jackson to include the extract on Joe Davies from *Journeyman, an autobiography* by Ewan MacColl; to Marion Shoard for use of an extract from her book *This Land is Our Land*; and Ann Beedham for use of George Willis Marshall photograph from *Days of Sunshine and Rain*.

Further reading

A Peak District Anthology - Roly Smith, Frances Lincoln Ltd 2012

Clem Beckett, Motorcycle Legend and War Hero - Robert Hargreaves, Pen & Sword Military 2022

A Right to Roam - Marion Shoard, Oxford University Press 1999 (See her website)

Clarion Call, Sheffield's access pioneers - Dave Sissons, Terry Howard & Roly Smith 2017

Days of Sunshine and Rain - Ann Beedham, published by the author 2011

Freedom to Roam - Howard Hill, Moorland Publishing 1980

High Peak Faces and Places - Keith Warrender, Willow Publishing 1978

Kinder People - Pam Gee, published by the author 1985

Kinder Scout, Portrait of a Mountain - Roly Smith, Derbyshire County Council 2002

Kinder Scout, the people's mountain - Ed Douglas and John Beatty, Vertebrate Publishing 2018

Kinder Scout with the footpaths and bridle roads about Hayfield - William Walker, 1877

Peakland Days - Roger Redfern, Robert Hale & Co 1970

Ramblers' Federation handbooks

Sheffield Clarion Ramblers' handbooks

The Battle For Kinder Scout - Roly Smith, Tom Waghorn, & Keith Warrender, Willow Publishing 2012

The Book of Trespass - Nick Hayes, Bloomsbury Circus 1920

The Land magazine

The Mysterious Case of William Walker - Bill Shaw (unpublished)

The Royal Forest of the Peak - IE Burton, Peak Park Planning Board 1966

This Land is Our Land - Marion Shoard, Gaia Books Ltd 1997

Walking Class Heroes - Roly Smith, Signal Books 2020

Who Owns England - Guy Shrubsole, HaperCollins 2020

Keith Warrender

Kinder

Appendix 1

Philip Poole

In Benny Rothman's published 1982 account of the Kinder Trespass he refers to a large demonstration at Leith Hill, Surrey, in support of countryside access. This had been organised by Philip Poole, a political activist and ally, of Benny who later went on to have a world-famous business in central London.

Born 1909 in Lambeth, Philip was an avid reader of books on socialism and got a job as office boy with Finsbury Labour Party where he was delegated to carry the box on which the speakers stood at outdoor meetings.

Poole was the secretary of a Workers' Theatre Group, a rapidly growing movement between 1929 and 1933, and acted in the Red Radio group in Hackney. They performed on the backs of lorries, outside factory gates and in public halls. The players wore overalls with just a hat or scarf to denote who were the workers and bosses. The shows were political in content and presentation, adopting modern drama techniques used by similar groups in Russian revolutionary theatre. By 1932 there were about sixty groups around Britain.

Poole did not take part in the Kinder Trespass but was a friend of Benny Rothman. He ran the Liberty Rambling Club which met at Meg's Cafe, Holborn, London, where poets and artists gathered. He founded and organised the Progressive Rambling Club in London, and was editor of its journal 'Progressive Rambler'. By 1939 the club had a hundred members and they were campaigning for reduced railway fares. That year Poole also began a series of regular articles on rambling matters for the Daily Worker newspaper.

Two thousand people attended the rally in the Tillingbourne Valley, Surrey in 1939 organised by Poole in support of greater access to the countryside. This was the largest rally of walkers ever seen in the south of England. There were speeches from Lewis Silkin MP criticising the rise in London Transport fares, and Tom

Poole family

Stephenson who explained why ramblers could not support the forthcoming Access to Mountains Bill. From leaving school in 1924, Poole later began his own stationery business in Bloomsbury Square. He moved to a shop on Drury Lane, Covent Garden in about 1976 where he opened 'His Nibs', described as an Aladdin's Cave of wooden drawers and cabinets filled with nibs, inks, quills and pens.

He became known internationally for his range of nibs which were bought by leading cartoonists, illustrators, calligraphers, animators and designers. Many of them sent him grateful letters of thanks for his friendly help, which he kept in a folder to show customers. The great cartoonist William Heath Robinson was one of his regular patrons, as well as cartoonist Ralph Steadman. A customer described going to his shop as like being measured for a suit in Saville Row because the perfect nib in exactly your size would be provided.

He was regarded as an expert on pen nibs and could date all his stock, some of which was one hundred and fifty years old. He reputedly stocked five thousand different types of fountain pen nibs and owned the world's biggest collection, many of them of historic value. Visitors to the shop mention how Poole, even in his eighties, used to ascend a ladder and perilously stretch out with a foot off the ladder rung to find an item in a drawer.

He was a man of few words but kind and enthusiastic. When a couple came from Canada to meet him in his shop he could barely utter a hello from the top of his ladder as he delved into the drawers.

From Drury Lane he moved his business to the premises nearby of art supplier L Cornelissen at Great Russell Street, near the British Museum, in 1990 where he worked six days a week until his death in 1999 at the age of 89. Cartoonists used to send him personalised birthday cards, and he often asked them to draw cartoons of him. Parts of his pen collection can be seen at London University's Museum of Writing and at the Pen Room Museum at the Argent Centre, Birmingham.

Appendix 2
Howard Hill

It is uncertain whether Hill took part in the Trespass. He was nineteen years old at the time and a friend of Benny Rothman. He was definitely involved in the later Abbey Brook trespass as he acknowledged in his book *Freedom to Roam*. The description of the Kinder Trespass is written, like the Abbey Brook incident, in the third person. Although he was a great supporter of direct action, he gives no indication he was present. His description of the Kinder Trespass is taken essentially from Rothman's account and various press reports, and has no fresh eye-witness details.

There have been suggestions that Hill's publishers wanted him to downplay his role in the protest. I've not been able to trace his family who may be able to throw more light on the matter.

Hill was born in 1913, the son of George, a herbalist, and Alice. He was an apprentice electrician before gaining employment at a steelworks. In the 1930s he joined the YCL and was a founder member of the Spartacus Rambling Club.

Between 1938 and 1946 he was a Labour councillor for Sheffield Brightside and also stood for parliamentary election as a Communist on seven occasions but was not successful. During the last World War he served in the RAF until he was invalided out. He was expelled from Labour in 1946 because of his association with the Communist Party.

After the War he became full-time secretary of Sheffield Communist Party until he retired in 1975 and was later elected to the Executive Committee of the Sheffield branch of the Ramblers Association for whom he was Access Officer.

In 1950 he led a protest at the Sheffield City Council when they met to approve an increase the rent of Council houses. He had not been allowed to address the meeting and shouted from the public gallery 'I wish to protest against the deputation not being relieved. It was on behalf of 30,000 people'. Hill continued 'Thousands of pounds are being spent preparing for war'. Following the Lord Mayor's request to either keep quiet or leave, he and twenty others left the public gallery.

In 1951 he was brought to court for causing obstruction while giving an open-air speech. He was defended by Lord Morris, a former Sheffield MP, who said that the summons had been brought under an act from 116 years ago. Why were they picking on him when making Communist speeches was legal? Morris pointed out that both Mr Attlee and Mr Churchill had therefore committed the same offence while giving speeches at outdoor gatherings. Hill was given an absolute discharge.

Hill died in 1980, the year his book *Freedom to Roam* was published which was the first comprehensive history of the open-air movement, outlining the history of the battle for access to the mountains and moors. In an interview with the Guardian that year, he was described as:

> unyielding as the massive rocks all around. I believe these moors and weather did more than anything else to shape the sturdy ruggedness of the northerner. His hair is as hardy as heather, his whiskers a Dickensian luxuriousness. He looks a chip off his blasted heath.

> We walked where ramblers have been chased by game-keepers for years - and sometimes still are. But now mass trespasses, inspired by such as Hill, have opened up the wide, passionate spaces. He suggested we go and look at Chatsworth, the Devonshire seat. We passed two or three notices on the road warning against entry. 'Don't worry about that,' he said firmly. 'I've been thrown out of here before'.

His death was particularly tragic, collapsing during a live broadcast on television. He was taking part in a discussion in the Yorkshire TV 'Calendar' programme when he suddenly fell ill. At first the studio staff thought he was reacting in a light-hearted way, then quickly realised the seriousness of the situation. He was taken to a local hospital where he was pronounced dead on arrival.

Hill had been a member of various unions, and later studied their history and that of the labour movement. All his papers, along with material on rambling and the countryside have been deposited at Hull University.

Appendix 3
Ramblers attacked with pitchforks

There are many recorded instances of ramblers being attacked by keepers and farmers over disputed walking routes. The example below illustrates a judge's attitude to walkers' rights of access.

On Sunday 10th October 1915, a party of thirteen from the Manchester Ramblers attempted to walk through Long Lea Farm, Rowarth as they thought it was on a right of way. (The public footpath can be seen on modern OS maps).

As they opened the gate to the farm, they were met by a boy with a stick who shouted at them to go back and struck Clara Richardson, one of the ramblers. They were then attacked by the farmer's three daughters who were using pitchforks to load hay into a loft. Richardson was stabbed with a pitchfork in the leg, thigh and abdomen as she struggled to take the pitchfork off one of the girls. Afterwards Richardson was told by her doctor to rest for 48 hours and was too ill to work for a week. Her dress had also been damaged in the incident.

The case was brought to Buxton County Court in February 1916 where Miss Richardson claimed damages for her injuries. Judge Alan Mcpherson said 'the party had some idea there was a right of way and went, but he could not bring himself to think that the defendant (the farmer and his wife) were liable for damages'. He thought 'these stupid people (the ramblers) had brought it on themselves'.

The judge said he didn't support farmers defending their property with pitchforks but nevertheless, the verdict was given to the defendant with costs.

Manchester Ramblers' picnic

Willow Publishing

Appendix 4

BWSF members listed in Benny Rothman's 'black book' c1932-3

Marshall Edmondson, Chapel St, Barnoldswick
CF Lynch, Socialist Hall, Briggate, Shipley
G Revill, Stothird Rd, Sheffield
Mr HL Barnford, Shakespeare St, Patricroft
L Helman, Waterloo Rd, M/c
Ralph Mason, Chapel St, Barnoldswick
Grace Siddon, Knowles Terrace, Pendlebury
Nellie Bellard, Aukland St, Salford
Will Evitty, Clarfields Rd, Wood Green, Wednesbury
G & W Shepherd, Foleshill Rd, Coventry
J Bate, Nursery Cottage, Padgate Lane, Warrington
M Goldberg, Queen St, Cheetham
M Caplan, Park Avenue, Cheetham
Clem Beckett, Swinton St, Cheetham
G Betts, Blackburn
Laura Dianer, Tabruck St
Ray Michaels, Little Turner St, London E1
Frank Johnson, Smith St, Oldham
Stanley Mitchell
JE Narker, The Terrace, Walsall
J Horrocks, Veal Street, Rochdale
RS Harris, Delamere St North, Ashton-u-Lyne
WH Gill, Forland Rd, Cheadle Heath, Stockport
FG Hulme, Stockport Rd, Cheadle Heath, Stockport
AR Halliday, New Road, Belper, Derbyshire
Mr P Rook, Greendale Rd, Port Sunlight
E Cowshaw, Crosters Rd, Bury
RR Sharpe, Carleton Ave, Moss Side
H Barmforth, Taurus St, Oldham

G Wilde, Regent St, Salford
S Taylor, Briggs Ave, Crewe
J Clementson, Greenbank Crescent, Darlington
H Hill, Manchester Rd, Castleton
E Moore, Rook St, Manchester
C Hulme, The Grange, Edgeley Rd, Stockport
W Mitchell, Uplands, Stoke Heath, Coventry
H Pickup, Moss St, Gt Harwood
A Rathmill, Yorkshire St, Ashton-u-Lyne
Frank Davidson, Grove St, Nelson
M Kershaw, Beech St, Barnoldswick
Alice Moores, c/o Oak St, Pendlebury
Mary Anderson, Oak St, Pendlebury
G Borrows, Crown St, Liverpool, Sec BWSF
H Brierley, Southbottom St, Rochdale
A Wolfe, c/o Rochdale Rd, M/c
S Burchill, Miles Hill Crescent, Leeds
Sadie Johnson, Sykes St, Castleford
M Herriott, Nightingale, Gt Ducie St, M/c
E Rhodes, Rochdale
S Gadian, Howarth St, Cheetham
Bill Jones, John St, Bolton
Thomas McDonald, Industry St, Sheffield
John Lynch, Cocker St, Bradford, M/c
Harold Sladen, Stockton St, Alexander Rd, M/c
Alice Fuller, The Crescent, Park Avenue, Haslingdon
Leslie Hutchinson, Charlton St, Collyhurst, M/c
E Pollitt, Duke St, Stockport

Interested in rambling:
(including) Nellie Wallace - Chatham Road, Swinton

Sympathetic to BWSF:
(including) AW Gillett, Dalton Hall, Victoria Park, M/c

Cheetham Hill YCL publicising the civil war in Spain, with known Kinder Trespassers Monty Rosenfield, Izzey Luft, Benny Rothman, George Westfield and Max and Jud Clynes' sisters Lily and Bella.

North East Labour History Society

Appendix 5
Bold boots of the Bogtrotters
By TOM WAGHORN

Look closely at this photo, taken nearly ninety years ago. It's the only known group picture of the Bogtrotters, Manchester's famous walking and climbing club of the 1930s, renowned for their long-distance endurance feats on the moors.

They wore heavy boots sprouting clinkers and hobnails, jackets, pullover and sometimes plus-fours. Some even sported collars and ties.

Note some are puffing at their pipes. In those days, pipe-smoking was supposed to indicate the manly, pensive, meditative mood apparently engendered by mountaineering.

All smiles, the Bogtrotters posed for the camera around 1934 at Tunstead House, the cafe on the lower slopes of Kinder Scout, a popular haunt at the end of the day for Peakland walkers.

The last of the Bogtrotters, Walter Riley of Withington, died in 2003, aged one hundred. The picture was found in his papers, together with fascinating syllabuses and well-thumbed and autographed dinner menus of the 1930s. Men-only, the Bogtrotters were a small but influential group. The 1934 syllabus lists thirty-five members, nearly all with Manchester or Salford addresses. Most of theiroutings were in the Peak by train for a thirty-mile tramp.

Favourite crags for climbing meets were Laddow, Stanage, Cratcliffe and the Roaches. The club owned a large patrol tent with good camping tackle, small lightweight tents, ropes and ice-axes together with a small map library.

Annual dinners were usually held at the Yorkshire Bridge Inn, at Bamford near the foot of Win Hill. 'Community songs' and a toast to the club were among the enjoyments. Sid Shallice spoke on one occasion on the theme of 'aspiration, perspiration, respiration and cremation.'

Influential? Alf Bridge, president in 1927, became one of Britain's leading rock-climbers, pioneering new routes in Lakeland and Snowdonia. Workwise, he helped the successful British Everest expedition of 1953 and became a close friend of leader John Hunt. His speciality was oxygen. Eddie Holliday was on the first ascent of Narrow Slab on Clogwyn du'r Arddu.

Walter Riley, a joiner, crafted the wooden runners for Britain's first mountain rescue stretcher, designed by Eustace Thomas of the Rucksack Club. And Bobby Burns was an outstanding manufacturer of hard-wearing rucksacks, under the slogan 'Better Built by Burns'.

Until the discovery of Riley's mementos, historians of the Peak and Pennine walking scene had assumed the Bogtrotters was merely a group of kindred spirits, rather than a club with the usual structure of president, secretary, committee, organised meets and annual dinners. We assume that the club started around 1926, but don't know when the group folded. Riley's papers were passed to the archivist of the city's Rucksack Club, since a number of Bogtrotters were also Rucksackers. They are a tribute to remarkable men.

Appendix 6
From King's Forest to Enclosure

The land divided

Land ownership was at the heart of the Kinder Scout Mass Trespass, and to understand the origins of the dispute we have to go back many centuries. People often talk of reclaiming the King's Land but half of Kinder had not been in the King's ownership since 1674 when Charles II sold it off, with the other half allocated to commoners. To understand this, we must look back to the hunting preserves of the Saxon period which were developed further by William the Conqueror. Kinder was part of the one hundred and-eighty-square-mile Royal Forest of the Peak, and commoners, by virtue of their holdings, exercised common rights of pasturage there.

In about 1635, commoners petitioned for the right to enclose it because of the severity of Forest Laws and the damage done to crops by the King's red deer. This resulted in a commission which advised the King to enclose the commons, giving half of it to the tenants. A survey was begun in 1635 which divided the land equally between the King and the tenants. This was completed in 1640 and the deer were either destroyed or wiped out by a severe winter. The survey map showed properties owned by John and Thomas Marriott, John Kinder, Mrs Bowdon and Mr Davenport. The moor where the Mass Trespass took place and the Kinder plateau were also divided between the Sovereign and the people. (See map page 200).

Eyre family

In 1674 Charles II, ever in need of finances, granted his share of the land to his loyal supporter Colonel Thomas Eyre of Gray's Inn, giving him 7331 acres in the High Peak. The Eyres were believed to have descended from the Saxon Le Heyre family who had been keepers of the hounds in the Royal Forest.

Over the centuries, the Eyres had close connections with the Royal Forest. William and Robert le Eyr were early foresters. In their hereditary office as 'Receivers' and 'Foresters of Fee' the Eyres collected the King's rents and fines from the tenants. They were later involved in lead mining as the land was cleared for mining and smelting. In 1570, Thomas and Christopher Eyre of Hope were known as the landed gentry of the Royal Forest. Thomas Eyre, who came from the North Lees branch of the family, had rented or sold some of the land granted by the king to help finance commoners' litigations by the time of his death in 1717.

Land redistribution

Enclosure of common land had been taking place for centuries, a process which benefited the bigger landowners. Riots and disturbances broke out in Derbyshire over enclosures. In 1569 owners were attacked with swords, daggers, pitchforks, clubs and bows at Maipstone Farm near Hayfield. Tenants at Over Haddon tore up fences and put their cattle in the fields.

The Parliamentary enclosures consolidated strips of land in open fields and enclosed surrounding pasture and common or 'waste' areas. Many ancient ways were lost during the process. The larger landowners obtained the biggest share of the awarded lands, with the smaller holders finding their plots isolated with no legal way of access to them, and in need of expensive walling off. As a result they were forced to sell off their few acres at a reduced rate, whereas the main landowners completed deals among themselves to consolidate their holdings, which increased their value. The changes in land ownership led to a population drift into the towns and cities as the dispossessed flooded into the urban centres. In turn, the newly-enlarged farming estates developed in efficiency and production to feed the growing number of mill and factory workers.

Hayfield enclosed

Hayfield in the parish of Glossop was divided into three hamlets: Great Hamlet, enclosed in 1829,

Phoeside, enclosed in 1829, and Kinder. In June 1839, a meeting for those interested in the allotment of open fields, pastures and moors in the Kinder Hamlet was called by major local landowners and main beneficiaries, John Marriott of Hayfield and Kinder, and Edward Bennett of Kinder, at Mrs Quarmby's George Inn, Hayfield.

They met again on 7th August 1839 at the George Inn, with Commissioners Adam Fox and Thomas Lomas to view the proposals of how the commons and waste lands were to be divided, allotted and enclosed, and to deal with any objections to the claims delivered. The claims had been on view at the offices of a solicitor in Stockport. The enclosures were incorrectly presented to the people as being of general benefit, and later they were described locally as a 'wholesale land grab'. Commissioner Fox farmed a 100-acre estate and owned the Martinside Estate. The finalised allotment of the enclosures was shown at the George Inn on 14 March 1840.

The Tithe map of 1854 showed that Bowden Bridge Quarry site, Kinder Bank and Kinder Low belonged to Micah Hall. Cluther Rocks and King's Piece were owned by Samuel Marriott, and Kinder Downfall including the old Smithy and shooters' refectory (See page 11) were in the ownership of John Marriott. William Walker of Farlands, writer of the local footpath guide, had four acres.

Poor Man's Piece

Hayfield villagers were particularly aggrieved that 'Poor Man's Piece' and 'Poor Man's Wood' had been removed in the Enclosures. This was a forty-acre site where people had the right of digging turf or peat on Leygate Moor, granted in perpetuity by the owner of the Park Hall Estate, Joseph Hague, in his 1781 will. The old turf road is marked on the map enclosed with the 1878 Kinder Scout and Hayfield footpaths guide, and the site is marked on current OS maps as 'Old Pits (Peat) Plantation'. The new 18ft wide road had been built by the landowner to give access to the workings. In the 1830s a passer-by recalled seeing a group on the site cutting and stacking turf for winter fuel.

It seems that the ancient rights to 'Poor Man's Piece' had been allowed to lapse, but the villagers were keen to reinstate it. Led by Ishmael Pursglove, a local stone merchant and campaigner for local rights, the villagers raised £5 1s to have walls which had been built across the old turf road pulled down, and a gate erected. This was destroyed in retaliation by the owner, Mr Sumner, in 1897 but Pursglove fought back and following a letter from the council, Sumner agreed to the re-erection of a gate with a key each for him and the villagers, two years later. Pursglove preserved this right of way by leading a procession along it once a year carrying sacks and turf-cutting spades. Later people turned to coal rather than peat to burn and the landowner quietly took over the plot and the road was walled off. In 1969 there was an unsuccessful attempt to re-establish the old rights to the turfery.

Farlands, later the residence of James Watts

William Walker who lived at Farlands, Kinder, gave a lecture to the Manchester Literary Club in 1880 in which he said the Enclosures had been *'a wicked Act, a wilfully ignorant Act, which gave thousands of acres of moorland which could not possibly be brought under agriculture, to rich owners for absolutely nothing. When a large part of King's Land on the Scout was surveyed, no one had the courage to ask even for their rights. Farmers seemed willing, on getting their share of allotment, to hold their peace, and the majority of the villagers were tenants of the larger landowners; and it is a significant fact that the individual who surveyed that part of the Scout apportioned to Park Hall … was at that time owner Captain White's agent. It seems now that even the road to this turfery is disputed and walled up. There are three causes for the present indifference of the people: first, village selfishness; second, fear of landlords; third, want of means in those willing to try to save the rights.'*

Walker memorably summed up the situation with his words in the 1878 guide:
'The award of acres may be thus tabulated:
To the rich according to their riches - 2000 acres
To the poor according to their poverty - 0 acres
Moreover, minus upwards of 40 acres'.

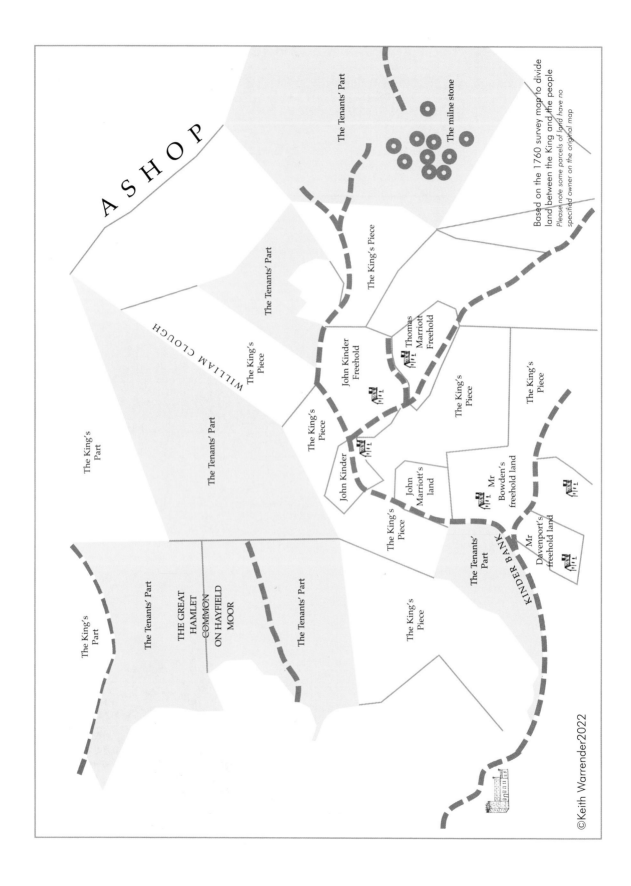

ASHOP

The Tenants' Part

The milne stone

The King's Piece

The Tenants' Part

WILLIAM CLOUGH

The Tenants' Part

The King's Piece

The King's Part

John Kinder Freehold

Thomas Marriott Freehold

The King's Piece

The King's Piece

The King's Piece

The Tenants' Part

The King's Piece

John Kinder

John Marriott's land

Mr Bowden's freehold land

The King's Piece

Mr Davenport's freehold land

The Tenants' Part

KINDER BANK

The King's Part

The Tenants' Part

THE GREAT HAMLET COMMON ON HAYFIELD MOOR

The Tenants' Part

The King's Piece

Based on the 1760 survey map to divide land between the King and the people
Please note some parcels of land have no specified owner on the original map

©Keith Warrender 2022